ISLAMIC FINANCE

ISLAMIC FINANCE

Between Religious Norms and Legal Practice

Wim Decock
Vincent Sagaert
(eds.)

intersentia
Cambridge – Antwerp – Chicago

Intersentia Ltd
Sheraton House | Castle Park
Cambridge | CB3 0AX | United Kingdom
Tel.: +44 1223 370 170 | Fax: +44 1223 370 169
Email: mail@intersentia.co.uk
www.intersentia.com | www.intersentia.co.uk

Distribution for the UK and Ireland:
NBN International
Airport Business Centre, 10 Thornbury Road
Plymouth, PL6 7 PP
United Kingdom
Tel.: +44 1752 202 301 | Fax: +44 1752 202 331
Email: orders@nbninternational.com

Distribution for Europe and all other countries:
Intersentia Publishing nv
Groenstraat 31
2640 Mortsel
Belgium
Tel.: +32 3 680 15 50 | Fax: +32 3 658 71 21
Email: mail@intersentia.be

Distribution for the USA and Canada:
Independent Publishers Group
Order Department
814 North Franklin Street
Chicago, IL60610
USA
Tel.: +1 800 888 4741 (toll free) | Fax: +1312 337 5985
Email: orders@ipgbook.com

Islamic Finance. Between Religious Norms and Legal Practice

ISBN 978-1-78068-619-6
ISBN 978-1-78068-869-5 (PDF)
D/2019/7849/77
NUR 827

GPRC
Guaranteed
Peer Reviewed
Content

British Library Cataloguing in Publication Data. A catalogue record for this book is available from the British Library.

CONTENTS

INTRODUCTION

Wim DECOCK and Vincent SAGAERT

This volume collects the papers presented at the Leuven Islamic Finance symposium on 7 December 2017. Organized jointly by UMT School of Law and Policy in Lahore (Pakistan) and the Faculties of Law and Theology at KU Leuven (Belgium), the conference brought together high-level practitioners and esteemed experts from different academic fields – theology, law, economics – for an inter-cultural and inter-disciplinary dialogue on Islamic finance. The conference was made possible thanks to a generous grant by the Flemish Research Foundation (FWO), the support of Katechetica, the alumni network of the Faculty of Theology, Leuven's Global Law School and Themis, the post-graduate training and congress centre at the Faculty of Law. Following an invitation by Dean Bernard Tilleman and Dean Mathijs Lamberigts, the general aim of this symposium was to explore the tension existing between the religious and legal principles underlying Islamic finance, on the one hand, and the actual legal practice of Islamic banking, on the other. While Islamic finance must allow the Muslim community to reconcile their economic needs with the principles of religion, there are increasingly signs that the practice of Islamic finance is forced to develop sophisticated legal devices to reconcile the original conception of Islamic finance with the dictates of the modern market. In his standard work on the subject, Ibrahim Warde, professor at the Fletcher School of Law and Diplomacy (Tufts), observes "*a gap between promise and performance*" in this regard.[1] Given the financial importance and development of Islamic finance, it should not surprise that several legal systems try to accommodate Islamic finance within their legal framework. Despite a declining trend in its growth rate, the business of Islamic finance is nevertheless thriving, the sector being worth more than $ 2,4 trillion at the end of 2017, according to estimates.[2]

The contributions in this volume highlight several aspects of the theory and practice of Islamic finance. The relationship between religion, ethics and finance in both the Islamic tradition and the Christian tradition is explored in *Rodney*

[1] I. Warde, *Islamic Finance in the Global Economy*, Edinburgh, Edinburgh University Press, 2010[2], 240.

[2] Global Islamic Finance Report 2018, https://www.astanafindays.org/storage/media/5b55d014d1e42.pdf.

Wilson's contribution on Christian and Islamic perspectives on contemporary finance. He confronts the functioning of canon law in the Christian churches with respect to financial management with the *shari'ah* governance of Islamic banking institutions. Different attitudes towards risk-taking and interest are explained, despite a shared commitment to moral values that are supposed to supplement secular laws on banking and finance. The rise of Islamic financial institutions since the 1960s is contrasted with the absence of explicitly Christian financial institutions, except for particular initiatives such as the Kingdom Bank and Ecclesiastical Insurance. Perhaps the most important difference Wilson observes is the lack of centrally administered authorities in the Islamic world, which leads to a wide variety of diverging and often conflicting opinions about legitimate banking activities among Muslims. For example, most Muslim majority countries have not introduced a complete ban on interest-taking, except for the Islamic Republic of Iran, and interpretations of the *riba*-prohibition differ from one country to the other. As a result, Wilson concludes, "*differences within religions may be greater than differences between religions, at least in the realm of finance.*"

This view on the variety of conceptions within Islamic finance is largely confirmed by the second contribution in this volume, in which *Mathias Rohe* assesses the legal aspects of Islamic finance in the contemporary world. He sets out the legal rules by analyzing the variety of interpretations of the prohibitions on interest-taking (*riba*) and high-risk transactions (*gharar*) which underlie Islamic banking activities. The possibilities for applying Islamic legal principles in international contracts, for instance through international private law, are explored. Rohe observes that conflict of law-clauses referring to the law of specific states, *e.g.* Pakistan, are more likely to be accepted in Europe than general references to Islamic law, at least with state courts. Arbitration mechanisms offer more flexibility. Within European jurisdictions, the notion of suppletive rules as opposed to mandatory substantive law also offers room for the introduction of financial transactions that meet the requirements of Islamic law, such as *ijara*, Islamic lease, *murabaha* and *musharaka*, Islamic partnerships, and *hawala*, a kind of bills of exchange. In conclusion, Rohe sees two main strategies for combining Muslim faith and financial practice. It is possible to try to stick to the traditional texts and invent more or less convincing strategies to reconcile tradition with modernity, for instance by appealing to approved circumvention techniques. Another option is to re-contextualize the old norms, re-interpret them according to the values underlying the *shari'ah* and integrate them with new ethical concerns such as fair trade, ecological impact and labour conditions. Examples are given how these strategies are applied to overcome the tension between the theory and practice of islamic finance.

The legal and economic technicalities of specific Islamic banking services are analysed in the following two contributions. The legal dimension of the subject matter is highlighted by *Syed Imad-ud-Din Asad*. He starts with an overview of the religious sources of Islamic law in general, including the *Qur'an*, the *Sunnah*, and their learned interpretation by scholars through individual reasoning by analogy (*Qiyas*) and the common opinion of learned experts (*Ijma*). After a basic introduction to the prohibitions on interest, excessive risk-taking and gambling underlying Islamic finance, a systematic overview of specific financial transactions is provided. Deposit-, equity-, debt- and fee-based products are analyzed in depth. A comparative analysis of the development of Islamic finance in the Muslim world, the UK and Luxembourg gives insight into the interaction between state policies, institutions and the practice of Islamic finance. At the end of his paper, the author notices that one of the great challenges today is to keep the religious inspiration behind the sophisticated legal devices alive, while the practical effects obtained by Islamic finance transactions have developed in such way that they are to resemble those of conventional banking. This tension is compounded by the fact that a major challenge for Islamic banks in non-Muslim-majority jurisdictions is to compete with conventional (non-Muslim) financial institutions.

The urgent problem of obtaining a level playing field with conventional banks is addressed by *Hans Visser* in a paper that concentrates on the regulatory aspects of Islamic finance in non-Muslim-majority countries. As a matter of fact, there are many regulatory hurdles preventing a faster rise of Islamic retail banks in European countries. A major issue concerns the question whether regulators follow what Visser calls an economic or a legal approach, viz. a substantive or formal approach. For tax purposes these approaches lead to very different outcomes. For example, if a strictly legal or formal perspective is applied, then Islamic banks cannot be considered as incurring financing costs (since they do not pay interest in the legal sense of the word, but markups), thus losing the opportunity to deduct those costs when paying taxes. Visser argues for an economic rather than for a legal approach, which would allow the markups to be considered from a substantial point of view as tantamount to interest, thus allowing Islamic banks to deduct them in their tax file. He recognizes, though, that, from a political point of view, there is currently little interest in promoting the substantial perspective. Other pressing issues dealt with by Visser are the differences in accounting standards set by the Accounting and Auditing Organization for Islamic Financial Institutions (AAOFI) and the International Accounting Standard Board (IASB). He also brings up the question of whether Basel III solvency and liquidity requirements apply to Islamic banks or not. More often than not, Islamic banks face a competitive disadvantage if they are to apply the rules of Basel III, since, for lack of a variety of high-quality liquid assets, they are obliged to meet the rules by holding cash.

Some of the complex legal arrangements that are put in place to make Islamic finance work in non-Muslim-majority jurisdictions are illustrated in great technical detail by *Martin Bünning* and *Aryanaz Rezaian*. They discuss the sophisticated legal constructions set up in Germany to allow for the introduction of Shari'ah compliant investment practices that are in line with the German regulatory framework. In this manner, these arrangements can benefit from the existing tax system, especially interest deduction in debt financing. This contribution provides first-hand evidence that, in day to day business, bridging the gap between the theory and practice of Islamic finance is a balancing act that requires sensitivity to cultural diversity as well as specialized knowledge about regulatory regimes.

Diverging views on the history, presence and future of Islamic finance are presented in the last papers of the volume. *Mahmoud El-Gamal* offers a critical account of the rise of Islamic banking since the 1970s from an economist's perspective. Thanks to the explosion of oil revenues in the Middle East, funds could be generated to fuel what El-Gamal calls "a state-sponsored capitalist-Islamism". Unlike earlier forms of socialist-Islamism, it did not threaten the post-colonial political order and allowed aspiring Muslims to affirm their identity while climbing the rungs of society. El-Gamal's thought-provoking analysis of the historical factors that contributed to the rise of Islamic finance leads to a pessimistic forecast. Decreasing revenues from petro-dollars mean that many of the states that took the lead in promoting Islamic finance are at risk of economic decline, which would inevitably compromise the future of Islamic finance, or, at least, make it evolve in different ways. El-Gamal observes a shift in paradigm from capitalist-Islamism to terrorist-Islamism, which needs to be carefully monitored by regulators. Neither aggressive anti-terror nor aggressive modernization policies should be pursued. The social and financial capital of Muslim populations struggling to reconcile tradition and modernity should not be lost, for instance by stimulating home grown models such as mutual housing cooperatives or credit unions that borrow the Islamic finance brand name. In an ideal world, El-Gamal thinks, Muslims should be taught "that there is nothing intrinsically un-Islamic about modern financial practices." A compromise view on the historical development and future perspectives for Islamic finance is nevertheless offered by *Amel Makhlouf*. She takes a longer view on the development of Islamic trade and finance, arguing that these faith-based forms of commerce and banking will continue to be successful, as they once did in the medieval period, long before the age of the petro-dollars.

In conclusion, this volume offers contributions by outstanding scholars and practitioners in the field that reveal the complexities involved in applying religious principles and legal theory to the daily practice of business and finance. A fruitful dialogue has been created between lawyers, theologians, and economists from academia and practice who hold diverging views about the present state and the future of Islamic finance. Many papers clearly show that there is still growth potential for Islamic finance in the Western world, not only among Muslim clients but also among non-Muslims looking for alternative investment instruments. As several speakers and attendants have indicated during the conference, Islamic finance has an important role to play in stimulating environmental and social impact investing.[3] From a European perspective, though, the "hype" about economic finance nevertheless appears to belong to the past. In the wake of the 2008 financial crisis, several political leaders in the UK, France and Luxemburg made big public statements about their desire to turn their financial centres into the European capital of Islamic finance. Islamic finance was at some point even thought to be crisis-proof, despite later evidence to the contrary.[4] A decade on, the political climate has shifted considerably, even if Western European countries such as Belgium continue to explore ways to integrate Islamic banking into the conventional financial system.[5] Prospects for Islamic finance in countries such as Malaysia, Iran, Saudi Arabia, Kuwait, United Arab Emirates, Indonesia, Pakistan and Egypt remain of a wholly different order, though, than in Europe or the United States. While the latest Global Islamic Finance Report indicates slowing growth rates for the sector even in those countries, the Islamic finance sector continues to flourish in large parts of Southern Asia, the Middle East and Northern Africa. Perhaps, then, there is not only a growing gap between promise and performance in the Islamic finance industry, as Ibrahim Warde noticed, but also between geopolitical areas in the world economy.

---

3 In this regard, see R. Jaufeerally, "Islamic Banking and Responsible Investment: Is a Fusion Possible?" in W. Vandekerckhove et al. (eds.), Responsible Investment in Times of Turmoil, Dordrecht, Springer, 2011, 151–164; and S. Farook and R.U. Shikoh, "Integration of Social Responsibility in Financial Communities", in K. Hassan and M. Mahlknecht (eds.), Islamic Capital Markets: Products and Strategies, Chichester, Wiley, 2011, 69–89.

4 S. Ongena, S. Zaheer and F. di Mauro (ed.), *Islamic Finance in Europe*, (European Central Bank Occasional Paper Series, 146), June 2013, 41–47.

5 See the presentations at the symposium "Islamic Banking: An Opportunity for Belgium" (Brussels, 5 December 2013), www.financialforum.be/sites/financialforum.be/files/media/1340.pdf.

CHRISTIAN AND ISLAMIC PERSPECTIVES ON CONTEMPORARY FINANCE

Rodney Wilson
Emeritus Professor

1. INTRODUCTION

Religious laws today mainly exist in parallel to secular national laws as states are no longer theocratic. Nevertheless religious dogma retains considerable influence over law making, especially in the area of family law, and to a much lesser extent in financial law and regulation. It is instructive to contrast how Canon Law functions in Christian churches with respect to financial management with the *Shari'ah* governance of Islamic financial institutions.

Christian institutions are centrally administered by ecclesiastical authorities whereas Islam is a decentralised religion resulting in much less authority for the religious leadership. Nevertheless there is some devolution of day to day financial management in Christian churches as Canon Law requires each diocese to establish a Finance Council, composed of at least three of the faithful expert in financial affairs and civil law, presided over by the diocesan bishop or his delegate. The assets of the Church are trust property for the benefit of its whole community. It is, therefore, only fair that the community should participate in the administration of those assets.[1]

There are few designated Christian financial institutions comparable to Islamic banks. Organisations such as Banco Espírito Santo or the Istituto per le Opere di Religione, the Vatican Bank, have been subject to financial irregularities and unfortunately cannot be regarded as upholding Christian values.[2] The distinguishing feature of Islamic banks is that their governance structure includes a *Shari'ah* board with responsibility for ensuring that all financial transactions

1 Margaret Lightbody, (2000) "Storing and shielding: financial management behaviour in a church organization", *Accounting, Auditing and Accountability Journal*, 13:2, 156–174.

2 Ernst A. Lewin, "The finances of the Vatican", *Journal of Contemporary History*, 18:2, 185–204.

are compatible with Islamic teaching. How this responsibility is exercised and the authority of the boards has been subject to much debate and criticism.[3]

2. FINANCIAL GOVERNANCE OF CHRISTIAN INSTITUTIONS

In Christian churches the day to day financial governance is devolved to parish level, with interested church wardens or elders comprising the finance committee, usually guided by the parish priest. Local initiatives include stewardship campaigns to raise funds to cover the stipend of the clergy and church maintenance and renovation.[4] The selection of charitable beneficiaries and the disbursement of donations are also handled locally, although the advice of the bishops may be sought. The church hierarchy is responsible for setting the financial contribution to the diocese, with more affluent parishes usually contributing more than those in low income areas. This redistribution to reflect differing needs is determined by the Diocesan Finance Council which advices the bishop on financial matters. Diocesan Finance Councils also serve to strengthen accountability and ensure that good financial practices are in place and followed. It is the Diocesan Finance Council which nominates new members, but the bishops who have the authority to appoint members.[5]

Membership is for a fixed term, usually five-years, with reappointment possible, but there is agreement that the council should be refreshed by the appointment of new members. Members of the Diocesan Finance Council must be Christians in good standing with the Church and Canon law requires that they be "truly expert in financial affairs and civil law, and outstanding in integrity."[6] Relatives of the diocesan bishop may not be appointed. With the exception of the Diocesan Finance Officer, employees of the Archdiocese or individuals with business interests with the Church may not serve on the Council.

Although the governance of Christian institutions is subject to Canon Law, governance practices have been increasingly influenced by best practice in corporate and national governance. Canon Law is viewed as complimentary to civil law, existing in parallel, but not a substitute. Disputes between Churches and their members are usually dealt with by national courts rather than the Ecclesiastical authorities. The churches recognise the supremacy of state secular law, but lobby to

---

3 Waemustafa, Waeibrorheem and Abdullah, Azrul, (2015) "Mode of Islamic bank financing: does the effectiveness of *Shari'ah* Supervisory Board matter?" *Australian Journal of Basic and Applied Science*, 9:37, 458–462.

4 Adrian Sargeant, (2005) "Church and parachurch fundraising in the United States: what can we learn?" *International Journal of Non-profit and Voluntary Sector Marketing*, 10:3, 133–136.

5 A.G. Farrelly, (1989), "The Diocesan Finance Council: functions and duties according to the Code of Canon Law", *Studia Canonica*, 23:1, 149–166.

6 C. 492, §1.

influence legal developments, such as restrictions on the opening hours for Sabbath trading. The retention of charitable status is important for the churches, as this ensures no tax is paid on income. Indeed in many jurisdictions the churches can reclaim taxes paid by donors. In the United Kingdom the Church of England is directly involved in law making, as the Bishops attend the House of Lords.[7]

3. FINANCIAL GOVERNANCE OF ISLAMIC INSTITUTIONS

The financial management of Mosques conforms to traditional Islamic teaching on *waqf*, Islamic charitable foundations. There is considerable diversity in how *waqfs* are managed as the wishes of the benefactor have to be respected, even after the benefactor has died. There are many parallels between the financial management of *waqf* foundations and the common law concept of charitable trusts, not least in the discretion given to the trustees acting on behalf of the benefactor. In the Ottoman Empire there was detailed legal provision for *waqf*, but with the emergence of the secular Turkish Republic many *waqf* were nationalised by the state, undermining the authority of the clergy.[8] Similar polices were pursued in many Arab countries, notably Egypt under Nasser, where religious institutions became subservient to the state.[9]

Waqf have been established in many non-Muslim countries, including in Europe, where they are in the form of trusts or charitable endowments. Many have been established with funding from the Gulf, potentially controversial given the lack of reciprocity, with church building prohibited in Saudi Arabia. There are also issues of inclusiveness, with Shia Muslims uncomfortable and unwelcome in Sunni funded mosques and Islamic educational establishments.

There is no central authority in Europe or individual European countries to direct *waqf*, most being established by local initiatives in areas with significant Muslim communities. The Muslim Council of Europe is an advisory body on Islamic arbitration, conciliation and mediation, but it largely deals with family matters such as divorce and has no power of enforcement.[10] This also applies with the Muslim Council of Britain, although it is also involved in political lobbying which was successful in getting equal tax treatment for Islamic financial

7 Anna Harlow, Frank Cranmer and Christopher Norman Doe, (2008), "Bishops in the House of Lords: a critical analysis", *Public Law*, 52:3, 490–509.

8 Oded Peri, (1992), "*Waqf* and Ottoman welfare policy: the poor kitchen of Hasseki Sultan in Eighteenth-Century Jerusalem", *Journal of the Economic and Social History of the Orient*, 35:2, 167–186.

9 Daniela Pioppi, (2004) "From religious charity to the welfare state and back: the case of Islamic endowments (*waqfs*) revival in Egypt", *European University Institute*, Working Paper RSCIS 2004/3.

10 Http://iceurope.org/.

contracts to their secular equivalents. It is strictly non-partisan however, and does not get involved in British politics.[11]

Family law matters can be dealt with by *Shari'ah* courts with the consent of the parties, but civil divorce or custody orders concerning children still have to be subject to national courts. Commercial disputes involving Islamic financial institutions and their clients are rarely dealt with by *Shari'ah* courts which lack the financial expertise needed in complex cases. The parties in dispute in *Shari'ah* courts have to be willing to abide by the rulings on a voluntary basis as the courts have no powers of enforcement. Islamic banks and their clients rely on national law enforcement in commercial disputes. National courts can call on *Shari'ah* scholars as expert witnesses in disputes involving Islamic financial institutions. The scholars can testify on the integrity of contracts from an Islamic perspective. Judges are not however obliged to follow any recommendations by expert witnesses and they can disregard their testimony. In practice it is only in Malaysia where Islamic scholars have been called as expert witnesses, and this precedent has not been followed in the Arab World or Europe.[12]

4. ALTERNATIVE PERSPECTIVES ON INTEREST, DEBT AND LENDING

Self-designated Islamic economists criticise conventional bank finance based on interest, equating interest with *riba*, which is explicitly condemned in the Koran. The justification for the prohibition is that interest charges are exploitative and amount to usury, a concern also from an historical Christian perspective best expressed in the writing of the medieval Saint, Thomas Aquinas.[13] In modern Christian teaching a distinction is drawn between interest and usury, with moderate interest regarded as normal, but the high rates charged by companies such as pay-day lenders as unacceptable. There is no clear guidance on when interest becomes usurious but rather than suggesting a rate, which would depend on factors such as inflation, the concern is with excessive and unfordable indebtedness. Biblical teaching is that debtors should pay what they owe[14] but lenders should be merciful and consider the plight of those who are unable to repay due to circumstances beyond their control such as ill heath, crop failures or natural disasters. The Old Testament advocates the cancellation of debt every

---

11 Www.mcb.org.uk/.

12 Ruzian Markom, Sharina Ali Pitchay, Zinatul Ashiqin Zainol, Anita Abdul Rahim and Rooshida Merican, (2013), "Adjudication of Islamic banking and finance cases in the civil courts of Malaysia", *European Journal of Law and Economics*, 36:1, 1–34.

13 Shaikh M. Ghazanfar, (2000), "The economic thought of Abu Hamid Al-Ghazali and St. Thomas Aquinas: some comparative parallels and links", *History of Political Economy*, 32:4, 857–888.

14 Numbers 30:2.

seven years, which if interpreted literally would preclude long term mortgage finance, although today this is conveniently ignored by the Christian churches.[15]

The churches have not advocated the establishment of designated Christian banks but rather urged that existing banks should be aware of Christian teaching. In contrast some Muslims regard conventional banking practices as incompatible with Islamic teaching. Some leading banks now, however, offer Islamic financial products, but scholars are concerned that there could be inadequate fire walls between conventional and Islamic assets and liabilities. Rather stand-alone Islamic banks are regarded as the better solution, with these institutions not offering interest based loans or paying interest on deposits.[16]

Islamic finance involves risk sharing with investment depositors earning a share in the bank's profits rather than receiving interest payments. Unlike shareholders however, depositors have no voting rights and they do not benefit from capital gains on their deposits. Much of their financing comes from trading transactions where the bank purchases a good on behalf of a client and subsequently re-sells the good to the client on a deferred payment basis with the bank charging a mark-up. Risks are shared as the bank owns the good initially and has legal liability if the good is defective. Leasing is also popular, where the bank receives rental income rather than interest.[17]

Islamic banks cannot offer interest based loans, but the wide variety of alternatives has proved viable and arguably offers clients more choices. The methods of financing are distinctive from those of secular banks and the cost of finance is usually competitive, but can be more expensive where the products are complex and the client has to bear some of the costs of risk sharing. In secular finance banks do not provide risk capital, which comes from equity finance, both public and private. Islamic banks cannot buy shareholdings in enterprises they support, largely because they are regulated as banks with current account depositors offered the same degree of protection as those with secular banks.[18]

In addition to national regulation Islamic banks are subject to assurance by *Shari'ah* boards. Each bank appoints its own board, which amounts to the privatisation of *Shari'ah* compliance, but in some jurisdictions, notably Malaysia, there are national boards accountable to the central bank. In nationalised systems only the central *Shari'ah* boards have the authority to issue *fatwa* or rulings on the legitimacy of particular Islamic products. In decentralised systems

15 Deuteronomy 15: 1–2.

16 Juan A. Solé, (2007), "Introducing Islamic banks into conventional banking systems", *IMF Working Paper* 07/175.

17 Mohammad Omar Farooq, (2009), "Partnership, equity financing and Islamic finance: whither profit and-loss sharing?" *Review of Islamic Economics*, 11, 67–88.

18 Dahlia El-Hawary, Wafik Grais and Zamir Iqbal, (2007), "Diversity in the regulation of Islamic financial institutions", *The Quarterly Review of Economics and Finance*, 46:5, 778–800.

each board has the authority to issue *fatwa*, some of which are conflicting. Nationalising *Shari'ah* compliance ensures consistency, but also stifles debate. Although having a *Shari'ah* board increases banking costs it has the merit of providing a further layer of client protection. Clients believe approved financial products are authentic and the judgement of *Shari'ah* boards commands respect and is viewed as adding value.[19]

5. RISK SHARING AND THE JUSTIFICATION OF REWARD

An important principle of contemporary Islamic finance is the justification of remuneration, whether in the form of income or capital gains. Salaries are justified by working through physical or mental effort and as in Christianity there is the belief that humans should work to the best of their abilities rather than being idle. Islamic teaching respects private property rights, and if tenants occupy and use lands, buildings or equipment the owners are entitled to receive rents. However ownership of property is conditional, as ultimately the owners are custodians on behalf of the Almighty, and they are responsible to ensure the property is well managed in a sustainable manner that benefits society and future generations. Leasing contracts should spell out the responsibilities of owners and lessees as in Islamic *ijarah* agreements, and mere financing leases where the owner is remunerated without any responsibility are prohibited under *Shari'ah*.[20]

In contrast to salaries or rental income, *riba* is viewed as an unjustified payment whereby the financier is simply being remunerated for providing money, with no interest in, or indeed knowledge of, how their money is utilised. The borrower bears sole liability for risk, whereas the financier expects to have their money returned plus interest regardless of economic circumstances. This corresponds with the terms of savings contracts with banks, as deposits are guaranteed with the state underwriting deposit protection schemes which results in depositors bearing no risks, with the entire burden of the risk being the liability of the savings bank or the state. Islamic banks are allowed to offer transactions accounts to depositors in which their funds are guaranteed, but depositors do not earn any interest from such deposits, the benefit of the accounts being the offer of a debit card and a cheque book and the ability to manage transfers and payments on-line through the internet or apps. To earn a

19 Azhar Abdul Raman and Abdullah Awadh Bukair, (2013), "The influence of the *Shari'ah* supervision board on corporate social responsibility disclosure by Islamic banks of Gulf Co-Operation Council countries", *Asian Journal of Business and Accounting*, 6:2, 65–104.

20 Mohammad Hisham Kamali, (2005), "*Shari'ah* Issues of Islamic Leasing: Perspective of the Lessor", Unpublished paper, *International Islamic Leasing Conference*, Kuwait, 24–25.

return on deposits Islamic banks offer investment accounts with the depositors sharing in the bank's profits rather than receiving interest.[21]

Investment deposits with Islamic banks cannot be equated with equity holdings as depositors are not owners and have no voting rights. Unlike conventional savings accounts, the value of the deposits cannot be guaranteed, as they are designated as profit and loss sharing. The risk sharing relates to not only rate of return risk, but also to capital at risk, as is the case with equity investment. However investors in equity are usually attracted because of the possibility of capital gains, but with Islamic investment deposits there is no upside, as the deposits do not increase in value. As with equity investment there is nevertheless a downside; hence the investment deposits are asymmetrical, a type of hybrid with some equity characteristics but also some of the features of conventional savings deposits. From a purely financial perspective investment deposits are rather unattractive as there is no benefit apart from a profit share, but there is the risk of capital loss. To compensate either the expected profit payouts have to exceed the expected rate of interest on savings deposits, or informal understandings given that in the event of a default the investment depositors will be higher in the pecking order than equity investors with regards to rights to compensation from the bank's remaining capital.

Such financial complexity is not covered in traditional *Shari'ah* teaching, but is covered by the contracts between the investment depositors and Islamic banks which have been approved by the banks *Shari'ah* boards. A broader issue is whether such contemporary *fiqh* is the best way of ensuring that Islamic values are upheld, or if the alternative of simply accepting savings contracts yielding modest returns to depositors to compensate for temporary liquidity sacrifices is preferable. Of course the *Shari'ah* scholars serving on the boards of Islamic financial institutions reject the latter approach, but many Muslims remain unconvinced that modest rates of interest equate with *riba*.

Arguably from a moral perspective risk sharing is more just than placing all the burdens on one party. However much depends on the ability of each party to carry risk. Most bank depositors want safe keeping as they have limited income and are reluctant to be exposed to the vagaries of equity markets. Those with variable return savings deposits are of course exposed to monetary policy which determines interest rates, but changes are more predictable and vary less than equity prices. Investment depositors with Islamic banks are in theory exposed to variable profit shares, but in practice these are less volatile than the dividends paid to bank shareholders. Furthermore many Islamic banks hold profit equalisation reserves with a portion of profits retained in good years which can be distributed to investment depositors when profitability is reduced or losses occur.

---

21 Simon Archer and Rifaat Ahmed Abdel Karim, (2009), "Profit-sharing investment accounts in Islamic banks: regulatory problems and possible solutions", *Journal of Banking Regulation*, 10.4: 300–306.

6. MORAL VALUES IN FINANCE

Both Christianity and Islam provide moral perspectives on finance which complement secular laws and regulations. There is no suggestion that religious teaching should replace national laws governing banks and capital markets. Islamic banks, for example, are required to be adequately capitalised and maintain sufficient liquidity under Basel III in order to protect depositors and avoid expensive government bail-outs in the case of defaults.[22] The religious concern is about access to the banking system for those in self-employment or on low income, or in other words the system's inclusiveness. In Muslim societies there are of course those who don't want to be included in secular systems, hence the role for Islamic banks in inclusion.

There has also been criticism by both Christians and Muslims of the excessive profits made by secular banks and the large pay disparities within the institutions, with the latter remaining an issue after the 2007 financial crisis when many banks suffered declining stock prices or even bankruptcy. An alternative was Christian and Muslim credit unions, non-profit making institutions often involved in charitable financing. Credit unions cannot provide a full range of banking services however, as they are regulated separately. Even church administrators have to use the services of secular banks, but mosque endowments are often managed, where possible, by Islamic banks.

In both Christian and Islamic thinking there is concern about how finance is used and what is supported. In Islam the financing of breweries, distilleries or companies producing pork products is prohibited, as well as investment in casinos facilitating gambling activities. There are an increasing number of Islamic funds that screen equity investment to ensure it is *halal* or permitted. There are even indices tracking *Shari'ah* compliant stock, most notably the S&P Dow Jones Islamic indices. Christian investment institutions have fewer prohibitions, but avoid financing gambling activities or tobacco companies. Both Christian and Islamic fund managers have been influenced by the international debate on economic sustainability, especially that on climate change. In 2016 the Dow Jones Islamic Market Sustainability Index was launched with 105 companies included in the index and management provided by Zurich based RobecoSAM, a pioneer in sustainability investing since 1995.[23]

---

22 Waeibrorheem Waemustafa and Suriani Sukri, (2015), "Bank specific and macroeconomics dynamic determinants of credit risk in Islamic banks and conventional banks", *International Journal of Economics and Financial Issues*, 5:2, 476–481.

23 Www.robecosam.com/.

7. ISLAMIC BANKING EXPERIENCES

Contemporary Islamic finance originated in Pakistan, Egypt and Malaysia in the 1960s with the foundation of credit unions where depositors would put their savings but receive no financial return. Instead depositors, as members of the union, were able to apply for interest free loans. The organisational structure was that of a cooperative, run on a not-for-profit basis, where the members were the shareholders. The institutions were unregulated, but as there was a high degree of trust between the members rather the lack of conventional equity funding did not prove a problem. Foremost among the credit unions was the Mit Ghamr Savings Bank which was opened in 1963 to finance agricultural and rural development projects in the Nile delta.[24] Almost 250,000 depositors opened accounts before the bank became a victim of political maneuverings as it was associated with Islamists who were opposed by the socialists. By 1971 it was nationalised and no longer emphasised its Islamic credentials.[25] Islamic banking was re-introduced into Egypt as part of Sadat's Open Door Policy when Saudi nationals were granted banking licenses, but the institutions created, the Faisal Islamic Bank and Al Baraka, failed to take-off as they lacked indigenous roots. Secular commercial banks remain dominant in Egypt with Islamic financial institutions' share of deposits being less than 20 percent of total deposits.

In Malaysia the political climate was more favourable for Islamic finance which was viewed by the government as a means of empowering the majority Muslim population as part of the New Economic Policy.[26] Muslims wanting to travel from Malaysia to Mecca and Medina for *Hajj* had to save for the visit, as in the 1960s airfares and accommodation was relatively expensive. Savings with a secular bank would earn interest, and it was seen as dubious to use *riba* to finance *Hajj*. In 1963 a pilgrims fund was established in Kuala Lumpur, Tabung Haji, which enabled participants to save for *Hajj* while earning returns which were *Shari'ah* compliant.[27] Today Tabung Haji continues to operate as an investment company with stakes in property, plantations and other *Shari'ah* compliant financial institutions.

Elsewhere Islamic finance has involved the establishment of *Shari'ah* compliant commercial banks which are privately owned or listed on stock markets as limited liability companies. Dubai Islamic Bank was the first of this

---

24 Abdelkader Chachi, (2005), "Origin and development of commercial and Islamic banking operations", *Islamic Economics* 18.2: 3–25.

25 Ann Elizabeth Mayer, (1985), "Islamic banking and credit policies in the Sadat era: the social origins of Islamic banking in Egypt", *Arab Law Quarterly*, 1.1:32–50.

26 Ho Khai Leong, (1992), "Dynamics of policy-making in Malaysia: the formulation of the New Economic Policy and the National Development Policy", *Asian Journal of Public Administration* 14.2 204–227.

27 Abdus Samad and M. Kabir Hassan, (1999), "The performance of Malaysian Islamic bank during 1984–1997: An exploratory study", *International Journal of Islamic Financial Services* 1.3: 1–14.

kind of institution, established in 1975, followed by Kuwait Finance House in 1977 and Bahrain Islamic Bank in 1978. These aimed to provide as wide a range of services as secular banks, but in a manner which was *Shari'ah* compliant. Much of the initial finance was trade related, with the Islamic banks purchasing goods from overseas exporters and reselling them to Gulf based importers for a mark-up. As the banks were temporary owners of the good, the mark-up was justified by the ownership risk, such contracts being designated as *murabaha*, the most used method of Islamic financing.

From the 1980s salaries for government employees and major private sector companies in the Gulf were increasingly paid by bank transfers rather than cash, which necessitated employees opening bank accounts. Many opted for having their salaries paid into Islamic rather than secular banks. This new business opportunity encouraged the Islamic banks to develop their retail operations and become more involved in personal finance.[28] As there was an increasing demand for mortgages for properties, including buy to rent finance, Islamic banks were able to offer *ijara* leasing mortgages and diminishing *musharaka* partnership mortgages. The latter was and remains extremely popular with banks paying eighty or even ninety percent of the purchase price and the client paying the remainder. The client pays rent to the bank for their use of the property, and over time purchases by instalments the bank's share of the property. As with secular mortgages, the repayments period can extend to fifteen or even twenty years.

Islamic vehicle finance is similarly structured, but uses three to five year *ijara* leasing contracts. The bank purchases the vehicle on behalf of the client who then pays rent for the use of the vehicle which remains the property of the bank. If the client wishes to own the vehicle at the end of the lease period then a hire purchase agreement is possible with the client making additional monthly payments or a terminal payment. As with Islamic mortgages the banks try to keep the charges in line with those offered by secular banks.

In Saudi Arabia Islamic finance was pioneered by the Al Rajhi family from 1957, but initially they were mainly focused on remittances and foreign exchange services, both for local citizens and the many foreign workers in the Kingdom. However by the 1970s Al Rajhi started taking deposits and providing other banking services, indeed it had the largest branch network in Saudi Arabia. Hence in 1988 it was incorporated as a bank subject to supervision by the Saudi Arabia Monetary Agency which serves as the Kingdom's central bank.[29] Its assets exceed US $80 billion, making it the largest Islamic bank in the world,

---

28 Rodney Wilson, (2005), "The growth of Islamic banking and product development among Islamic retail banks", in Jaffer Sohail, (ed.), *Islamic Retail Banking and Finance: Global Challenges and Opportunities, Euromoney Books*, London, 18–28.

29 Abdulmonem Alzalabani and Reji D. Nair, (2013), "Financial recession, credit crunch and Islamic banks: a case study of Al Rajhi Bank in the Kingdom of Saudi Arabia", *East-West Journal of Economics and Business*, 1: 15–36.

with over 500 branches, including 118 dedicated ladies branches. In recent years Al Rajhi has expanded abroad with branches in Kuwait, Jordan and Malaysia.[30]

The retail Islamic banking model has proved very exportable with Dubai Islamic Bank establishing branches in Pakistan, Kuwait Finance House opening branches throughout Turkey[31] and Al Rayan of Qatar acquiring Islamic Bank of Britain. This foreign expansion was driven by both push and pull factors, the former being the limited size of Gulf markets and the saturation by Islamic financial institutions. In the case of Dubai Islamic Bank many Pakistani expatriates already used its facilities, and there were low risks in granting mortgages in Pakistan when the applicants had their salaries paid into the bank in Dubai.[32] In the case of Al Rayan there was the potential to offer second home finance to Qataris acquiring luxury apartments or houses in London.[33]

8. CHRISTIAN PERSPECTIVES ON FINANCE

The spread of explicitly Islamic financial institutions has not been replicated in Christianity but contemporary Christian debates have influenced financial thinking, not least attitudes to banking practices and what is acceptable in terms of long term asset management. The critique of financial malpractice before and during the global financial crisis has prompted much discussion amongst both the clergy and the Christian laity about whether financial institutions are serving the public good.[34] Some churches, notably the Greek Orthodox, have done much to help the victims of the financial crisis through philanthropic work and charity meals, but have avoided getting involved in political discourse on the crisis.[35] Other religious leaders, notably Justin Welby, the Archbishop of Canterbury, have been much more forceful in their critique of unrestricted capitalism and the behaviour of financiers.[36] Welby admits progress has been made since the financial crisis in promoting ethical standards in banking, but fuller recognition of social values remains a work in progress.[37]

---

30 Www.alrajhibank.com.sa/en/investor-relations/about-us/pages/about-us.aspx.

31 Https://www.kuveytturk.com.tr/en/.

32 Https://www.dibpak.com/.

33 Https://www.alrayanbank.co.uk/home-finance/home-purchase-plan/.

34 Andy Mullineux, (2014), "Banking for the public good", *International Review of Financial Analysis*, 36: 87–94.

35 Gerasimos Makris and Dimitris Bekridakis, (2013), "The Greek Orthodox Church and the economic crisis since 2009", *International Journal for the Study of the Christian Church*, 13.2: 111–132.

36 Marika Rose, (2016), "It's not the money but the love of money that is the root of all evil: social subjection, machinic enslavement and the limits of Anglican social theology", *Religions* 7.8: 103–115.

37 Justin Welby, (2014), "The future of banking standards and ethics", *Address to the House of Lords*, *http://newcityagenda.co.uk/wp-content/uploads/2014/06/Archbishop-of-Canterbury-transcript-2014.06.17-for-web.pdf.*

Encouraging established financial institutions to adhere to higher ethical standards will arguably have more social impact than opening new institutions based on specific religious values. Whether the church gets the credit for its efforts in promoting such a discourse is another matter, as the established financial institutions remain secular, indeed regardless of the religious faith of their employees, it would be unacceptable to be seen to promote any particular religion or denomination. The United Kingdom based Cooperative Bank[38] and the Netherlands based Triodos Bank[39] are examples of financial institutions that profess adherence to ethical values, with an emphasis on backing sustainable activities which are environmentally friendly and socially responsible investment that benefits employees and the wider community. Both banks are relatively small compared with major retail banks, but the emphasis on ethical values attracts customers who share their values and who care at least as much about how their savings are utilised rather than merely financial returns.

The few examples of explicitly Christian financial institutions include the Kingdom Bank[40] and Ecclesiastical Insurance[41], both based in the United Kingdom. Although the Kingdom Bank was only founded in 2005 it was preceded by the Assemblies of God charitable trust that financed the building of new Pentecostal Churches which the major banks were reluctant to fund. Congregations were encouraged to place funds with the charity so that they could in turn benefit from the charity. Incorporation as a bank enabled Kingdom to offer personal finance and compete with other retail banks. Ownership remains with the Assemblies of God Property Trust, but the bank is regulated by the Financial Conduct Authority in the same manner as secular banks. Ecclesiastical Insurance has provided insurance services for Anglican churches for one hundred and thirty years. In recent years it has widened its range of products to include home, educational and health care insurance for individuals as well as services for charities and the Church of England. Like the Kingdom Bank they are wholly owned by a charity, the Allchurches Trust, which invests in communities to change peoples' lives for the better. Profits not re-invested are donated to charity rather than paying dividends to shareholders as with secular financial institutions.

9. LEGAL AND REGULATORY ISSUES

Religious financial institutions have to operate within existing legal and regulatory frameworks and even in majority Muslim states, national law in

38 Https://www.co-operativebank.co.uk/.
39 Https://www.triodos.nl/nl/particulieren/.
40 Https://www.kingdom.bank/.
41 Https://www.ecclesiastical.com/.

practice takes precedent over *Shari'ah*. For the most part there is no conflict, as banking laws are designed to protect customers and ensure that tax payers do not have to fund expensive bail-outs of the type which arose during the global financial crisis due to regulatory failure. Islamic and Christian banks accept the need to comply with Basel III capital and liquidity requirements governing what is prudent. In Islamic banking circles there has been some debate about whether investment deposits can count as capital, but the Islamic Financial Services Board, the international standard setting body for the industry, has indicated that they should not, their treatment therefore being similar to that of savings accounts with secular banks.

Even in countries such as Iran and Malaysia which have enacted Islamic banking and finance laws the provisions are the same as for secular institutions with a few add-ons, notably the provision for *Shari'ah* governance. In countries such as Kuwait and the United Arab Emirates Islamic financial institutions operate under existing law with minor modification to allow for *Shari'ah* governance. It should be noted that the *Shari'ah* boards only deal with religious matters, with bank strategy and operations the continued responsibility of the Board of Directors, to which the *Shari'ah* board is accountable. The Kingdom Bank has no separate Christian board to ensure its operations comply with Biblical teaching, rather the Board of Directors comprises members with considerable banking and finance experience, while the chief executive has served as an Anglican Church warden and Baptist deacon.

In Europe discussion of *Shari'ah* is greeted by suspicion and indeed hostility by populist politicians. In the field of finance however it should not be viewed as a threat, but rather a business opportunity. There is no demand or need for Islamic financial laws, rather minor changes to existing laws to ensure a level playing field for Islamic finance is sufficient. In the United Kingdom provisions for alternative finance were made so that there was no double stamp duty on *murabaha* or diminishing *musharaka* as hitherto stamp duty was imposed on banks acquiring assets as well as on their sale. These minor legal amendments opened up the Islamic financial potential in the City of London, attracting new entrants without causing damage to existing financial institutions.[42]

Litigation as a result of financial disputes is usually the prerogative of national courts rather than the religious authorities or religious courts. Canon law in the Christian church does not cover disputes over terms of employment or remuneration of the clergy. Disputes between Islamic banks and their clients are dealt with by national courts rather than *Shari'ah* courts. In Malaysia there has been a considerable amount of litigation involving repayments to

42 Her Majesty's Treasury, (2008), "The development of Islamic finance in the UK: the Government's perspective", *Bank of England*, London.

Islamic financial institutions where clients are in breach of contract.[43] Islamic financial institutions adopt the same procedures to recover debts as their secular equivalents, and this is not regarded as being inappropriate. As many Islamic financing contracts are cross border agreements, provision is often made in the contracts for independent litigation in third party countries rather than the domiciles of the bank or the client. Law firms in London have dealt with this litigation, and high profile cases have been heard by the High Court and Court of Appeal, the first being the Shamil Bank of Bahrain dispute with Beximco Pharmaceuticals of Bangladesh in 2005 which set a precedent in English law.[44] This was followed by litigation in the English courts between the Islamic Investment Company of the Gulf and Symphony Gems of the Netherlands in 2008.

10. CONCLUSION

Although there are many organisations promoting Christian Muslim dialogue, there has been no discussion of interfaith approaches to financial management.[45] There are commonalities between the scope and remit of Canon Law and the management of *waqf* endowments in Islam. Each could learn from the other's experiences, especially in common jurisdictions, where they have to deal with issues such as attaining or maintaining charitable status as not-for-profit organisations. Swapping knowledge of dealing with secular legal authorities could be beneficial. Good practices in financial reporting can be discussed, particularly the desirability of having independent audits systems. Sound financial governance for religious institutions is imperative if the trust of the faithful is to be maintained, as any rumour of misbehaviour or corruption will soon be detrimental to the willingness to donate.

The remit of *Shari'ah* is much wider than Canon Law, as it governs not only Islamic institutions but every aspect of the lives of believers, including their day to day business and financial affairs. It is the contemporary interpretation of interest as *riba* which has propelled the development of Islamic banking, for which there is no Christian equivalent. It should be noted however that many devout Muslims do not agree with this interpretation, and hence in most Muslim majority countries, with the notable exception of the Islamic Republic of Iran, there has been no attempt to introduce comprehensive Islamic banking

43 Adnan Trakic, (2013), "The adjudication of *Shari'ah* issues in Islamic financial contracts: Is Malaysian Islamic finance litigation a solution?" *Humanomics* 29.4: 260–275.

44 Julio C. Colon, (2010), "Choice of law and Islamic finance", *Texas International Law Journal*, 46: 411–435.

45 Douglas Pratt, (2015), "Theology after Dialogue: Christian-Muslim Engagement Today and Tomorrow", *Islam and Christian-Muslim Relations*, 26:1, 89–101.

laws prohibiting interest based financial transactions.[46] Rather adherence to the prohibition of interest is by consent and cannot be forced. Secular banks paying interest to depositors and charging interest on lending continue to thrive in the Islamic world. This illustrates that differences within religions may be greater than differences between religions, at least in the realm of finance.

BIBLIOGRAPHY

Alzalabani, Abdulmonem and Reji D. Nair, (2013), "Financial recession, credit crunch and Islamic banks: a case study of Al Rajhi Bank in the Kingdom of Saudi Arabia", *East-West Journal of Economics and Business*, 1: 15–36.

Archer, Simon and Rifaat Ahmed Abdel Karim, (2009), "Profit-sharing investment accounts in Islamic banks: regulatory problems and possible solutions", *Journal of Banking Regulation*, 10.4: 300–306.

Chachi, Abdelkader, (2005), "Origin and development of commercial and Islamic banking operations", *Islamic Economics* 18.2: 3–25.

Colon, Julio C. (2010), "Choice of law and Islamic finance", *Texas International Law Journal*, 46: 411–435.

El-Hawary, Dahlia, Wafik Grais and Zamir Iqbal, (2007), "Diversity in the regulation of Islamic financial institutions", *The Quarterly Review of Economics and Finance*, 46:5, 778–800.

Farooq, Mohammad Omar, (2009), "Partnership, equity financing and Islamic finance: whither profit and-loss sharing?" *Review of Islamic Economics*, 11, 67–88.

Farrelly, A.G., (1989), "The Diocesan Finance Council: functions and duties according to the Code of Canon Law", *Studia Canonica*, 23:1, 149–166.

Ghazanfar, Shaikh M., (2000), "The economic thought of Abu Hamid Al-Ghazali and St. Thomas Aquinas: some comparative parallels and links", *History of Political Economy*, 32:4, 857–888.

Harlow, Anna, Frank Cranmer and Christopher Norman Doe, (2008), "Bishops in the House of Lords: a critical analysis", *Public Law*, 52:3, 490–509.

Her Majesty's Treasury, (2008), "The development of Islamic finance in the UK: the Government's perspective", *Bank of England*, London.

Kamali, Mohammad Hisham, (2005), "*Shari'ah* Issues of Islamic Leasing: Perspective of the Lessor", Unpublished paper, *International Islamic Leasing Conference*, Kuwait, 24–25.

Khan, Mohsin S., and Abbas Mirakhor, (1990), "Islamic banking: experiences in the Islamic Republic of Iran and in Pakistan", *Economic Development and Cultural Change*, 38:2, 353–375.

46 Mohsin S. Khan, and Abbas Mirakhor, (1990), "Islamic banking: experiences in the Islamic Republic of Iran and in Pakistan", *Economic Development and Cultural Change*, 38:2, 353–375.

Leong, Ho Khai, (1992), "Dynamics of policy-making in Malaysia: the formulation of the New Economic Policy and the National Development Policy", *Asian Journal of Public Administration*14.2 204–227.

Lewin, Ernst A. "The finances of the Vatican", *Journal of Contemporary History*, 18:2, 185–204.

Lightbody, Margaret, (2000) "Storing and shielding: financial management behaviour in a church organization", *Accounting, Auditing and Accountability Journal*, 13:2, 156–174.

Makris, Gerasimos and Dimitris Bekridakis, (2013), "The Greek Orthodox Church and the economic crisis since 2009", *International journal for the Study of the Christian Church*, 13.2: 111–132.

Markom, Ruzian, Sharina Ali Pitchay, Zinatul Ashiqin Zainol, Anita Abdul Rahim and Rooshida Merican, (2013), "Adjudication of Islamic banking and finance cases in the civil courts of Malaysia", *European Journal of Law and Economics*, 36:1, 1–34.

Mayer, Ann Elizabeth, (1985), "Islamic banking and credit policies in the Sadat era: the social origins of Islamic banking in Egypt", *Arab Law Quarterly*, 1.1:32–50.

Mullineux, Andy, (2014), "Banking for the public good", *International Review of Financial Analysis*, 36: 87–94.

Peri, Oded, (1992), "*Waqf* and Ottoman welfare policy: the poor kitchen of Hasseki Sultan in Eighteenth-Century Jerusalem", *Journal of the Economic and Social History of the Orient*, 35:2, 167–186.

Pioppi, Daniela, (2004) "From religious charity to the welfare state and back: the case of Islamic endowments (*waqfs*) revival in Egypt", *European University Institute*, Working Paper RSCIS 2004/3.

Pratt, Douglas, (2015), "Theology after dialogue: Christian–Muslim engagement today and tomorrow", *Islam and Christian–Muslim Relations*, 26:1, 89–101.

Raman, Azhar Abdul and Abdullah Awadh Bukair, (2013), "The influence of the *Shari'ah* supervision board on corporate social responsibility disclosure by Islamic banks of Gulf Co-Operation Council countries", *Asian Journal of Business and Accounting*, 6:2, 65–104.

Rose, Marika, (2016), "It's not the money but the love of money that is the root of all evil: social subjection, machinic enslavement and the limits of Anglican social theology", *Religions* 7.8: 103–115.

Samad, Abdus and M. Kabir Hassan, (1999), "The performance of Malaysian Islamic banks during 1984–1997: an exploratory study", *International Journal of Islamic Financial Services* 1.3: 1–14.

Sargeant, Adrian, (2005) "Church and parachurch fundraising in the United States: what can we learn?" *International Journal of Non-profit and Voluntary Sector Marketing*, 10:3, 133–136.

Solé, Juan A., (2007), "Introducing Islamic banks into conventional banking systems", *IMF Working Paper* 07/175.

Trakic, Adnan, (2013), "The adjudication of *Shari'ah* issues in Islamic financial contracts: Is Malaysian Islamic finance litigation a solution?" *Humanomics* 29.4: 260–275

Waeibrorheem, Waemustafa, and Abdullah, Azrul, (2015) "Mode of Islamic bank financing: does the effectiveness of *Shari'ah* Supervisory Board matter?" *Australian Journal of Basic and Applied Science*, 9:37, 458–462.

Waemustafa, Waeibrorheem and Suriani Sukri, (2015), "Bank specific and macroeconomics dynamic determinants of credit risk in Islamic banks and conventional banks", *International Journal of Economics and Financial Issues*, 5:2, 476–481.

Welby, Justin, (2014), "The future of banking standards and ethics", Address to the House of Lords, http://newcityagenda.co.uk/wp-content/uploads/2014/06/Archbishop-of-Canterbury-transcript-2014.06.17-for-web.pdf

Wilson, Rodney, (2005), "The growth of Islamic banking and product development among Islamic retail banks", in Jaffer Sohail, (ed.), *Islamic Retail Banking and Finance: Global Challenges and Opportunities, Euromoney Books*, London, 18–28.

WEB REFERENCES (ALL ACCESSED 2–4TH JANUARY 2018)

http://iceurope.org/
www.alrajhibank.com.sa/en/investor-relations/about-us/pages/about-us.aspx
www.mcb.org.uk/
www.robecosam.com/
https://www.alrayanbank.co.uk/home-finance/home-purchase-plan/
https://www.co-operativebank.co.uk/
https://www.dibpak.com/
https://www.ecclesiastical.com/
https://www.kingdom.bank/
https://www.kuveytturk.com.tr/en/
https://www.triodos.nl/nl/particulieren/

RELIGIOUS AND ETHICAL FINANCE IN A GLOBALISED WORLD – CONTEMPORARY DEVELOPMENTS AND LEGAL ASSESSMENTS

Mathias ROHE
Director Erlangen Centre for Islam and Law in Europe

1. INTRODUCTION

Which role can religious or ethical norms play in the field of legally structured economics? To which extent are the applicable laws driven by religious or ethical principles? In the past, religious provisions enforced by legal means in particular had considerable impact on economies in several parts of the world. Transactions based on interest were prohibited in Judaism, Christianity and Islam alike regarding fellow believers.[1] For example, the Bishop of Milan Ambrosius (339–397) equated taking interest and theft.[2] The same goes for the prohibition of possessing or dealing with goods which were not recognised to be merchantable from a religious point of view, e.g. alcohol or pork. Insofar, laws regulating finance had a strong religious or ethical flavour in the past.[3]

---

1 For Christianity (based on Luke 6:35) cf. the short summary in Hans Peter Schwintowski, Legitimation und Überwindung des kanonischen Zinsverbots, in Norbert Brieskorn et al. (ed.), *Vom mittelalterlichen Recht zur neuzeitlichen Rechtswissenschaft*, Ferdinand Schöningh, Paderborn et al. 1994, pp. 261ff.; for Islam (based on Qur'ān 2, 275 et al.) cf. Christian Wichard, *Zwischen Markt und Moschee*, Ferdinand Schöningh, Paderborn et al. 1995, pp. 182ff.; cf. also Abū L-Walīd Muḥammad ibn Aḥmad ibn Rushd, *Al-Muqaddimat al-mumahhida*, vol. 2, Cairo 1325/1907, p. 178f., with references for the opinion according to which the prohibition of interest would not be valid in relations with non-Muslims.

2 S. Ambrosii *De Bono Mortis* 12.56 "si quis usuram accipit, rapinam facit, vita non vivit"; ("if anyone accepts usury, or commits theft, life does not live in him") translated by William Theodore Wiesner William, The Catholic University of America Press, Washington, D.C. 1970, p. 151, available at https://books.google.de/books?id=QjjlAAAAMAAJ&printsec=frontcover&hl=de&source=gbs_ge_summary_r&cad=0#v=onepage&q&f=false (last accessed 19.06.2018).

3 For an outline of ethical aspects in legal contractual relations cf. Howard Kahane, *Contract Ethics: Evolutionary Biology and the Moral Sentiments*, Rowman & Littlefield, Boston/London 1995; for the links between Christianity and the law cf. e.g. Gerhard Dilcher and Ilse Staff (eds.), *Christentum und modernes Recht*, Suhrkamp, Frankfurt a.M. 1984; regarding Islam cf.

At the same time, we know that strong restrictions on transactions which were considered to be economically favourable, if not necessary, almost certainly led to strategies of circumvention: the prohibition of interest was bypassed by agreements on instalment payments, which were summing up to an amount practically including interest.[4] In Islam, the instrument of such at least in part legally accepted strategies – in the Ḥanafī school of law in particular – was called "*ḥiyal*".[5] In addition, strict prohibitions of interest simply caused high interest rates in practice, since in case of conflict the claims of the lender were not enforceable by official means. On the basis of records from seventeenth-century Kayseri in Anatolia, Ronald Jennings[6] has shown that annual interest of 20% was common practice even for legal and administrative bodies in the regular course of business.

The secularisation of many legal orders since the 19th century has certainly diminished the immediate influence of religion on the respective law of the countries. Nevertheless, the religio-ethical flavour is still remarkable in basic legal principles such as "good morals" or "good faith". In addition, within the sphere of default contract and investment law rules, ethical reflections have regained ground especially in Western societies since the 1970s, e.g. with respect to "fair trade" or ecological sustainability. In many Islamic countries, phenomena of formally re-Islamising the economy have increased after the decline of secular regimes and ideologies particularly in the Arabic-Islamic world and the rise of Saudi-Arabian Wahhabism.

In the following, we will first briefly describe the main legal aspects of Islamic provisions regarding finance. We will then discuss the legal levels on which religious or ethical norms may apply. The application of Islamic norms in Germany and Europe will be in the focus of this discussion.

2. RELIGIOUS ECONOMY AND FINANCE AND THE LAW: THE EXAMPLE OF ISLAM

Islamic contract and commercial law evolved in an environment that was comparatively advanced. Sura 4:29 contains the central basis: 'O believers, consume not your goods between you in an unlawful fashion, unless you are

---

e.g. Mathias Rohe, *Islamic Law in Past and Present*, Brill, Leiden/Boston 2015, pp. 133–135 with further references.

4 For the involvement of the Order of the Knights Templar in such transactions with the Christian nobility in Western Europe cf. Nachum T. Gidal, *Die Juden in Deutschland von der Römerzeit bis zur Weimarer Republik*, Könemann Verlag, Köln 1997, p. 40.

5 Cf. Ahmad Alkhamees, *A Critique of Creative Sharīʿah Compliance in the Islamic Finance Industry*, Brill, Leiden/Boston 2017, pp. 37–66 in particular. For examples cf. Mathias Rohe, *op.cit.*, pp. 142–149.

6 Ronald C. Jennings, *Studies on Ottoman Social History in the Sixteenth and Seventeenth centuries*, Isis press, Istanbul 1999, pp. 201, 213ff.

trading, [agreeing together].'[7] All of this, however, must not take place in an unlawful fashion; as a consequence, it becomes necessary to supervise economic transactions. If the supervision grows too strict, people – in the Islamic world as well – will start looking for ways of evading its constraints wherever possible.

The first issue to be tackled is the prohibition *ribā*, which is often translated as 'usury' or 'interest'. The Quran[8] sets out the opposition of permitted trade and prohibited *ribā*. What exactly it refers to is not defined, and consequently open to interpretation.[9] The classical doctrine leads to results which exclude not only any discrepancy between the service and the consideration (quid pro quo), but effectively every kind of interest[10] including the so-called *ribā al-nasī'a* (interest-bearing credit).[11] In consequence, legal stratagems were developed to functionally achieve the result of interest payments while making use of accepted forms of transactions (*ḥiyal*, sg. *ḥīla*). Such stratagems are recognised by the Hanafite school in particular.[12] At present, major sections of 'Islamic Banking' – which formally does not allow interest – rest on these: instead of interest, 'fees' (*ḍarā'ib*) are raised, which have the same economic effect. Purists, of course, do not approve of this procedure. This may be why some mock Islamic Banking as 'Islamic whisky'.

On the other hand, since the twentieth century, many Islamic countries have enacted regulations which diverge from the classical doctrine. In the UAE, commercial transactions are distinguished from private credit agreements: while in the latter case interest on credit is prohibited, the commercial code of 1993 stipulates a legal interest rate of 12% for the former, which may even be exceeded for default interest.[13]

---

7 When Rudi Paret (*Der Koran, Übersetzung*, W., Kohlhammer, 10 ed. Stuttgart 2007) translates the term *bi-l-bāṭil* as 'in a deceitful way' or 'with intent to defraud', this is too narrow. The author agrees with Johannes Wichard's (*op.cit.*, p. 89, n. 1) criticism; *bāṭil* is what is void, contravenes the law, and indeed has a place in legal terminology according to this meaning.

8 Suras 2:275f., 278, 280; 3:130; 4:160f.; 30:39; cf. in detail Johannes Wichard, *op.cit.*, pp. 182ff.

9 Cf. M. Muslehuddin, *Islamic Jurisprudence and the Rule of Necessity and Need*, IND, New Delhi 1982, pp. 40f. with further references.

10 Cf. e.g. Johannes Wichard, *op.cit.*, pp. 190ff.; Florian Amereller, *Hintergründe des "Islamic Banking"*, Duncker&Humblot, Berlin 1995, pp. 133ff.; Rüdiger Lohlker, *Das islamische Recht im Wandel*, Waxmann, Münster et al. 1999; N. A. Saleh, *Unlawful Gain and Legitimate Profit in Islamic Law*, Graham & Trotman, 2 ed. London et al. 1992, pp. 39ff., all containing numerous references.

11 Regarding the variety of definitions and the classification in groups cf. only Wizārat Al-Awqāf Wa L-Shu''n Al-Islāmiyya Kuwayt, al-mawsū'a al-fiqhiyya, vol. 22, Kuwayt pp. 50, 53 and ff.; Johannes Wichard, *op.cit.*, pp. 189ff. with further references.

12 Cf. Muḥammad ibn Al-Ḥasan Al-Shaybānī, *Kitāb al-makhārij fī l-ḥiyal*, ed. by Joseph Schacht, Leipzig 1930; Abū Bakr Aḥmad ibn 'Umar Al-Shaybānī, *Kitāb al-ḥiyal wa-l-makhārij*, ed. by Joseph Schacht, reprint of the 1923 Hanover edition, Olms, Hildesheim 1968.

13 Cf. Hilmar Krüger, Vermögensrechtliches Privatrecht und Shari'a am Beispiel der Vereinigten Arabischen Emirate, *ZVglRWiss* 97 (1998), pp. 360–386 (382).

The Egyptian civil code contains provisions on interest (art. 226 Civil Code: statutory interest rate in case of delayed payment 4%, in commercial transactions 5%).[14] The then mufti of Egypt al-Ṭanṭāwī followed a similar line of reasoning in an expert legal opinion he composed in 1989, according to which interest-bearing government bonds are not contrary to the prohibition of *ribā*. However, there was some vehement protest against al-Ṭanṭāwī's opinion.[15] According to a press report from 1994, an Egyptian Islamist terrorist organisation called all customers of banks to cancel their interest-bearing accounts because of Islam's prohibition of any interest.[16]

Besides the broadly interpreted prohibition of *ribā*, contractual freedom of scope is limited in classical Islamic law by the prohibition of speculative/high-risk transactions[17] (*gharar*). Instances of this are found, e.g., in sura 2:219; 5:90f.; 4:29, as well as in the sunna.[18] In places, the argumentation coincides with the prohibition of *ribā*, e.g. regarding the restriction of exchange transactions of raw and processed fruit.[19] As a general rule, contractual services must be sufficiently defined and performable.[20] This is another area in which an extensive casuistry has developed. On the other hand, there is fundamental agreement on the permissibility of hedging transactions such as surety or guarantee[21], even though, in these cases, it is impossible that all circumstances could be known at the time of the conclusion of the contract. This is especially true of the decisive aspect of whether there is a risk of default. The extent of the prohibition of *gharar* becomes significant especially with regard to modern forms of commercial transactions.

According to the broad classical interpretation, the prohibition of *gharar* prevents types of contract which do not specify the services to be performed. This affects a multitude of banking transactions (futures transactions etc.) as well as complex contracts with the performance not specified in detail, which are also customary in international trade and commerce (franchise agreements,

---

14 Cf. Omaia Elwan, Der Scheck im ägyptischen Recht, in Ulrich Huber and Erik Jayme (eds.), *Festschrift für R. Serick*, Recht und Wirtschaft, Heidelberg 1992, pp. 82f. with further references; Holger Jung, Ägyptisches internationales Vertragsrecht, in Herbert Kronke, Gert Reinhart and Nika Witteborg (eds.), *Islamisches und arabisches Recht als Problem der Rechtsanwendung*, Peter Lang, Frankfurt a.M. et al. 2001, pp. 58f. with further references.

15 Cf. Jakob Skøvgaard-Petersen, *Defining Islam for the Egyptian State. Muftis and Fatwas of the Dar al-Ifta*, Brill, Leiden/Boston 1997, pp. 295ff.

16 Cf. 'Neue Drohung ägyptischer Fundamentalisten', Frankfurter Allgemeine Zeitung, 22.02.1994, p. 6. In order to emphasise its demands, the 'Jamaʿa Islamiya' planted bombs outside banks.

17 Cf. e.g. Christian Wichard, *op.cit.*, pp. 148ff. with further references.

18 Mālik ibn Anas, Al-muwaṭṭaʾ, ed. by Muḥammad Fu'ād Abd al-Bāqī, vol. 2, dār iḥyāʾ al-kutub al-arabiyya, no place or date, p. 664, no. 75.

19 Thus Mālik ibn Anas, *op.cit.*, vol. 2, pp. 665f., who discusses this issue in connection with the prohibition of *gharar*.

20 Cf. the summarising remarks in Christian Wichard, *op.cit.*, p. 148f.

21 *Op.cit.*, p. 162f. with further references.

contracts concerning major construction projects etc.). Multiple-stage marketing of goods and services can also be restricted, as selling an item before one has taken possession of it is considered to be inadmissible as a rule. Under a strict interpretation, doubts are also cast on insurance contracts.[22] Genuine factoring is also regarded as inadmissible.[23]

There are modern attempts at reinterpretation by means of *ijtihād* in this area as well.[24] In accordance with them, the prohibition of *gharar* is limited to contractual relationships within which the uncertainty regarding a service or performance is comparable to a gamble due to its aleatory character. Investment or risk protection transactions taking into account the fair value of capital or the economic background of risk spreading would not fall under this category. Under Kuwaiti law, for instance[25], futures trading is permissible. In the UAE, there is remarkable divergence between the legislation of the more traditionally inclined Abu Dhabi (negative) and the economically prospering and more open Dubai (positive).[26] This demonstrates the variety of interpretations which, more or less, take into account the given circumstances of the contemporary world economy.

In addition, some goods are declared not to be merchantable, or at least dealing with them is considered to be sinful. Items forbidden for religious reasons are alcohol and pork, as well as games of chance.[27] Trading in tobacco or arms is rejected, as is investment in prostitution or other 'impure' actions and items such as, e.g., pornographic films. The investment principles of Islamic investment funds often rule out such participation explicitly.

Sometimes subtle questions have to be resolved, such as whether it is permissible to invest in real estate which is then rented to companies which sell alcohol products.[28] Under the new rules of the board of the Dow Jones Islamic Index, for instance, it is prohibited to hold shares in corporations which are in debt to the amount of more than 33% of their own capital resources, which draw more than 5% of their profits from non-operating interest revenue or whose receivables amount to more than 45% of their own capital resources.[29] There is a wide spectrum of opinions when it comes to details. Consequently, attempts

22 Cf. Kilian Bälz, *Versicherungsvertragsrecht in den arabischen Ländern*, VVW, Karlsruhe 1997, pp. 9ff., 20ff. in particular.

23 Cf. Gerhard Wegen/Christian Wichard, Islamische Bankgeschäfte, *R.I.W.* 41 (1995), p. 829.

24 Cf. only the remarks on the subject in Abdullah M. Binladin, Negotiability of Financial Instruments in Contemporary Financial Markets: An Islamic Legal Analysis, Diss. (Harvard University), Cambridge/Mass 2000, pp. 289ff. and passim.

25 Cf. 'Kuwait Introduces Futures Trading', Al Sharif Advocates & Legal Consultants, Legal Bulletin 3/1998 (Dubai), p. 8.

26 References in Hilmar Krüger, *op.cit.*, pp. 383ff.

27 Cf. 'Islamischer Aktienfonds in Deutschland', Freitagsblatt 2/2 February 2003, 13; Angelo Venardos, *Islamic Banking and Finance in Southeast Asia*, World Scientific, New Jersey et al. 2005, p. 70 with further references.

28 Cf. 'Muslimische Anleger in der City bleiben gelassen', Frankfurter Allgemeine Zeitung, 22.07.2005, p. 21.

29 Cf. Angelo Venardos, *op.cit.*, pp. 70f.

are being made to establish generally binding standards[30] in order to guarantee sufficient legal security. One such attempt may be seen, for instance, in the Sharia Standard of the Accounting Organisation for Islamic Financial Institutions (AAOIFI) based in Bahrain.[31]

3. ISLAMIC FINANCE IN EUROPE: RELEVANT LEGAL LEVELS

3.1. PRIVATE INTERNATIONAL LAW (PIL)

Islamic private commercial law may apply in Europe as long as the statutes of Private International Law (PIL) make this possible. Regarding cross-border transactions, European countries grant freedom of choice in this area ('party autonomy'; for the EU cf. art. 3 Rome I Regulation[32]). In commercial relations with certain Islamic countries, the law governing the contract is frequently inspired by Islamic law. On the other hand, Islamic conflict of laws governing contracts may limit the choice of legal system. The Islamic *ordre public* (public policy) – in some countries – objects to agreements or regulations which include interest.[33] In the case of international contracts, Western contractual partners frequently attempt to rule out the applicability of Islamic contractual law, or, at the very least, to assign conflict solution to 'neutral' institutions such as arbitration courts outside the Islamic world. However, some Muslim partners have found these not to be universally reliable in the past. This is one reason why countries such as Saudi Arabia insist as a rule that Saudi institutions be appointed to resolve conflicts.[34]

Nevertheless, in many cases, European jurisdiction is given on such transactions. As long as (e.g. Iranian, Saudi, Pakistani etc.) state law is concerned, its provisions can be applied under the rules of PIL within the limits of public policy (cf. art. 21 Rome I Regulation). In general, the specific norms regarding Islamic finance do not contradict European laws, thus conflicts are rare in this field.[35] But what about choice of law-clauses referring to "Sharia" or

30 For the difficulties of establishing such standards and some suggestions cf. Aminath Amany Ahmed, Azhar Mohamad and Aghilasse Kashi, Does an Islamic Finance Industry Need a Unification of Standards? A Qualitative Discussion, Arab Law Quarterly 31 (2017), pp. 336–362.

31 See Kilian Bälz, Das islamische Recht als Vertragsstatut?, IPrax 25 (2005), p. 46. Further information may be found at www.aaoifi.com.

32 Regulation (EC) No 593/2008 of the European Parliament and the Council of 17 June 2008 on the law applicable to contractual obligations (Rome I), text available at https://eur-lex.europa.eu/LexUriServ/LexUriServ.do?uri=OJ:L:2008:177:0006:0016:en:PDF (last accessed 19.06.2018).

33 Regarding present-day Egypt see Holger Jung, *Ägyptisches internationales Vertragsrecht*, Mohr (Siebeck), Tübingen 1999, pp. 98ff. For a limited application under European conflict of laws rules cf. Kilian Bälz, *Zinsbeschränkungen*, pp. 277ff.

34 Cf. Hilmar Krüger, *op cit*, pp. 485, 499ff.

35 Cf. Mathias Rohe, Europäisches Kollisionsrecht und religiöses Recht, in: Stefan Arnold (ed.), *Grundfragen des Europäischen Kollisionsrechts*, Mohr (Siebeck), Tübingen 2016, pp. 67–86.

"Islamic law" instead of a particular state law? Here, we have to distinguish with respect to the institutions to be involved in conflict resolution. In arbitral institutions, such clauses may well be accepted[36], given the fact that even the "ars aequi et boni" (the art of deciding in a just and appropriate manner) might be chosen by the litigants as a basis for decision-making.

Regarding conflict resolution by state courts, however, the prevailing opinion in European courts and among scholars[37] holds that only a particular national law may be selected, not 'the Sharia' per se, since it is too unspecific and contains a broad variety of possibly conflicting positions, which renders decision-making extremely difficult if not impossible. The same goes for "Jewish law" according to English courts.[38] Nonetheless, such invalid choice on the PIL level might have an impact on the interpretation of contractual terms, e.g. if there are clear indications that the parties intended to avoid interest payments by this choice of law. In any case, when formulating cross-border contracts, it is highly advisable to include precise provisions regarding such aspects. A possible tool to achieve the result of interest payments by resorting to functionally comparable and religiously acceptable solutions would be the agreement on paying fixed additional instalments. This is also used now for internal needs in the UK, where the government has developed plans to offer study loans avoiding interest payment clauses. Instead, the students will have to pay back fixed amounts to a fund for further finance of such loans.[39] This demonstrates the importance of Islamic finance beyond the sphere of international transactions in Europe: Islam and Islamic ethics have become a part of European societal life.

3.2. DEFAULT RULES OF SUBSTANTIVE LAW

An increasingly relevant level of (indirect) application of Islamic norms is in the area of the default rules (as opposed to mandatory rules) of substantive law.[40]

---

36 Cf. Jens Adolphsen and Franziska Schmalenberg, Islamisches Recht als materielles Recht in der Schiedsgerichtsbarkeit?, SchiedsVZ 5 (2007), pp. 57–64; Walid Ben Hamida, La finance islamique devant le juge étatique: étude comparée, *R.I.D.C.* 4/2015, pp. 923–940 (939f.).

37 Concerning how to handle a contract intending to implement the 'principles of the Glorious Shari'a' cf. the decisions in Shamil Bank of Bahrain vs. Beximco Pharmaceuticals and Others (Judgment of the High Court of Justice 2002 Folio 1172, QBD Commercial Court; Court of Appeal (Civil Division) [2004] EWCA Civ 19); cf. also Kilian Bälz, Das islamische Recht als Vertragsstatut?, *IPRax* 25 (2005), pp. 44ff.; Walid Ben Hamida, La finance islamique devant le juge étatique: étude comparée, *R.I.D.C.* 4/2015, pp. 923ff.

38 Halpern v. Halpern: zur Anwendbarkeit nicht-staatlichen Rechts und "Rom I" in England, C.A. [2007] 3 All ER 478 regarding an inheritance case. Cf. also Maren Heidemann, ZEuP 16 (2008), 618–632.

39 Cf. the report "Shariah law compliance gets green light from UK government with new halal student loan" from 17.05.2016, available at https://www.express.co.uk/news/uk/671092/Sharia-law-student-loan-UK-Government (last accessed 20.06.2018).

40 For different approaches in Europe in this field cf. Andrea Büchler, *Islamic Law in Europe?* Ashgatex, Farnham 2011, pp. 57ff.

To the extent that the system of private law allows freedom of scope, private preferences could play a part in shaping the law. Those who wish to avoid interest-bearing and speculative transactions will have ample freedom to conclude finance contracts meeting such requirements.

The financial sector has taken into account the needs of Muslims with a traditional outlook, on a relatively broad basis in the UK with its very tradition-oriented Muslim population, but, so far, on a relatively low level in Germany.[41] European banks distribute 'Islamic' equity fund shares for financial investments which rule out any involvement with companies dealing in games of chance, alcohol, tobacco, interest-bearing loans or illicit sex.[42] The Kuveyt Türk Beteiligungsbank (investment bank) in Frankfurt obtained a full banking license in 2015.[43] Stock exchange values are being listed, e.g., in the Dow Jones Islamic Market Indexes[44] or in the FTSE Global Islamic Index.

If these investments take place with religious authorities involved, some points of regulatory law[45] must be clarified, such as the documented definition of the investment principles, the lawful cooperation with Islamic expert panels, or the limits of applications by appealing to 'good Muslims'. The customary, if not entirely unproblematic at the regulatory level, determining or monitoring of company policy by sharia boards is likely to be unavoidable if the necessary trust of the religious clients is to be retained. It is the only way in which the desired 'exonerating effect', i.e. safeguarding activity according to religious norms in a subjectively satisfying fashion, can be achieved. The advantages of domestic providers subject to regulatory laws are obvious, as the author is aware

---

41 Cf. the instructive report by Azadeh Faroush and Michael Mahlknecht, A critical view on Islamic Finance in Germany, in Valentino Cattelan (ed.), *Islamic Finance in Europe: Towards a Plural Financial System*, Elgar, Cheltenham 2013, pp. 203ff.; for the challenges of the existing legal framework and the market conditions in Germany cf. the collective volume edited by Abdurrahim Kozali, Ibrahim Salama and Souheil Thabti, *Das islamische Wirtschaftsrecht*, Peter Lang, Frankfurt a.M. 2016. For other European countries cf. the other reports in Valentino Cattelan (ed.), *op.cit.*, 143ff.

42 Cf. 'Islamischer Aktienfonds in Deutschland', Freitagsblatt 2/2 Feb. 2000, 13; regarding legal issues cf. Kilian Bälz, Islamic Investment Funds in Germany, Akhbar – Newsletter of the Arab Regional Forum of the International Bar Association on Business Law, vol. 7 no. 2 (2000); ID., Islamische Aktienfonds in Deutschland?, BKR 2 (2002), pp. 449ff.

43 Cf. Mathias Rohe, Islamic Banking und Finance in Europa – ein Testfall für europäische Privatautonomie und ihre Grenzen, in: Cordula Stumpf, Friedemann Kainer and Christian Baldus (eds.), *Festschrift für Peter-Christian Müller-Graff zum 70. Geburtstag*, Nomos, Baden-Baden 2015, pp. 784–790; cf. also Peter Becker, Islamic Banking and Finance – (zukünftige) Herausforderung der notariellen Praxis, RNotZ 14 (2014) pp. 22–34 and following regarding the challenges for the practice of notaries involved.

44 For details cf. the information available at https://us.spindices.com/index-family/shariah/dow-jones-islamic-market (last accessed 26.06.2018).

45 For the European scene cf. Ahmed Belouafi and Abderrazak Belabes, Islamic Finance and the Regulatory Challenge: The European case, in Jonathan Langton, Christina Trullols and Abdullah Q. Turkistani (eds.), *Islamic Economics and Finance: A European Perspective*, Palgrave Macmillan, Basingstoke 2011, pp. 149ff.

of numerous Muslims in Europe having lost considerable sums with suspicious providers, e.g., from Turkey.[46] Even the state of Saxony-Anhalt has launched an Islamic bond (*sukuk*[47], 100 million euro to begin with), issued by a Dutch holding company.[48]

In addition, financing the purchase of real estate might be based on the traditional Islamic instrument of the *murābaḥa* (a chain of sales contracts disclosing the amount of profit of the respective contract partner). The client is at the same time the owner of the item 'financed', but also has to bear its obligations (including possible insurance); on the other hand the 'funder' receives real securities that are easily recoverable, and claims with comparatively small risks attached. Disadvantages may be due to a higher tax rate, and also to a lack of flexibility with regard to the fluctuating cost of refunding or the desire to terminate contracts ahead of term. Regarding taxes, the legislation in the UK has facilitated the practical implementation of traditional models of acquisition avoiding interest, which are compatible with Islamic law. New rules have been implemented to levy the stamp duty only once in cases of 'Islamic mortgage'.[49] HSBC Amanah offers such Islamic mortgages, other banks have followed suit.

The same transaction can also be used for the purchase of goods. The bank providing the funds takes on the function of interim purchaser of the goods, with its profit margin formally resulting from a – permitted – sales transaction and not from a – prohibited – interest-bearing credit. By means of skillful contract design, the risks arising from the position – never desired by the bank – as purchaser or seller can be minimised in such a way that in actual fact a funded transaction results. This result may be achieved, for instance, by the bank as the first purchaser shifting the risk of non-delivery by the seller onto the ultimate purchaser.[50] If the amount of the agreed profit margin or the agreed lump-sum

---

46 Cf. reports of suspicious investments by such organisations in Turkey in 'Neuer Markt auf Türkisch' (Michael Fröhlingsdorf), Spiegel Online, 29.01.2004 (available at at http://magazin.spiegel.de/EpubDelivery/spiegel/pdf/29787309, last accessed 19.06.2018).

47 Based on a combination of leasing contracts which relate to the state's real estate property. Muslims emphasise that this kind of loan is much more advantageous to future generations than simple credits which have to be paid back, as it is limited by the value of the real estate which will be passed on to future generations; cf. 'Finanzmarkt: Islam-Anleihe aus Magdeburg', Die Bank, 01.01.2004.

48 Cf. 'Sachsen-Anhalt bereitet erste islamische Anleihe vor', Frankfurter Allgemeine Zeitung, 06.11.2003, p. 31; 'Anlegen mit Allahs Segen', Handelsblatt, 14.07.2004, p. 29. Cf. also the thorough study by Osman Sacarcelik, *Rechtsfragen islamischer Zertifikate*, Nomos; Baden-Baden 2013.

49 Cf. 'Chancellor abolishes double stamp duty', Muslim News, 25 Apr. 2003, 4; Iqbal Azaria, Islamic home finance arrives on UK's high streets, Muslim News 25 July 2003 (no. 171), 6. Regarding the situation in the USA cf. Bill Maurer, *Pious property. Islamic Mortgages in the United States*, Russell Sage Foundation, New York 2006.

50 Concerning a relevant case decided by the English High Court on 13 Feb. 2002 (applying English law as chosen by the parties involved) cf. Kilian Bälz, Islamische Bankgeschäfte (*op. cit.*); ID., Das islamische Recht als Vertragsstatut? (*op.cit.*), 44.

compensation for delay are calculated with reference to interest rates such as LIBOR, the resulting transactions are even more similar to credit transactions.[51]

The *murābaḥa* was also able to establish itself as a type of export funding, with the export goods sold to the bank as an intermediary who then sells it on to the (Muslim) importer with an additional charge. The fact that this is a credit transaction is illustrated by the purchase price given in the first contract being payable instantly, while that given in the second contract – including the additional charge – is deferred until receipt of the goods or later.[52] Negative consequences arising from the prohibition of selling items before one has taken possession of them may be minimised by interposing only one 'virtual second' between the two 'purchase contracts' (i.e. defining the duration of the contracts in such a way that the second one comes into force only one second after the first one expires). Thus, the importer is hardly able to reject the goods; furthermore, he may be subject to a corresponding fine. Overall this construction is very close to the letter of credit.

The forms of so-called *ijāra*, which is similar to leasing, with or without the option to purchase, have the advantage – compared to the *murābaḥa* as well – that payment can be adapted according to the amount and the payment term; as the 'funder' has to be the owner, he can use the item for asset-backed securities when refinancing. Disadvantages are that clients are less than fond of the funder's position as the owner and of his resultant obligations which cannot always be covered by insurance. The more recent type of the diminishing *mushāraka* – a corporate partnership depending on the progress of repayment – avoids the abovementioned disadvantages and offers shared property with flexible payments.[53] The purchaser would rent the bank's share until the final repayment. Legal problems may arise with respect to the wording of the purpose of the partnership ('financing' or 'possessing' the item), the possible need for formal requirements in the partnership agreement under sec. 311b German Civil Code, the application of the provisions on consumer credits (e.g. regarding termination of the contract, sec. 499 German Civil Code), and the possible liability of the bank. In addition, the double tax rate remains.

Islamic understanding can also be significant when applying laws, especially when interpreting contractual relationships. The author's own experience as a judge at the Court of Appeals of Nuremberg yields the example that the prohibition to take interest may define transactions among Muslims. Thus it would be possible for this kind of understanding to conclude that a sum of money given to a contract partner on an oral agreement basis without specifying any details should be regarded as a silent partnership rather than a loan. The

51 As rightly pointed out by Kilian Bälz, ibid.
52 See Kilian Bälz, Das internationale Vertragsrecht der islamischen Banken, *WM* 53 (1999), 2444f.
53 Cf. Peter Becker, *op.cit.*, pp. 22, 28ff.

result would be that, in case of business failure, the money is lost due to the shared risk between the contract partners.

A specific issue of international finance inspired by Islamic rules is the establishment of so-called *Ḥawāla* banks. The *ḥawāla*[54] is a form of remittance similar to a bill of exchange.[55] It is a basic model of cashless transactions[56] and was exported with great success to Europe in the Medieval and Early Modern periods. Using such cashless forms of transactions is permitted under European laws in general. The economic justification seems to be, on the one hand, the desire to transfer money abroad quickly and cheaply – with a fee of only 1–2% of the transaction amount.[57] In view of the very high fees still customary among commercial banks, this is entirely understandable. Furthermore, employing such mechanisms becomes almost unavoidable when it comes to transfers to countries without a functioning banking sector. In some Asian countries, cashless transactions are possible only in this way. It is also possible to avoid restrictive regulations of currency imports.[58] IMF experts conclude that in 15 selected states (among them Iran, Pakistan, Bangladesh, Algeria, India and Turkey) $760,000 million have flowed through these channels over the past 20 years.[59]

Legal difficulties arise if these transaction types take place in an institutionalised fashion and go through bank-like organisations. If these *ḥawāla* banks are used to launder dirty money[60] or maintain the infrastructure of terrorist organisations, the dangers are obvious. It is for this reason that the Islamic world is taking initiatives for improved monitoring, such as the obligation to register with the central bank in the UAE.[61]

Due to the dangers attendant on these transfers, in 1998, the German legislative authority included the money transfer transaction in sec. 1 para. 1a p. 2 no. 6 German Banking Act (KWG) in the list of financial services subject to prior approval; penalties for breaches are found in sec. 54 para. 1 no. 2 German Banking Act (statutory offence) and in sec. 37, 50 German banking Act (if need be, suspension of business activity). According to information provided by the

---

54 On research into legal facts cf. Michael H. Thung, Written Obligations from the 2nd/8th to the 4th/10th Century, *ILAS* 3 (1996), pp. 1, 4ff.; cf. also Abdalaziz Duri, *Arabische Wirtschaftsgeschichte*, Artemis, Zürich 1979, p. 89 with further references.

55 Cf. e.g. Abū Bakr Muḥammad ibn Aḥmad Al-Sarakhsī, Kitāb al-mabsūṭ, vol. 20, Dār al-maʿrifa; Beirut 1406/1986, pp. 52ff.; Christian Wichard, *op.cit.*, pp. 177f., 247 with further references.

56 Cf. Abdalaziz Duri, *op.cit.*, pp. 89 and n. 77, 179.

57 Profits are probably made mainly from differences between currency rates, cf. Michael Findeisen, 'Underground Banking' in Deutschland, *WM* 54 (2000), p. 2127.

58 Cf. 'Hawala-System verliert an Gewicht', Frankfurter Allgemeine Zeitung, 12.06.2002, p. 27.

59 Ulrich Schneckener, Strukturen des islamistischen Terrorismus: Das Netzwerk 'Al-Qaʿida', in Berlin, Senatsabteilung für Inneres (ed.), *Islamismus. Diskussion eines vielschichtigen Phänomens*, Berlin 2005, pp. 33, 41.

60 Cf. *op.cit.*, pp. 2129f.

61 Cf. 'Hawala-System verliert an Gewicht', Frankfurter Allgemeine Zeitung, 12.06.2002, p. 27.

regulatory authority Bundesanstalt für Finanzwesen (BaFin), ca 350 companies have reported such activity. Breaches of the duty to keep records called for by commercial and tax law have also been mentioned.[62]

In sum, there is ample space for financial transactions meeting the traditional understanding of Islamic economic law and religious commands. Of course, such transactions have to meet the mandatory rules governing all sorts of transactions. Thus, consumer protection laws have to be considered. Some new sorts of questions may arise here: What about liability for non-Shari'ah-compliance of a product? Regarding investment regulations, a clear description of strategies and warning from low performance is required. The law of associations demands to avoid external leadership, which would distort the relevant liability regulations. Thus, the right of last decision must not be assigned to external Shari'ah boards.[63] Islamic charities would equally fall under the relatively strict state control regarding the use of the charities' capital. Furthermore, competition law would restrict aggressive advertisement on the basis of undue religious or ethical pressure.

4. STRATEGIES: WHAT RENDERS FINANCE ISLAMIC?

Regarding Muslims in Europe who care about religion in financial issues, two different strategies of defining transactions to be compatible with Islam are to be discerned. Some would simply stick to the wording of Islamic legal or religious provisions and their traditional interpretation. In this context, we must refer to the developing culture of expert opinions, which deals with matters of economy among other things. Especially Muslims with an Arab background are active in this field, but also a number of European converts to Islam. Traditionally, devout Muslims are concerned even outside the borders of the Islamic world with arranging their everyday activities in a fashion compatible with their faith, and consequently feel themselves bound by the rules prohibiting *ribā* and *gharar*. There are individuals who resolve such issues as well as, more recently, institutions such as the European Council for Fatwa and Research which was founded in 1997.[64]

As regards interest-bearing transactions, we generally find a very strict position which does not refer to modern considerations of credit economy with

62 Cf. Michael Findeisen, *op.cit.*, p. 2127.

63 Cf. Matthias Caspers, Islamische Aktienfonds – eine kapitalmarktrechtliche Herausforderung? In: Ulrich Burgard et al. (eds.), *Festschrift für Uwe H. Schneider zum 70. Geburtstag*, Dr. Otto Schmidt, Köln 2011, pp. 229–246.

64 Cf. Al-Majlis Al-Aurubī Li –L-Iftā' Wa L-Buḥūth, *Fatāwā*, vol. 1, Cairo n.d. (1999), pp. 19f.

a single word, even among Muslim scholars – clearly every type of interest, including default interest, is considered to be prohibited.[65]

This is the basis for the market of re-invented Islamic finance, including more or less convincing strategies to reconcile traditional thinking with present day economic exigencies. Some instruments resort to traditionally accepted strategies of factual circumvention of norms by formally sticking to the wording (*ḥiyal*). A contemporary Muslim scholar trained in Islamic and Western law and specialised in Islamic finance harshly criticises this approach: "Insisting on justifying the use of some *ḥīlah* because it was mentioned in the classical literature would only harm the industry of Islamic finance. Ultimately, people would come to realise that there is no difference between conventional products and so-called Shari'ah-compliant products except that the latter are more expensive."[66]

The other strategy is a re-interpretation of such rules in the light of the given circumstances of life on the basis of independent reasoning (*ijtihād*) in search for the higher objectives of Shari'ah rules (*maqāṣid al-Šarīah*). This would include the consideration of new scientific knowledge, e.g. the various functions of interest which might differ from usury (e.g. the compensation of inflation, the function of a lump sum for damages or the time value of capital).[67] After all, the prohibition of interest mostly results in particularly high rates of interest – as additional charges are added due to uncertainty – independently of the guise in which they appear.

In addition, religio-ethical principles[68] are considered here to be more crucial than medieval interpretations of the laws, e.g. acceptable working conditions, environment-friendly production or fair trade relations.[69] Two scholars at George Washington University have developed an "Economic Islamicity Index" on the basis of 113 measurable variables derived from the Qur'an and the sunna of the prophet of Islam Muhammad. The principal goals for an Islamic economic system are defined as achievement of economic justice and achievement of sustained economic growth, broad-based prosperity and job creation, and

---

65 In detail regarding the Council and its expert opinions Mathias Rohe, The Formation of a European Shari'a, in Jamal Malik (ed.), *Muslims in Europe: From the Margin to the Center*, LIT Verlag, Münster 2004, pp. 161, 173ff.

66 Ahmad Alkhamees, *op.cit.*, p. 233.

67 Cf. M. Charfi, *Islam and Liberty*, pp. 82ff.

68 For new approaches regarding ecological issues cf. the collective volume *Islam and Ecology*, eds. Richard C. Foltz, Frederick M. Denny and Azizan Baharuddin, Harvard University Press, Cambridge/Mass 2003.

69 Cf. e.g. Mahmoud A. El-Gamal, *Islamic Finance, Law, Economics, and Practice*, Cambridge University Press, Cambridge et al. 2006; Sherin Kunhibava, Sustainable Financing and Enhancing the Role of Banks in Malaysia, *Arab Law Quarterly* 32 (2018), pp. 129–157; Kilian Bälz, Islamisches Kreditwesen – Religion, Wirtschaft und Recht im Islam, *ZVglRWiss* 109 (2010), pp. 272–292 (289f.).

adoption of Islamic economic and financial practices.[70] On this basis, they have compared the "Islamicity" of 208 states. The top of the list is marked by Ireland, Denmark and Luxembourg. Belgium ranks at 10, Germany at 26 followed by Israel; the first country of the so-called Islamic world is Malaysia ranked 33rd. Saudi-Arabia only reaches rank 91, Egypt rank 128, Iran rank 139, Pakistan rank 145, Somalia rank 199.[71]

Such approaches result in an ethicisation of Shari'ah, being then the basis for guidance rather than governance. While European laws open broad space for Islamic finance on a more or less traditional basis, the ethical approach would perfectly reconcile the religious needs and creeds not only with the indispensable and well-argued legal environment in Europe and elsewhere, but also fit into the debate on sustainable economy in European societies as a whole.

70 Scheherazade S. Rehman/Hossein Askari, An Economic Islamicity Index (EI2), Global Economy Journal vol 10/3 (2010), pp. 1–37 (11ff. in particular with more detailed indicators).

71 Ibid., pp. 17–22.

ISLAMIC FINANCE: CONCEPTS, TRANSACTIONS, DEVELOPMENTS, AND CRITIQUE

Syed Imad-ud-Din ASAD

1. ISLAMIC LAW

Islamic law or Sharia, as the Muslims believe, is the collection of rules that were revealed by Allah[1] to Muhammad, the last of His prophets, whereby mankind is directed to lead their lives.[2]

Revelation is the primary source of Islamic law. Revelation can be classified into manifest revelation and internal revelation.[3] Manifest revelation comprises "the communications made by Gabriel, under the direction of God, to the Prophet, either in the very words of God or by hints and of such knowledge as occurred in the mind of the Prophet through the inspiration from God."[4] Internal revelation signifies "the opinion of the Prophet, embodied in the form of ratiocination, delivered from time to time, on the questions that happened to be raised before him."[5]

1 "Allah" is the Arabic word for God. See Maurice Bucaille, *The Bible, the Qur'an and Science*, Elmhurst, NY, Tahrike Tarsile Qur'an 1978, pp.112–113; Seyyed Hossein Nasr, *Islam: Religion, History, and Civilization*, San Francisco, HarperOne 2003, p. 4; Natalie Schoon, *Modern Islamic Banking*, West Sussex, Wiley 2016, p. 16.

2 Syed Riazul Hassan, *The Reconstruction of Legal thought in Islam*, Law Pub. Co 1974, p. 2; Bernard Lewis, *The Political Language of Islam*, Chicago, University of Chicago Press 2002, p. 28; William Montgomery Watt, *Islam: A Short History*, Oxford, Oneworld Publications Ltd 2006, p. 88; Ahmad Hasan, *The Early Development of Islamic Jurisprudence XIII*, Islamic Research Institute 1988; Muhammad Asad, *The Principles of State and Government in Islam*, Whitefish, Mont, Literary Licensing, LLC 2011, p. 3; C. G. Weeramantry, *Islamic Jurisprudence: An International Perspective*, Basingstoke, Palgrave Macmillan 2001, p. 1.

3 Sir Abdur Rahim, *The Principles of Muhammadan Jurisprudence*, Lahore, All Pakistan Legal Decisions 1963, p. 69.

4 Sir Abdur Rahim, *The Principles of Muhammadan Jurisprudence*, Lahore, All Pakistan Legal Decisions 1963, p. 69.

5 Sir Abdur Rahim, *The Principles of Muhammadan Jurisprudence*, Lahore, All Pakistan Legal Decisions 1963, p. 69.

Thus, the Quran and the Sunnah of the Prophet contain the entire final revelation.[6] The Quran embodies only those manifest revelations that were made in the exact words of Allah; the rest of the revelations, both manifest and internal, form the corpus of the Sunnah.[7]

1.1. LEGAL SIGNIFICANCE OF THE QURAN

The Quran is the principal source of Islamic law.[8] However, the Quran is not a code of law in the western sense.[9] It does not prescribe every possible rule regarding every possible aspect of human life and activity.[10] In other words, instead of laying down the law in detail, it generally indicates the fundamental principles that lead people in a certain direction and help them achieve certain goals.[11] Where the Quran has laid down detailed rules in respect of certain issues, there are instances where it only gives an idea as to how a thing should be dealt with.[12] The concerned authorities have been empowered to determine these details according to the circumstances.[13]

---

6 Sir Abdur Rahim, *The Principles of Muhammadan Jurisprudence*, Lahore, All Pakistan Legal Decisions 1963, p. 69.

7 Sir Abdur Rahim, *The Principles of Muhammadan Jurisprudence*, Lahore, All Pakistan Legal Decisions 1963, p. 69.

8 Allama Muhammad Iqbal, *The Reconstruction of Religious Thought in Islam*, New Delhi, Kitab Bhavan 2010, p. 145; William Montgomery Watt, *Islam: A Short History*, Oxford, Oneworld Publications Ltd 2006, p. 90; Tahir Wasti, *The Application of Islamic Criminal Law in Pakistan*, Brill Nijhoff 2009, p. 24; Natalie Schoon, *Modern Islamic Banking*, West Sussex, Wiley 2016, p. 16; Jamal Badawi, 'Muslim/Non-Muslim Relations: An Integrative Approach' (2003) 8 *JILC (The Journal of Islamic Law and Culture)* 23, 25.

9 Allama Muhammad Iqbal, *The Reconstruction of Religious Thought in Islam*, New Delhi, Kitab Bhavan 2010, p. 145; Sidrah Unis, *Quran as a Legal Guide*, Dawn News, June. 25, 2004; Tahir Wasti, *The Application of Islamic Criminal Law in Pakistan*, Brill Nijhoff 2009, p. 24.

10 Allama Muhammad Iqbal, *The Reconstruction of Religious Thought in Islam*, New Delhi, Kitab Bhavan 2010, p. 145; Sidrah Unis, *Quran as a Legal Guide*, Dawn News, June. 25, 2004; N. J. Coulson, *A History of Islamic Law*, New Brunswick, N.J, Aldine Transaction 2004, pp. 11–13.

11 Allama Muhammad Iqbal, *The Reconstruction of Religious Thought in Islam*, New Delhi, Kitab Bhavan 2010, pp. 145–149; NJ Coulson, *A History of Islamic Law*, New Brunswick, N.J, Aldine Transaction 2004, pp. 11–13; Sidrah Unis, *Quran as a Legal Guide*, Dawn News, June. 25, 2004; Tahir Wasti, *The Application of Islamic Criminal Law in Pakistan*, Brill Nijhoff 2009, pp. 24–25.

12 Sidrah Unis, *Quran as a Legal Guide*, Dawn News, June. 25, 2004.

13 Sidrah Unis, *Quran as a Legal Guide*, Dawn News, June. 25, 2004.

1.2. LEGAL SIGNIFICANCE OF THE SUNNAH

The Sunnah[14] is the second source of Islamic law.[15] While the Quran describes, answers, and deals with the fundamental issues of life, the responsibility of furnishing a further exposition was entrusted upon Muhammad.[16] In other words, the Quran and the Sunnah constitute one complete whole and are fundamentally interdependent.[17]

Unlike the Quran, the entire existing body of the Sunnah is not considered to be authentic.[18] While the Quran was available in written form during the lifetime of Muhammad[19], the whole corpus of the Sunnah was not preserved in the same way.[20] Whereas some of his companions did prepare written compilations[21] of his sayings and deeds, others just memorized them.[22] Thus, there was no single, authentic document containing the whole Sunnah at the time of Muhammad's death.

---

14 "Hadith and the Sunnah were initially different but they are now synonymous... The expression Hadith and Sunnah denote both the words and deeds of the Prophet (peace be upon him). The difference between the two has practically disappeared." Muhammad Hamidullah, *The Emergence of Islam,* Adam Publishers 2004, p. 44. "It must be mentioned that the two Arabic terms Hadith and Sunnah are generally taken to be synonymous, but there is a vast difference between the two. Hadith literally means "tale" or "narrative"; whereas, Sunnah literally means "trodden path" or "busy path." Hadith refers to a tradition or story of the Prophet, and Sunnah signifies the law deduced from it. In other words, Sunnah, with reference to Islamic law, denotes a rule derived from the sayings or conduct of the Prophet as narrated in a Hadith." Sidrah Unis, *Significance of Sunnah,* Dawn News, June. 3, 2005. In the present article, Hadith and Sunnah have been used synonymously.

15 Allama Muhammad Iqbal, *The Reconstruction of Religious Thought in Islam,* New Delhi, Kitab Bhavan 2010, p. 149; Muhammad Asad, *Islam at the Crossroads,* New Delhi, Kitab Bhavan 1991, p. 61; William Montgomery Watt, *Islam: A Short History,* Oxford, Oneworld Publications Ltd 2006, p. 90; Natalie Schoon, *Modern Islamic Banking,* West Sussex, Wiley 2016, p. 16; Tahir Wasti, *The Application of Islamic Criminal Law in Pakistan,* Brill Nijhoff 2009, p. 25.

16 For a further explanation of Sunnah, see Sir Abdur Rahim, *The Principles of Muhammadan Jurisprudence,* Lahore, All Pakistan Legal Decisions 1963, pp. 69–77; Syed Riazul Hassan, *The Reconstruction of Legal thought in Islam,* Law Pub. Co 1974, pp. 25–35; Sidrah Unis, *Significance of Sunnah,* Dawn News, June. 3, 2005; Habib Ahmed, *Product Development in Islamic Banks,* Edinburgh, Edinburgh University Press 2011, p. 19; C. G. Weeramantry, *Islamic Jurisprudence: An International perspective,* Basingstoke, Palgrave Macmillan 2001, pp. 34–39.

17 Sidrah Unis, *Significance of Sunnah,* Dawn News, June. 3, 2005.

18 Maurice Bucaille, *The Bible, the Qur'an and Science,* Elmhurst, NY, TahrikeTarsile Qur'an 1978, pp. 242–252.

19 C. G. Weeramantry, *Islamic Jurisprudence: An International Perspective,* Basingstoke, Palgrave Macmillan 2001, p. 5.

20 C. G. Weeramantry, *Islamic Jurisprudence: An International Perspective,* Basingstoke, Palgrave Macmillan 2001, p. 35.

21 For example, Sahifae Sadiqa, Sahifae Ali, Sahifae Abu Bakr, Sahifae Jebir, Sahifae Samra bin Jundal, and Sahifae Sahia. Syed Riazul Hassan, *The Reconstruction of Legal thought in Islam,* Law Pub. Co 1974,p. 30; Muhammad Hamidullah, *The Emergence of Islam,* 2004, p. 57.

22 See Syed Riazul Hassan, *The Reconstruction of Legal thought in Islam,* Law Pub. Co 1974, pp. 28–30; Maurice Bucaille, *The Bible, the Qur'an and Science,* Elmhurst, NY, Tahrike Tarsile Qur'an 1978, pp. 242–248; C. G. Weeramantry, *Islamic Jurisprudence: An International Perspective,* Basingstoke, Palgrave Macmillan 2001, pp. 35–38.

After Muhammad, during the reign of the Pious Caliphs or the Rightly Guided Caliphs[23], while the Quran was available in a consolidated form, the Sunnah was scattered in different compilations and memories of different individuals. This allowed individuals and groups to create statements favouring their interests and then attribute them to Muhammad.[24]

In order to keep the situation from becoming totally chaotic, Muslim scholars, more than a century after Muhammad's death, set out to systematically compile the Sunnah.[25] These compilations started appearing in the ninth century.[26] Unfortunately, despite all the caution that was observed by the compilers, numerous sayings, which they believed to be true, later turned out to be false.[27] The criterion employed by them – i.e., their focus on the trustworthiness of the reporters of those sayings – was an important one, but it was insufficient.[28] In fact, Muhammad himself gave the essential criterion: "After I am gone differences will arise among you. Compare whatever is reported to be mine with the Book of God; that which agrees therewith you may accept as having come from me; that which disagrees you will reject as a fabrication."[29]

Unfortunately, not all compilers applied this criterion sincerely and strictly.[30] However, there is nothing that prohibits Muslims from applying it today while studying the Sunnah.

1.3. LEGAL SIGNIFICANCE OF QIAS AND IJMA

Muslims believe that legislative power belongs exclusively to Allah.[31] Consequently, no man or body of men can ever be capable of or allowed to make laws for other men.[32]

23 Abu Bakr, Umar, Uthman, and Ali; William Montgomery Watt, *Islam: A Short History*, Oxford, Oneworld Publications Ltd 2006, p. 35.

24 William Montgomery Watt, *Islam: A Short History*, Oxford, Oneworld Publications Ltd 2006, p. 89; Muhammad Husayn Haykal, *The Life of Muhammad*, Indianapolis, IN, American Trust Publications 1997, pp. LXXXI, LXXXIII-LXXXIV.

25 C. G. Weeramantry, *Islamic Jurisprudence: An International Perspective*, Basingstoke, Palgrave Macmillan 2001, p. 35.

26 Seyyed Hossein Nasr, *Islam: Religion, History, and Civilization*, San Francisco, HarperOne 2003, p. 55.

27 Muhammad Husayn Haykal, *The Life of Muhammad*, Indianapolis, IN, American Trust Publications 1997, pp. LXXXI, LXXXIII-LXXXIV.

28 Muhammad Husayn Haykal, *The Life of Muhammad*, Indianapolis, IN, American Trust Publications 1997, p. LXXXII.

29 Muhammad Husayn Haykal, *The Life of Muhammad*, Indianapolis, IN, American Trust Publications 1997, p. LXXXII.

30 Muhammad Husayn Haykal, *The Life of Muhammad*, Indianapolis, IN, American Trust Publications 1997, pp. LXXXII-LXXXVI.

31 Dr. S. M. Haider, *Constitutional Principles and Islamic State*, *in* Shariah and Legal Profession 129–130 (Dr. S. M. Haider ed., 1985).

32 Syed Imad-ud-Din Asad, *Development of Islamic Law*, Dawn News, May 24, 2002.

However, where there is no room for the making of new laws, there is also no prohibition on the extension and re-interpretation of existing laws.[33] This very process, which is highly encouraged by Allah and His Messenger, of extension and re-interpretation of laws given in the Quran and the Sunnah, in order to explain and analyse the legality of the latest issues, is denoted by Ijtehad.[34] It is the method of Ijtehad by which Allah has enabled the Muslim jurists to (1) make provisions for the developing circumstances, and (2) prove Islam as a system of life practical for all times.[35]

When Ijtehad is conducted by a single jurist, it is called Qiyas; and when it is conducted by a body of jurists, it is named Ijma.[36] If a Qiyas and an Ijma, both conducted at the same time regarding the same thing, contradict each other, then Ijma is preferred over Qiyas.[37] This is done on the basis of the presumption that the jurists acting as a body are less likely to arrive at an erroneous decision than a jurist acting alone.[38]

2. ISLAMIC FINANCE

2.1. DEFINITION AND SCOPE

Islamic finance signifies financial services, mechanisms, practices, transactions, and instruments that comply with the provisions given in the fundamental Islamic texts.[39] Islamic finance not only includes banking,

---

33 Sidrah Unis, *An Indispensable Tool*, Dawn News, Nov. 18, 2005.

34 Sidrah Unis, *An Indispensable Tool*, Dawn News, Nov. 18, 2005. For a detailed explanation of Ijtehad, Ijma, and Qias, see Amin Ahsan Islahi, *Islamic Law: Concept and Codification*, Islamic Publications 1989, pp. 27–29; C. G. Weeramantry, *Islamic Jurisprudence: An International Perspective*, Palgrave Macmillan, Basingstoke 2001, pp. 39–45; Sir Abdur Rahim, *The Principles of Muhammadan Jurisprudence*, Lahore, All Pakistan Legal Decisions 1963, pp. 115–163; Muhammad Asad, *This Law of Ours and other Essays*, Kuala Lumpur, Islamic Book Trust 2000, pp. 41–65; Muhammad Asad, *The Principles of State and Government in Islam*, Whitefish, Mont, Literary Licensing, LLC 2011, pp. 11–15, 24–27; Allama Muhammad Iqbal, *The Reconstruction of Religious Thought in Islam*, New Delhi, Kitab Bhavan 2010, pp. 151–157.

35 C. G. Weeramantry, *Islamic Jurisprudence: An International Perspective*, Basingstoke, Palgrave Macmillan 2001, p. 41.

36 Sidrah Unis, *An Indispensable Tool*, Dawn News, Nov. 18, 2005; Amin Ahsan Islahi, *Islamic Law: Concept and Codification*, Islamic Publications 1989, pp. 27–29.

37 Sidrah Unis, *An Indispensable Tool*, Dawn News, Nov. 18, 2005.

38 Sidrah Unis, *An Indispensable Tool*, Dawn News, Nov. 18, 2005. For details, see C. G. Weeramantry, *Islamic Jurisprudence: An International Perspective*, Basingstoke, Palgrave Macmillan 2001, pp. 39–40.

39 Syed Imad-ud-Din Asad, *The Business of Shariah Advice*, Dawn News, Oct. 11, 2009. For further definitions, see *Chartered Institute of Management Accountants, An Introduction to Islamic Finance* 6 (2014); Alfred Kammer et al., *International Monetary Fund, Islamic Finance: Opportunities, Challenges, and Policy Options* 9 (2015); Clifford Chance, Introduction to Islamic Finance 1 (2013); Usman Hayat and Adeel Malik, *Islamic Finance: Ethics, Concepts, Practice*, CFA Institute Research Foundation 2014, p. 1; Mohammed Obaidullah, *Islamic Financial Services*, 2005, p. 21; Muhammad Ayub, *Understanding Islamic Finance*, Hoboken, NJ, Wiley 2007, pp. 73, 96.

but also capital formation, capital markets, and all types of financial intermediation.[40]

It must be pointed out that, from broad to narrow, there are numerous definitions of Islamic finance.[41] This is due to the fact that there is immense diversity within Islam.[42] The different religious practices, beliefs, and groups are not only due to the Shia-Sunni divide.[43] There are various Islamic traditions, such as, Indo-Pakistani, Indonesian, Malay, Persian, Turkic, etc., that often diverge from the practices prevalent in the Arabian Peninsula.[44] Consequently, there is immense diversity within Islamic finance.[45]

2.2. BASIC CONCEPTS

While there are similarities between Islamic and western financial systems[46], certain norms and transactions are exclusive to Islam.[47] For instance, in Islamic finance, money is treated as a means of exchange, not as a commodity.[48] Profit-and-loss-sharing is the basis of Islamic finance.[49] In any business venture, the provider of capital must share the risks with the user of capital.[50]

Some Islamic financial restrictions are severe enough to render certain western financial practices and transactions absolutely void.[51] These prohibitions are based on the Quran and the Sunnah.[52] The main prohibitions are:

---

40 Zamir Iqbal, 'Islamic Financial Systems' (1997) 34 *F&D (Finance and Development)* 42.

41 Ibrahim Warde, *Islamic Finance in the Global Economy*, Edinburgh, Edinburgh University Press 2010, p. 7.

42 Ibrahim Warde, *Islamic Finance in the Global Economy*, Edinburgh, Edinburgh University Press 2010, p. 14.

43 Ibrahim Warde, *Islamic Finance in the Global Economy*, Edinburgh, Edinburgh University Press 2010, p. 14.

44 Ibrahim Warde, *Islamic Finance in the Global Economy*,Edinburgh, Edinburgh University Press 2010, p. 14.

45 Ibrahim Warde, *Islamic Finance in the Global Economy*, Edinburgh, Edinburgh University Press 2010, pp. 2, 4.

46 Frank E. Vogel and Samuel L. Hayes, *Islamic Law and Finance: Religion, Risk, and Return*, Boston, Springer 1998, p. 2.

47 Syed Imad-ud-Din Asad, *The Business of Shariah Advice*, Dawn News, Oct. 11, 2009.

48 Brian Kettell, *Introduction to Islamic Banking and Finance*, London, Harriman House 2011, p. 34; Tariq Alrifai, *Islamic Finance and the New Financial System*, Hoboken, Wiley 2015, p. 121.

49 Brian Kettell, *Introduction to Islamic Banking and Finance*, London, Harriman House 2011, p. 33; Natalie Schoon, *Modern Islamic Banking*, West Sussex, Wiley 2016, p. 43; and Tariq Alrifai, *Islamic Finance and the New Financial System*, Hoboken, Wiley 2015, p. 119.

50 Brian Kettell, *Introduction to Islamic Banking and Finance*, London, Harriman House 2011, pp. 33–34; Tariq Alrifai, *Islamic Finance and the New Financial System*, Hoboken, Wiley 2015, p. 119.

51 Syed Imad-ud-Din Asad, *The Business of Shariah Advice*, Dawn News, Oct. 11, 2009; Natalie Schoon, *Modern Islamic Banking*, West Sussex, Wiley 2016, pp. 49–50.

52 Usman Hayat and Adeel Malik, *Islamic Finance: Ethics, Concepts, Practice*, CFA Institute Research Foundation 2014, p. 26.

2.2.1. *Prohibition of Riba*

The prohibition of Riba is often referred to as the most distinguishing feature of Islamic finance.[53] While the literal meaning of Riba is increase or excess[54], scholars believe that it signifies any unjustified gain.[55]

The Quran has expressly prohibited Riba in very strong terms.[56] However, the Quran does not define Riba.[57] While the Sunnah provides more details about Riba, it still does not provide a clear definition.[58]

Similarly, the Quran and the Sunnah do not provide detailed reasons for the prohibition of Riba, except that charging Riba amounts to injustice.[59] However, contemporary scholars have tried to provide detailed explanations for the prohibition of Riba.[60]

All Muslims agree that Riba is prohibited; however, there are disagreements regarding the scope of Riba.[61] While there are scholars that believe that Riba includes both interest and usury; there are scholars that believe that Riba only includes usury.[62] There are scholars who do not restrict the concept of unjustified gain to interest and usury; they extend its scope to other practices as well, for

---

53 Hans Visser, *Islamic Finance: Principles and Practice*,Northampton, MA, Edward Elgar Pub 2013, p. 36.

54 Mahmoud A. El-Gamal, *Islamic Finance: Law, Economics, and Practice*, Cambridge, Cambridge University Press 2006, p. 49; Bala Shanmugam and Zaha Rina Zahri, *A Primer on Islamic Finance*, Charlottesville, VA, The Research Foundation of CFA Institute 2009, p. 8; Hans Visser, *Islamic Finance: Principles and Practice*, Northampton, MA, Edward Elgar Pub 2013, p. 36; Zamir Iqbal and Abbas Mirakhor, *An Introduction to Islamic Finance*, Singapore, Wiley 2011, p. 58; Mohammed Obaidullah, *Islamic Financial Services*, 22 2005; Habib Ahmed, *Product Development in Islamic Banks*, Edinburgh, Edinburgh University Press 2011, p. 30; Natalie Schoon, *Modern Islamic Banking*, West Sussex, Wiley 2016, p. 17; Ibrahim Warde, *Islamic Finance in the Global Economy*, Edinburgh, Edinburgh University Press 2010, p. 52.

55 Hans Visser, *Islamic Finance: Principles and Practice*, Northampton, MA, Edward Elgar Pub p. 36 2013; Zamir Iqbal and Abbas Mirakhor, *An Introduction to Islamic Finance*, Singapore, Wiley 2011, p. 58; Ibrahim Warde, *Islamic Finance in the Global Economy*, Edinburgh, Edinburgh University Press 2010, p. 52.

56 Ibrahim Warde, *Islamic Finance in the Global Economy*, Edinburgh, Edinburgh University Press 2010, p. 52.

57 Frank E. Vogel and Samuel L. Hayes, *Islamic Law and Finance: Religion, Risk, and Return*, Springer, Boston 1998, p. 72.

58 Frank E. Vogel and Samuel L. Hayes, *Islamic Law and Finance: Religion, Risk, and Return*, Springer, Boston 1998, p. 73.

59 Zamir Iqbal and Abbas Mirakhor, *An Introduction to Islamic Finance*, Singapore, Wiley 2011, p. 63.

60 Zamir Iqbal and Abbas Mirakhor, *An Introduction to Islamic Finance*, Singapore, Wiley 2011, p. 63.

61 Muhammad Ayub, *Understanding Islamic Finance*, Hoboken, NJ, Wiley 2007, p. 44; Natalie Schoon, *Modern Islamic Banking*, West Sussex, Wiley 2016, pp. 19, 35.

62 Hans Visser, *Islamic Finance: Principles and Practice*, Northampton, MA, Edward Elgar Pub 2013, pp. 36–41; Muhammad Ayub, *Understanding Islamic Finance*, Hoboken, NJ, Wiley 2007, pp. 49–51; Natalie Schoon, *Modern Islamic Banking*, West Sussex, Wiley 2016, pp. 19, 35, 44; Usman Hayat and Adeel Malik, *Islamic Finance: Ethics, Concepts, Practice*, CFA Institute Research Foundation 2014, p. 27.

instance, imposition of late fee.[63] While the scope of Riba is an ongoing debate, the majority of scholars believe that interest, usury, and all other practices that result in unjustified gain constitute Riba.[64]

2.2.2. Prohibition of Gharar

Gharar signifies uncertainty.[65] Gharar includes "ambiguity/uncertainty about the end result of a contract and the nature and/or quality and specifications of the subject matter of the contract or the rights and obligations of the parties, possession and/or delivery of the item of exchange."[66]

Riba is expressly prohibited by the Quran and the Sunnah[67], Gharar is not expressly prohibited by the Quran[68]; however, it is expressly prohibited by the Sunnah[69]; there is more literature on Riba than on Gharar.[70] While the presence of Riba invalidates a transaction, the presence of some Gharar does not invalidate a transaction.[71] In other words, a small amount of Gharar is acceptable.[72] This

---

63 Ibrahim Warde, *Islamic Finance in the Global Economy*, Edinburgh, Edinburgh University Press 2010, p. 52.

64 Ibrahim Warde, *Islamic Finance in the Global Economy*, Edinburgh, Edinburgh University Press 2010, pp. 53–55; Natalie Schoon, *Modern Islamic Banking*, West Sussex, Wiley 2016, p. 19.

65 Usman Hayat and Adeel Malik, *Islamic Finance: Ethics, Concepts, Practice*, CFA Institute Research Foundation 2014, p. 28; Bala Shanmugam and Zaha Rina Zahri, *A Primer on Islamic Finance*, Charlottesville, VA, The Research Foundation of CFA Institute 2009, p. 9; Mohammed Obaidullah, *Islamic Financial Services*, 2005, p. 29; Brian Kettell, *Introduction to Islamic Banking and Finance*, London, Harriman House 2011, pp. 35, 152; Habib Ahmed, *Product Development in Islamic Banks*, Edinburgh, Edinburgh University Press 2011, p. 33; Muhammad Yusuf Saleem, *Islamic Commercial Law*, Singapore, Wiley 2013, p. 3; Noripah Kamso, *Investing in Islamic Funds*, Wiley 2013, p. 53; Natalie Schoon, *Modern Islamic Banking*, West Sussex, Wiley 2016, p. 44; Hans Visser, *Islamic Finance: Principles and Practice*, Northampton, MA, Edward Elgar Pub 2013, p.52.

66 Muhammad Ayub, *Understanding Islamic Finance*, Hoboken, NJ, Wiley 2007, p. 58.

67 Habib Ahmed, *Product Development in Islamic Banks*, Edinburgh, Edinburgh University Press 2011, p. 30.

68 Maha-Hanaan Balala, *Islamic Finance and Law: Theory and Practice in a Globalized World*, 2011, p. 35; Habib Ahmed, *Product Development in Islamic Banks*, Edinburgh, Edinburgh University Press 2011, p. 34.

69 Usman Hayat and Adeel Malik, *Islamic Finance: Ethics, Concepts, Practice*, CFA Institute Research Foundation 2014, p. 28; Habib Ahmed, *Product Development in Islamic Banks*, Edinburgh, Edinburgh University Press 2011, p. 34.

70 Muhammad Ayub, *Understanding Islamic Finance*, Hoboken, NJ, Wiley 2007, p. 58.

71 Bala Shanmugam and Zaha Rina Zahri, *A Primer on Islamic Finance*, Charlottesville, VA, The Research Foundation of CFA Institute 2009, p. 9; Maha-Hanaan Balala, *Islamic Finance and Law: Theory and Practice in a Globalized World*, New York, I.B.Tauris 2011, pp. 39–40; Habib Ahmed, *Product Development in Islamic Banks*, Edinburgh, Edinburgh University Press 2011, p. 34; Muhammad Ayub, *Understanding Islamic Finance*, Hoboken, NJ, Wiley 2007, p. 58.

72 Mohammed Obaidullah, *Islamic Financial Services*, 2005, p. 29; Habib Ahmed, *Product Development in Islamic Banks*, Edinburgh, Edinburgh University Press 2011, p. 34; Maha-Hanaan Balala, *Islamic Finance and Law: Theory and Practice in a Globalized World*, New York, I.B.Tauris 2011, pp. 39–40.

is because uncertainty cannot be completely avoided in any business.[73] Thus, scholars are of the opinion that transactions that involve extreme uncertainty regarding the subject matter or the price should be forbidden.[74]

2.2.3. *Prohibition of Maysir*

Maysir signifies gambling or speculation.[75] Maysir refers to "easily available wealth or acquisition of wealth by chance."[76]

Maysir is involved in certain conventional financial transactions, which Muslims have to avoid.[77] For instance, a lottery is prohibited.[78] Similarly, conventional insurance not only involves Riba, but also Maysir; therefore, it is prohibited.[79]

2.2.4. *Prohibited Goods and Services*

Islamic financial institutions cannot enter into transactions that involve prohibited goods and services.[80] For instance, they cannot deal with entities dealing in alcohol, pork, gambling, pornography, prostitution, etc.[81]

3. ISLAMIC FINANCIAL TRANSACTIONS

Islamic financial transactions can be classified as deposit products, equity-based financing products, debt-based financing products, fee-based services, and

---

73 Muhammad Ayub, *Understanding Islamic Finance*, Hoboken, NJ, Wiley 2007, p. 58.

74 Mohammed Obaidullah, *Islamic Financial Services*, 2005, p. 29; Muhammad Ayub, *Understanding Islamic Finance*, Hoboken, NJ, Wiley 2007, p. 58.

75 Hans Visser, *Islamic Finance: Principles and Practice*, Northampton, MA, Edward Elgar Pub 2013, p. 52; Muhammad Yusuf Saleem, *Islamic Commercial Law*, Singapore, Wiley 2013, p. 4; Brian Kettell, *Introduction to Islamic Banking and Finance*, London, Harriman House 2011, p. 153.

76 Muhammad Ayub, *Understanding Islamic Finance*, Hoboken, NJ, Wiley 2007, p. 61.

77 Muhammad Ayub, *Understanding Islamic Finance*, Hoboken, NJ, Wiley 2007, p. 62.

78 Muhammad Ayub, *Understanding Islamic Finance*, Hoboken, NJ, Wiley 2007, p. 62.

79 Muhammad Ayub, *Understanding Islamic Finance*, Hoboken, NJ, Wiley 2007, p. 62.

80 Alsadek H. Gait and Andrew C. Worthington, *A Primer on Islamic Finance: Definitions, Sources, Principles and Methods* 12 (University of Wollongong, Working Paper No. 07/05, 2007); Usman Hayat and Adeel Malik, *Islamic Finance: Ethics, Concepts, Practice*, CFA Institute Research Foundation 2014, p. 26; Muhammad Yusuf Saleem, *Islamic Commercial Law*, Singapore, Wiley 2013, p. 5; Bala Shanmugam and Zaha Rina Zahri, *A Primer on Islamic Finance*, Charlottesville, VA, The Research Foundation of CFA Institute 2009, p. 4.

81 Alsadek H. Gait and Andrew C. Worthington, *A Primer on Islamic Finance: Definitions, Sources, Principles and Methods* 12 (University of Wollongong, Working Paper No. 07/05, 2007); Bala Shanmugam and Zaha Rina Zahri, *A Primer on Islamic Finance*, Charlottesville, VA, The Research Foundation of CFA Institute 2009, p. 4; Usman Hayat and Adeel Malik, *Islamic Finance: Ethics, Concepts, Practice*, CFA Institute Research Foundation 2014, p. 26; Tariq Alrifai, *Islamic Finance and the New Financial System*, Hoboken, Wiley 2015, pp. 117–118; Muhammad Yusuf Saleem, *Islamic Commercial Law*, Singapore, Wiley 2013, p. 5.

miscellaneous products and services.[82] It must be clarified that this section does not cover all Islamic financial transactions.

3.1. DEPOSIT PRODUCTS

The main deposit products are current deposit, savings deposit, and investment deposit.[83]

3.1.1. Current deposit

Generally, the banks give no return on these accounts.[84] This account provides for the safekeeping of one's money.[85] These accounts are usually structured as Wadiah or as Qard.[86]

Under Wadiah, the bank holds the money as Amana or in trust and utilizes that money at its own risk.[87] The depositor neither shares the profit nor the loss.[88]

Under Qard, the bank holds the money as Qard or benevolent loan and utilizes that money at its own risk.[89] The depositor neither shares the profit nor the loss.[90]

3.1.2. Savings deposit

This account provides for the safekeeping of one's surplus money while providing a modest return.[91] These accounts are usually structured as Wadiah or as Mudaraba.[92]

---

82 Mohammed Obaidullah, *Islamic Financial Services*, 2005, pp. xi-xiv, 17.

83 Mohammed Obaidullah, *Islamic Financial Services*, 2005, pp. 49–54.

84 Tariq Alrifai, *Islamic Finance and the New Financial System*, Hoboken, Wiley 2015, p. 141; Muhammad Ayub, *Understanding Islamic Finance*, Hoboken, NJ, Wiley 2007, p. 189.

85 Mohammed Obaidullah, *Islamic Financial Services*, 2005, p. 49; Tariq Alrifai, *Islamic Finance and the New Financial System*, Hoboken, Wiley 2015, p. 141; Natalie Schoon, *Modern Islamic Banking*, West Sussex, Wiley 2016, p. 78; Brian Kettell, *Case Studies in Islamic Banking and Finance*, West Sussex, UK, Wiley 2011, p. 49.

86 Natalie Schoon, *Modern Islamic Banking*, West Sussex, Wiley 2016, p. 78; Mohammed Obaidullah, *Islamic Financial Services*, 2005, pp. 49–50.

87 Mohammed Obaidullah, *Islamic Financial Services*, 2005, p. 50; Brian Kettell, *Case Studies in Islamic Banking and Finance*, West Sussex, UK, Wiley 2011, p. 50.

88 Natalie Schoon, *Modern Islamic Banking*, West Sussex, Wiley 2016, p. 44; Mohammed Obaidullah, *Islamic Financial Services*, 2005, p. 50.

89 Mohammed Obaidullah, *Islamic Financial Services*, 2005, p. 50; Natalie Schoon, *Modern Islamic Banking*, West Sussex, Wiley 2016, p. 78; Brian Kettell, *Case Studies in Islamic Banking and Finance*, West Sussex, UK, Wiley 2011, p. 50.

90 Natalie Schoon, *Modern Islamic Banking*, West Sussex, Wiley 2016, p. 78; Mohammed Obaidullah, *Islamic Financial Services*, 2005, p. 50.

91 Usman Hayat and Adeel Malik, *Islamic Finance: Ethics, Concepts, Practice*, CFA Institute Research Foundation 2014, p. 34; Mohammed Obaidullah, *Islamic Financial Services*, 2005, p. 51.

92 Usman Hayat and Adeel Malik, *Islamic Finance: Ethics, Concepts, Practice*, CFA Institute Research Foundation 2014, p. 34; Mohammed Obaidullah, *Islamic Financial Services*, 2005, p. 51.

Under Wadiah, the bank holds the money as Amana or in trust and utilizes that money at its own risk.[93] However, the bank gives a return to the depositor, solely at its discretion, as a gift, which is not part of the contract.[94] The return given by the bank is variable in nature as it is based on the profit made by the bank and as it is in the bank's discretion.[95]

Under Mudaraba, the depositor authorizes the bank to use the money, as Mudarib, for investment.[96] Thus, the profit is shared between the bank and the depositor.[97]

3.1.3. *Investment Deposit*

This is similar to the conventional fixed deposit that does not allow the depositor to withdraw the money prior to a maturity period.[98] This account is based on the concept of Mudaraba, i.e., the depositor authorizes the bank to use the money, as Mudarib, for investment.[99] For Islamic banks, these accounts are an important source of funds.[100]

3.2. EQUITY-BASED FINANCING PRODUCTS

The main equity-based financing products are Musharaka and Mudaraba.[101]

3.2.1. *Musharaka*

It is an arrangement in which all parties provide the capital as well as the skills or labour for a venture.[102]

---

93 Mohammed Obaidullah, *Islamic Financial Services*, 2005, p. 51; Brian Kettell, *Case Studies in Islamic Banking and Finance*, West Sussex, UK, Wiley 2011, p. 51.

94 Mohammed Obaidullah, *Islamic Financial Services*, 2005. p. 51.

95 Mohammed Obaidullah, *Islamic Financial Services*, 2005, p. 51; Brian Kettell, *Case Studies in Islamic Banking and Finance*, West Sussex, UK, Wiley 2011, p. 51.

96 Mohammed Obaidullah, *Islamic Financial Services*, 2005, p. 51.

97 Mohammed Obaidullah, *Islamic Financial Services*, 2005, p. 51.

98 Mohammed Obaidullah, *Islamic Financial Services*, 2005, p. 52.

99 Bala Shanmugam and Zaha Rina Zahri, *A Primer on Islamic Finance*, Charlottesville, VA, The Research Foundation of CFA Institute 2009, p. 26; Usman Hayat and Adeel Malik, *Islamic Finance: Ethics, Concepts, Practice*, CFA Institute Research Foundation 2014, p. 34; Brian Kettell, *Case Studies in Islamic Banking and Finance*, West Sussex, UK, Wiley 2011, p. 51; Mohammed Obaidullah, *Islamic Financial Services*, 2005, p. 52.

100 Bala Shanmugam and Zaha Rina Zahri, *A Primer on Islamic Finance*, Charlottesville, VA, The Research Foundation of CFA Institute 2009, p. 26; Mohammed Obaidullah, *Islamic Financial Services*, 2005, p. 52.

101 Mohammed Obaidullah, *Islamic Financial Services*, 2005, p. 17.

102 Zamir Iqbal and Abbas Mirakhor, *An Introduction to Islamic Finance*, Singapore, Wiley 2011, p. 86; Frank E. Vogel and Samuel L. Hayes, *Islamic Law and Finance,* Boston, Mass, Springer 1998,p. 195; Natalie Schoon, *Modern Islamic Banking*, West Sussex, Wiley 2016, p. 54; Habib

The parties share the profit according to a predetermined formula.[103] It is not necessary for the parties to share the profit in proportion to their capital contributions.[104] However, the parties do share the loss in proportion to their capital contributions.[105]

According to the majority of scholars, the Musharaka capital should preferably be in the form of money.[106] Where the capital contribution of a party is in a form other than money, it must be quantified and specified.[107]

Contemporary scholars have come up with the concept of Diminishing Musharaka.[108] A party to a Diminishing Musharaka, after participating in the venture, can liquidate its share in the venture.[109] A Diminishing Musharaka contains a provision according to which a party promises to periodically sell its share to the other party.[110]

3.2.2. Mudaraba

It is an arrangement in which one party, i.e., Rab-al-Mal, provides the capital and the other, i.e., Mudarib, provides the skills or labor regarding a venture.[111]

Ahmed, *Product Development in Islamic Banks*, Edinburgh, Edinburgh University Press 2011, p. 92; Muhammad Ayub, *Understanding Islamic Finance*, Hoboken, NJ, Wiley 2007, p. 308.

103 Bala Shanmugam and Zaha Rina Zahri, *A Primer on Islamic Finance*, Charlottesville, VA, The Research Foundation of CFA Institute 2009, p. 34; Brian Kettell, *Introduction to Islamic Banking and Finance*, London, Harriman House 2011, p. 78; Noureddine Krichene, *Islamic Capital Markets: Theory and Practice*, Singapore, Wiley 2013, p. 634; Natalie Schoon, *Modern Islamic Banking*, West Sussex, Wiley 2016, p. 54; Muhammad Ayub, *Understanding Islamic Finance*, Hoboken, NJ, Wiley 2007, p. 308.

104 Bala Shanmugam and Zaha Rina Zahri, *A Primer on Islamic Finance*, Charlottesville, VA, The Research Foundation of CFA Institute 2009, p. 34; Muhammad Ayub, *Understanding Islamic Finance*, Hoboken, NJ, Wiley 2007, p. 320.

105 Bala Shanmugam and Zaha Rina Zahri, *A Primer on Islamic Finance*, Charlottesville, VA, The Research Foundation of CFA Institute 2009, p. 34; Brian Kettell, *Introduction to Islamic Banking and Finance*, London, Harriman House 2011, p. 78; Natalie Schoon, *Modern Islamic Banking*, West Sussex, Wiley 2016, p. 54; Muhammad Ayub, *Understanding Islamic Finance*, Hoboken, NJ, Wiley 2007, p. 320.

106 Muhammad Ayub, *Understanding Islamic Finance*, Hoboken, NJ, Wiley 2007, p. 313.

107 Muhammad Ayub, *Understanding Islamic Finance*, Hoboken, NJ, Wiley 2007, p. 314.

108 Muhammad Ayub, *Understanding Islamic Finance*, Hoboken, NJ, Wiley 2007, p. 337.

109 Muhammad Ayub, *Understanding Islamic Finance*, Hoboken, NJ, Wiley 2007, p. 337; Natalie Schoon, *Modern Islamic Banking*, West Sussex, Wiley 2016, p. 54; Bala Shanmugam and Zaha Rina Zahri, *A Primer on Islamic Finance*, Charlottesville, VA, The Research Foundation of CFA Institute 2009, p. 35.

110 Muhammad Ayub, *Understanding Islamic Finance*, Hoboken, NJ, Wiley 2007, p. 337; Natalie Schoon, *Modern Islamic Banking*, West Sussex, Wiley 2016, p. 54; Bala Shanmugam and Zaha Rina Zahri, *A Primer on Islamic Finance*, Charlottesville, VA, The Research Foundation of CFA Institute 2009, p. 35.

111 Mahmoud A. El-Gamal, *Islamic Finance: Law, Economics, and Practice*, Cambridge, Cambridge University Press 2006, p. 120; Zamir Iqbal and Abbas Mirakhor, *An Introduction to Islamic Finance*, Singapore, Wiley 2011, p. 90; Mohammed Obaidullah, *Islamic Financial Services*, 2005, p. 57; Ibrahim Warde, *Islamic Finance in the Global Economy*, Edinburgh, Edinburgh University Press 2010, p. 145; Frank E. Vogel and Samuel L. Hayes, *Islamic Law and*

The parties share the profit according to a pre-determined formula.[112] In the case of loss incurred in the normal course of business, the party providing the capital bears the loss; the party providing the skills or labor does not bear the loss, it only loses all or part of the return for its skills or labor.[113] The party providing the skills or labour is only held liable for the loss if it is the result of any breach of trust, misconduct, or negligence on its part.[114]

The Mudaraba capital should preferably be in the form of money.[115] Where the capital contribution of a party is in a form other than money, it must be quantified and specified.[116]

Finance, Boston, Mass, Springer 1998, pp. 193–194; Hans Visser, *Islamic Finance: Principles and Practice*, Northampton, MA, Edward Elgar Pub 2013, p. 63; Brian Kettell, *Introduction to Islamic Banking and Finance*, London, Harriman House 2011, p. 63; Muhammad Yusuf Saleem, *Islamic Commercial Law*, Singapore, Wiley 2013, p. 112; Noureddine Krichene, *Islamic Capital Markets: Theory and Practice*, Singapore, Wiley 2013, p. 634; Natalie Schoon, *Modern Islamic Banking*, West Sussex, Wiley 2016, pp. 55–56; Maha-Hanaan Balala, *Islamic Finance and Law: Theory and Practice in a Globalized World*, New York, I.B.Tauris 2011, pp. 27–28; Tariq Alrifai, *Islamic Finance and the New Financial System*, Hoboken, Wiley 2015, p. 125; Muhammad Ayub, *Understanding Islamic Finance*, Hoboken, NJ, Wiley 2007, pp. 320–321.

112 Frank E. Vogel and Samuel L. Hayes, *Islamic Law and Finance,* Boston, Mass, Springer 1998, p. 194; Ibrahim Warde, *Islamic Finance in the Global Economy*, Edinburgh, Edinburgh University Press 2010, p. 145; Mohammed Obaidullah, *Islamic Financial Services*, 2005, p. 57; Bala Shanmugam and Zaha Rina Zahri, *A Primer on Islamic Finance*, Charlottesville, VA, The Research Foundation of CFA Institute 2009, p. 37; Hans Visser, *Islamic Finance: Principles and Practice*, Northampton, MA, Edward Elgar Pub 2013, p. 63; Brian Kettell, *Introduction to Islamic Banking and Finance*, London, Harriman House 2011, p. 63; Noureddine Krichene, *Islamic Capital Markets: Theory and Practice*, Singapore, Wiley 2013, p. 634; Natalie Schoon, *Modern Islamic Banking*, West Sussex, Wiley 2016, p. 56; Maha-Hanaan Balala, *Islamic Finance and Law: Theory and Practice in a Globalized World*, New York, I.B.Tauris 2011, p. 28; Tariq Alrifai, *Islamic Finance and the New Financial System*, Hoboken, Wiley 2015, p. 125; Muhammad Ayub, *Understanding Islamic Finance*, Hoboken, NJ, Wiley 2007, pp. 320–321.

113 Frank E. Vogel and Samuel L. Hayes, *Islamic Law and Finance,* Boston, Mass, Springer1998, p. 194; Zamir Iqbal and Abbas Mirakhor, *An Introduction to Islamic Finance*, Singapore, Wiley 2011, pp. 90–91; Ibrahim Warde, *Islamic Finance in the Global Economy*, Edinburgh, Edinburgh University Press 2010, p. 146; Mohammed Obaidullah, *Islamic Financial Services*, 2005, p. 57; Muhammad Ayub, *Understanding Islamic Finance*, Hoboken, NJ, Wiley 2007, p. 321; Hans Visser, *Islamic Finance: Principles and Practice*, Northampton, MA, Edward Elgar Pub 2013, p. 63; Brian Kettell, *Introduction to Islamic Banking and Finance*, London, Harriman House 2011, p. 63; Noureddine Krichene, *Islamic Capital Markets: Theory and Practice*, Singapore, Wiley 2013, p. 634; Natalie Schoon, *Modern Islamic Banking,* West Sussex, Wiley 2016, p. 56; Maha-Hanaan Balala, *Islamic Finance and Law: Theory and Practice in a Globalized World*, New York, I.B.Tauris 2011, p. 28; Tariq Alrifai, Islamic Finance and the New Financial System, Hoboken, Wiley 2015, p. 126; Bala Shanmugam and Zaha Rina Zahri, *A Primer on Islamic Finance*, Charlottesville, VA, The Research Foundation of CFA Institute 2009, p. 37.

114 Ibrahim Warde, *Islamic Finance in the Global Economy*, Edinburgh, Edinburgh University Press 2010, p. 146; Zamir Iqbal and Abbas Mirakhor, *An Introduction to Islamic Finance*, Singapore, Wiley 2011, p. 91; Hans Visser, *Islamic Finance: Principles and Practice*, Northampton, MA, Edward Elgar Pub 2013, p. 63; Natalie Schoon, *Modern Islamic Banking*, West Sussex, Wiley 2016, p. 56; Muhammad Ayub, *Understanding Islamic Finance*, Hoboken, NJ, Wiley 2007, p. 323.

115 Muhammad Ayub, *Understanding Islamic Finance*, Hoboken, NJ, Wiley 2007, p. 323.

116 Muhammad Ayub, *Understanding Islamic Finance*, Hoboken, NJ, Wiley 2007, p. 314.

There is neither any restriction on the number of parties providing the capital nor on the number of parties providing the skills or efforts.[117] The party providing the capital has the right to lay down conditions regarding the Mudaraba and the party providing the skills or labor is obligated to follow these conditions.[118]

Most the traditional scholars are of the view that the party providing the capital is not allowed to work for the Mudaraba.[119] However, it has the right to oversee the Mudaraba and has the right to monitor if the party providing the skills or labor is performing its responsibilities efficiently.[120] Some modern scholars are of the view that it should be left to the parties to decide whether or not the Rab-al-Mal should work for the Mudaraba and to what extent.[121]

Like Diminishing Musharaka, there is Diminishing Mudaraba.[122]

3.3. DEBT-BASED FINANCING PRODUCTS

The main debt-based financing products are Murabaha, Ijara, Salam, and Istisna.[123]

3.3.1. Murabaha

Murabaha is the transaction in which the "parties bargain on the margin of profit over the known cost price."[124] The party selling the asset must honestly state its original price and any additional expenses incurred on it.[125] The seller and the buyer must mutually agree on the margin of profit charged by the seller.[126]

---

117 Muhammad Ayub, *Understanding Islamic Finance*, Hoboken, NJ, Wiley 2007, p. 321; Mahmoud A. El-Gamal, *Islamic Finance: Law, Economics, and Practice*, Cambridge, Cambridge University Press 2006, p. 121.

118 Muhammad Ayub, *Understanding Islamic Finance*, Hoboken, NJ, Wiley 2007, p. 324; Natalie Schoon, *Modern Islamic Banking*, West Sussex, Wiley 2016, p. 55.

119 Zamir Iqbal and Abbas Mirakhor, *An Introduction to Islamic Finance*, Singapore, Wiley 2011, p. 90; Brian Kettell, *Introduction to Islamic Banking and Finance*, London, Harriman House 2011, p. 63; Natalie Schoon, *Modern Islamic Banking*, West Sussex, Wiley 2016, p. 55; Muhammad Ayub, *Understanding Islamic Finance*, Hoboken, NJ, Wiley 2007, p. 325.

120 Muhammad Ayub, *Understanding Islamic Finance*, Hoboken, NJ, Wiley 2007, p. 325; Brian Kettell, *Introduction to Islamic Banking and Finance*, London, Harriman House 2011, p. 63.

121 Muhammad Ayub, *Understanding Islamic Finance*, Hoboken, NJ, Wiley 2007, p. 325.

122 Ibrahim Warde, *Islamic Finance in the Global Economy*, Edinburgh, Edinburgh University Press 2010, p. 146.

123 Mohammed Obaidullah, *Islamic Financial Services*, 2005, p. 17.

124 Muhammad Ayub, *Understanding Islamic Finance*, Hoboken, NJ, Wiley 2007, p. 213; Zamir Iqbal and Abbas Mirakhor, *An Introduction to Islamic Finance*, Singapore, Wiley 2011, p. 83.

125 Muhammad Ayub, *Understanding Islamic Finance*, Hoboken, NJ, Wiley 2007, p. 217; Brian Kettell, *Introduction to Islamic Banking and Finance*, London, Harriman House 2011, p. 43.

126 Hans Visser, *Islamic Finance: Principles and Practice*, Northampton, MA, Edward Elgar Pub 2013, p. 67; Zamir Iqbal and Abbas Mirakhor, *An Introduction to Islamic Finance*, Singapore, Wiley 2011, p. 83; Bala Shanmugam and Zaha Rina Zahri, *A Primer on Islamic Finance*,

As a method of financing, Murabaha assumes significance when it is conducted on a deferred payment basis.[127] At present, Murabaha is conducted by banks in the form of Murabaha to Purchase Orderer.[128] That is, in response to a formal request by a client, the bank buys an asset from a third party and sells it to the client on a deferred payment basis.[129] In other words, the bank buys an asset through a contract and then sells it to the client, on a deferred payment basis, through a separate contract.[130]

The client can specify the supplier from whom the asset is to be procured by the bank.[131] The bank can itself buy the asset, or it can appoint an agent to buy the asset on its behalf, or it can appoint the client as its agent to buy the asset on its behalf.[132]

The bank can ask the client to provide a security for the timely payment of the deferred price.[133]

3.3.2. *Ijara*

Ijara is a transaction in which a party enjoys, for a particular or known time period, the usufruct of an asset or the services of a person in return for a consideration.[134] The lessor is called "Ajir" or "Mujir."[135] The lessee is called "Mustajir."[136]

In the case of usufruct of an asset, the consideration is rent; in the case of services of a person, the consideration is wages.[137] Thus, the subject of Ijara can be assets or services.[138]

Charlottesville, VA, The Research Foundation of CFA Institute 2009, p. 32; Muhammad Ayub, *Understanding Islamic Finance*, Hoboken, NJ, Wiley 2007, p. 218.

127 Muhammad Ayub, *Understanding Islamic Finance*, Hoboken, NJ, Wiley 2007, p. 219.

128 Muhammad Ayub, *Understanding Islamic Finance*, Hoboken, NJ, Wiley 2007, p. 222; Bala Shanmugam and Zaha Rina Zahri, *A Primer on Islamic Finance*, Charlottesville, VA, The Research Foundation of CFA Institute 2009, p. 32; Usman Hayat and Adeel Malik, *Islamic Finance: Ethics, Concepts, Practice*, CFA Institute Research Foundation 2014, p. 33.

129 Muhammad Ayub, *Understanding Islamic Finance*, Hoboken, NJ, Wiley 2007, p. 222; Maha-Hanaan Balala, *Islamic Finance and Law: Theory and Practice in a Globalized World*, New York, I.B.Tauris 2011, p. 28.

130 Muhammad Ayub, *Understanding Islamic Finance*, Hoboken, NJ, Wiley 2007, p. 239.

131 Muhammad Ayub, *Understanding Islamic Finance*, Hoboken, NJ, Wiley 2007, p. 223.

132 Mohammed Obaidullah, *Islamic Financial Services*, 2005, pp. 68–69; Muhammad Ayub, *Understanding Islamic Finance*, Hoboken, NJ, Wiley 2007, pp. 221–222.

133 Zamir Iqbal and Abbas Mirakhor, *An Introduction to Islamic Finance*, Singapore, Wiley 2011, p. 84; Mohammed Obaidullah, *Islamic Financial Services*, 2005, p. 77; Muhammad Ayub, *Understanding Islamic Finance*, Hoboken, NJ, Wiley 2007, p. 229.

134 Muhammad Ayub, *Understanding Islamic Finance*, Hoboken, NJ, Wiley 2007, p. 279; Brian Kettell, *Introduction to Islamic Banking and Finance*, London, Harriman House 2011, pp. 89–90.

135 Mohammed Obaidullah, *Islamic Financial Services*, 2005, p. 79; Brian Kettell, *Introduction to Islamic Banking and Finance*, London, Harriman House 2011, pp. 89–90.

136 Mohammed Obaidullah, *Islamic Financial Services*, 2005, p. 79; Brian Kettell, *Introduction to Islamic Banking and Finance*, London, Harriman House 2011, pp. 89–90.

137 Mohammed Obaidullah, *Islamic Financial Services*, 2005, p. 279; Brian Kettell, *Introduction to Islamic Banking and Finance*, London, Harriman House 2011, pp. 89–90.

138 Muhammad Ayub, *Understanding Islamic Finance*, Hoboken, NJ, Wiley 2007, p. 280; Brian Kettell, *Introduction to Islamic Banking and Finance*, London, Harriman House 2011, pp. 89–90.

In the case of assets, it must be things that can be utilized without the consumption of their corpus.[139] For instance, foodstuff and fuel cannot be the subject of Ijara.[140]

All liabilities related to the ownership of the asset are borne by the lessor; all liabilities related to the use of the asset are borne by the lessee.[141] If any harm comes to the leased asset, it is also borne by the lessor unless it is established that the lessee's misuse or negligence caused it.[142]

The lessor cannot unilaterally increase the rent after the agreement is finalized.[143] However, during the lease period, there can be different rates, based on an agreed benchmark, for different phases.[144] Also, the parties can mutually agree to review the lease period or the rent or both.[145] It is allowed to sub-lease the asset with the approval of the lessor.[146]

When the rent becomes due, it is deemed a debt payable by the lessee.[147] Therefore, the lessor can demand a security from the lessee.[148]

A bank and its client can structure Ijara in three different ways. Firstly of all, the client can take on lease an asset owned by the bank, which is the least used structure, as banks generally do not deal in assets.[149] Secondly, the bank can itself purchase the asset, on the client's request, and then give it to the client on lease.[150] Thirdly, the bank can appoint the client as its agent to purchase the asset, required by the client.[151] In the third scenario, the client becomes the bank's agent while purchasing the asset; after taking the delivery of the asset, the client becomes the bank's lessee.[152]

---

139 Muhammad Ayub, *Understanding Islamic Finance*, Hoboken, NJ, Wiley 2007, p. 281; Zamir Iqbal and Abbas Mirakhor, *An Introduction to Islamic Finance*, Singapore, Wiley 2011, p. 81.

140 Muhammad Ayub, *Understanding Islamic Finance*, Hoboken, NJ, Wiley 2007, p. 281.

141 Bala Shanmugam and Zaha Rina Zahri, *A Primer on Islamic Finance*, Charlottesville, VA, The Research Foundation of CFA Institute 2009, p. 32; Mohammed Obaidullah, *Islamic Financial Services*, 2005, p. 89; Natalie Schoon, Modern Islamic Banking, West Sussex, Wiley 2016, p. 58; Muhammad Ayub, *Understanding Islamic Finance*, Hoboken, NJ, Wiley 2007, p. 285.

142 Mohammed Obaidullah, *Islamic Financial Services*, 2005, p. 89; Muhammad Ayub, *Understanding Islamic Finance*, Hoboken, NJ, Wiley 2007, p. 285.

143 Muhammad Ayub, *Understanding Islamic Finance*, Hoboken, NJ, Wiley 2007, p. 283.

144 Mohammed Obaidullah, *Islamic Financial Services*, 2005, p. 91; Muhammad Ayub, *Understanding Islamic Finance*, Hoboken, NJ, Wiley 2007, p. 283.

145 Muhammad Ayub, *Understanding Islamic Finance*, Hoboken, NJ, Wiley 2007, p. 283.

146 Muhammad Ayub, *Understanding Islamic Finance*, Hoboken, NJ, Wiley 2007, p. 284.

147 Mohammed Obaidullah, *Islamic Financial Services*, 2005, p. 91; Muhammad Ayub, *Understanding Islamic Finance*, Hoboken, NJ, Wiley 2007, p. 287.

148 Muhammad Ayub, *Understanding Islamic Finance*, Hoboken, NJ, Wiley 2007, p. 285.

149 Mohammed Obaidullah, *Islamic Financial Services*, 2005, p. 80.

150 Mohammed Obaidullah, *Islamic Financial Services*, 2005, p. 80.

151 Mohammed Obaidullah, *Islamic Financial Services*, 2005, p. 81.

152 Mohammed Obaidullah, *Islamic Financial Services*, 2005, p. 81.

3.3.3. *Salam*

Salam is the transaction in which the price of a specified asset is paid at the time of making the contract while the asset is delivered at a specified future date.[153] Originally, Salam was a financing method for small traders and farmers.[154]

The asset does not need to exist at the time of the contract.[155] The party selling the asset does not need to be the owner or the producer of the asset.[156] Scholars hold that "all goods that can be standardized into identical units can become the subject of Salam."[157] In other words, Salam can be conducted regarding fungible goods only.[158] For instance, rice, wheat, iron, copper, oil, etc.[159]

While the party selling the asset gets the money to satisfy its liquidity needs, the buyer gets the benefit of cheap price.[160] As the spot price paid by the bank is pegged lower than the expected future price, Salam results in a profit for the bank.[161]

The party purchasing the asset may enter into a Parallel Salam.[162] This way, it does not have to wait for the actual delivery of the asset in order to get back its money and the profit.[163] For instance, there will be a Salam in which the bank will buy the asset from the client; there will be another Salam in which the bank

153 Ibrahim Warde, *Islamic Finance in the Global Economy*, Edinburgh, Edinburgh University Press 2010, p. 143; Zamir Iqbal and Abbas Mirakhor, *An Introduction to Islamic Finance*, Singapore, Wiley 2011, pp. 79–80; Muhammad Ayub, *Understanding Islamic Finance*, Hoboken, NJ, Wiley 2007, p. 240; Frank E. Vogel and Samuel L. Hayes, III, *Islamic Law and Finance*, 1998, p. 183; Bala Shanmugam and Zaha Rina Zahri, *A Primer on Islamic Finance*, Charlottesville, VA, The Research Foundation of CFA Institute 2009, p. 37; Hans Visser, *Islamic Finance: Principles and Practice*, Northampton, MA, Edward Elgar Pub 2013, p. 71; Brian Kettell, *Introduction to Islamic Banking and Finance*, London, Harriman House 2011, p. 117; Natalie Schoon, *Modern Islamic Banking*, West Sussex, Wiley 2016, p. 58; Mohammed Obaidullah, *Islamic Financial Services*, 2005, p. 95.

154 Mohammed Obaidullah, *Islamic Financial Services*, 2005, p. 95; Brian Kettell, *Introduction to Islamic Banking and Finance*, London, Harriman House 2011, pp. 117, 121.

155 Hans Visser, *Islamic Finance: Principles and Practice*, Northampton, MA, Edward Elgar Pub 2013, p. 71.

156 Muhammad Ayub, *Understanding Islamic Finance*, Hoboken, NJ, Wiley 2007, p. 255.

157 Muhammad Ayub, *Understanding Islamic Finance*, Hoboken, NJ, Wiley 2007, p. 244.

158 Brian Kettell, *Introduction to Islamic Banking and Finance*, London, Harriman House 2011, p. 117; Hans Visser, *Islamic Finance: Principles and Practice*, Northampton, MA, Edward Elgar Pub 2013, p. 72; Natalie Schoon, *Modern Islamic Banking*, West Sussex, Wiley 2016, p. 58.

159 Muhammad Ayub, *Understanding Islamic Finance*, Hoboken, NJ, Wiley 2007, p. 244.

160 Zamir Iqbal and Abbas Mirakhor, *An Introduction to Islamic Finance*, Singapore, Wiley 2011, p. 80; Brian Kettell, *Introduction to Islamic Banking and Finance*, London, Harriman House 2011, p. 119; Muhammad Ayub, *Understanding Islamic Finance*, Hoboken, NJ, Wiley 2007, p. 242.

161 Mohammed Obaidullah, *Islamic Financial Services*, 2005, p. 96; Brian Kettell, *Introduction to Islamic Banking and Finance*, London, Harriman House 2011, p. 121.

162 Mohammed Obaidullah, *Islamic Financial Services*, 2005, p. 96; Brian Kettell, *Introduction to Islamic Banking and Finance*, London, Harriman House 2011, p. 121; Hans Visser, *Islamic Finance: Principles and Practice*, Northampton, MA, Edward Elgar Pub 2013, p. 72.

163 Mohammed Obaidullah, *Islamic Financial Services*, 2005, p. 96; Hans Visser, *Islamic Finance: Principles and Practice*, Northampton, MA, Edward Elgar Pub 2013, p. 72.

will sell the asset.[164] However, the original Salam and the Parallel Salam must be kept independent of each other.[165]

3.3.4. *Istisna*

Istisna is the transaction in which a party engages another party to manufacture or construct a particular asset, in return for a consideration, to be delivered at a specified future date.[166]

Any asset that needs to be manufactured or constructed can be the subject of Istisna.[167] For instance, parties can enter into Istisna regarding infrastructure and real estate development[168], manufacturing of aircrafts and ships, etc.[169] Istisna is not valid for natural things or products.[170] For instance, parties cannot enter into Istisna regarding livestock, vegetables, etc.[171]

The consideration in Istisna can be in the form of money, tangible goods, or usufruct of particular assets.[172] It is not necessary for the consideration to be paid in advance.[173] It can be paid in full at the end of the time period[174]; it can be paid in instalments, within the mutually agreed time period; or it can also be linked with the stages of completion.[175] Where the construction of a huge project

---

164 Muhammad Ayub, *Understanding Islamic Finance*, Hoboken, NJ, Wiley 2007, p. 256; Brian Kettell, *Introduction to Islamic Banking and Finance*, London, Harriman House 2011, p. 120; Hans Visser, *Islamic Finance: Principles and Practice*, Northampton, MA, Edward Elgar Pub 2013, p. 72.

165 Muhammad Ayub, *Understanding Islamic Finance*, Hoboken, NJ, Wiley 2007, pp. 252, 256; Brian Kettell, *Introduction to Islamic Banking and Finance*, London, Harriman House 2011, p. 120.

166 Frank E. Vogel and Samuel L. Hayes, *Islamic Law and Finance*, Boston, Mass, Springer 1998, p. 146; Ibrahim Warde, *Islamic Finance in the Global Economy*, Edinburgh, Edinburgh University Press 2010, p. 143; Mohammed Obaidullah, *Islamic Financial Services*, 2005, p. 99; Zamir Iqbal and Abbas Mirakhor, *An Introduction to Islamic Finance*, Singapore, Wiley 2011, p. 82; Brian Kettell, *Introduction to Islamic Banking and Finance*, London, Harriman House 2011, p. 103; Muhammad Ayub, *Understanding Islamic Finance*, Hoboken, NJ, Wiley 2007, p. 263.

167 Hans Visser, *Islamic Finance: Principles and Practice*, Northampton, MA, Edward Elgar Pub 2013, p. 73; Muhammad Ayub, *Understanding Islamic Finance*, Hoboken, NJ, Wiley 2007, p. 264.

168 Bala Shanmugam and Zaha Rina Zahri, *A Primer on Islamic Finance*, Charlottesville, VA, The Research Foundation of CFA Institute 2009, p. 36; Muhammad Ayub, *Understanding Islamic Finance*, Hoboken, NJ, Wiley 2007, p. 264; Zamir Iqbal and Abbas Mirakhor, *An Introduction to Islamic Finance*, Singapore, Wiley 2011, p. 83; Mohammed Obaidullah, *Islamic Financial Services*, 2005, p. 99.

169 Zamir Iqbal and Abbas Mirakhor, *An Introduction to Islamic Finance*, Singapore, Wiley 2011, p. 82; Muhammad Ayub, *Understanding Islamic Finance*, Hoboken, NJ, Wiley 2007, p. 269; Mohammed Obaidullah, *Islamic Financial Services*, 2005, p. 99.

170 Muhammad Ayub, *Understanding Islamic Finance*, Hoboken, NJ, Wiley 2007, p. 264.

171 Muhammad Ayub, *Understanding Islamic Finance*, Hoboken, NJ, Wiley 2007, p. 264.

172 Muhammad Ayub, *Understanding Islamic Finance*, Hoboken, NJ, Wiley 2007, p. 265.

173 Zamir Iqbal and Abbas Mirakhor, *An Introduction to Islamic Finance*, Singapore, Wiley 2011, p. 82; Brian Kettell, *Introduction to Islamic Banking and Finance*, London, Harriman House 2011, p. 108; Muhammad Ayub, *Understanding Islamic Finance*, Hoboken, NJ, Wiley 2007, p. 265.

174 Mohammed Obaidullah, *Islamic Financial Services*, 2005, p. 99; Zamir Iqbal and Abbas Mirakhor, *An Introduction to Islamic Finance*, Singapore, Wiley 2011, p. 82.

175 Muhammad Ayub, *Understanding Islamic Finance*, Hoboken, NJ, Wiley 2007, p. 265; Zamir Iqbal and Abbas Mirakhor, *An Introduction to Islamic Finance*, Singapore, Wiley 2011, p. 82.

is involved, over a long period of time, the parties may mutually agree to readjust the consideration if there are unforeseen contingencies.[176]

It is not necessary for the party selling the asset to itself manufacture the same, unless stated otherwise in the contract.[177] If the seller is not required to manufacture or construct the asset itself, the seller may get it manufactured or constructed by another party under a Parallel Istisna.[178] For instance, there will be an Istisna, between the bank and a manufacturer, in which the bank will be the buyer; there will be another Istisna between the bank and its client, in which the bank will be the seller.[179] However, both the contracts must be kept independent of each other.[180] The difference between the price received by the bank from the client and the price paid by the bank to the manufacturer constitutes the profit for the bank.[181]

The bank, whether acting as the buyer or the seller, may appoint an agent, "with the consent of the other party, to supervise the manufacturing process or to sell the asset when received."[182] The bank, whether acting as the buyer or the seller, may demand a security from the other party.[183]

3.4. FEE-BASED SERVICES

The main fee-based services are Wakala and Kafala.[184]

3.4.1. Wakala

Wakala signifies agency.[185] The scope of the agency must be clearly defined.[186] The task to be performed by the agent must be one that permits representation.[187]

176 Muhammad Ayub, *Understanding Islamic Finance*, Hoboken, NJ, Wiley 2007, p. 265.

177 Muhammad Ayub, *Understanding Islamic Finance*, Hoboken, NJ, Wiley 2007, p. 264; Mohammed Obaidullah, *Islamic Financial Services*, 2005, p. 99.

178 Muhammad Ayub, *Understanding Islamic Finance*, Hoboken, NJ, Wiley 2007, p. 267.

179 Frank E. Vogel and Samuel L. Hayes, *Islamic Law and Finance*, Boston, Mass, Springer 1998, p. 147; Muhammad Ayub, *Understanding Islamic Finance*, Hoboken, NJ, Wiley 2007, p. 267.

180 Muhammad Ayub, *Understanding Islamic Finance*, Hoboken, NJ, Wiley 2007, p. 267.

181 Mohammed Obaidullah, *Islamic Financial Services*, 2005, p. 99.

182 Muhammad Ayub, *Understanding Islamic Finance*, Hoboken, NJ, Wiley 2007, p. 267.

183 Muhammad Ayub, *Understanding Islamic Finance*, Hoboken, NJ, Wiley 2007, p. 267; Marifa Academy, *Islamic Banking and Finance: Principles and Practices*, p.58; Mohammed Obaidullah, *Islamic Financial Services*, 2005, p. 99.

184 Mohammed Obaidullah, *Islamic Financial Services*, 2005, p. 17.

185 Zamir Iqbal and Abbas Mirakhor, *An Introduction to Islamic Finance*, Singapore, Wiley 2011, p. 92; Bala Shanmugam and Zaha Rina Zahri, *A Primer on Islamic Finance*, Charlottesville, VA, The Research Foundation of CFA Institute 2009, pp. 22, 101; Brian Kettell, *Introduction to Islamic Banking and Finance*, London, Harriman House 2011, p. 156; Muhammad Yusuf Saleem, *Islamic Commercial Law*, Singapore, Wiley 2013, p. 68; Hans Visser, *Islamic Finance: Principles and Practice*, Northampton, MA, Edward Elgar Pub 2013, p. 74; Natalie Schoon, *Modern Islamic Banking*, West Sussex, Wiley 2016, p. 62; Muhammad Ayub, *Understanding Islamic Finance*, Hoboken, NJ, Wiley 2007, p. 347.

186 Muhammad Ayub, *Understanding Islamic Finance*, Hoboken, NJ, Wiley 2007, p. 348.

187 Muhammad Ayub, *Understanding Islamic Finance*, Hoboken, NJ, Wiley 2007, p. 348.

For instance, an agent cannot be appointed for praying, fasting, etc.[188] An agent can be appointed for sale, purchase, borrowing, lending, payments, litigation, bailment, pledge, etc.[189]

Measures taken by the agent on behalf of the principal are deemed to be measures taken by the principal.[190] An agent must exercise due care in the performance of its responsibilities.[191]

Wakala stands terminated by mutual consent, unilateral termination, discharge of responsibilities, death, loss of legal capacity, etc.[192]

Banks extensively use Wakala.[193] It must be pointed out that banks charge a fee whenever they provide agency services to their clients.[194] However, banks usually do not pay any fee to their clients if the clients provide agency services to the banks.[195]

3.4.2. Kafala

Kafala signifies guarantee.[196] At times, a client requires its bank to be an intermediary in a transaction in order to create confidence in the parties.[197] The bank does so by acting as the guarantor of its client's liability towards the other parties to the transaction.[198] The bank charges a fee to cover the expenses incurred in this process.[199]

3.5. OTHER SERVICES AND PRODUCTS

Other important services and products are sukuk and Takaful.

3.5.1. Sukuk

Sukuk is the plural of Sakk, which means certificate.[200] Sukuk signify certificates of equal value representing undivided shares in the ownership of tangible assets,

---

188 Muhammad Ayub, *Understanding Islamic Finance*, Hoboken, NJ, Wiley 2007, p. 348.
189 Muhammad Ayub, *Understanding Islamic Finance*, Hoboken, NJ, Wiley 2007, p. 348.
190 Muhammad Ayub, *Understanding Islamic Finance*, Hoboken, NJ, Wiley 2007, p. 348.
191 Muhammad Ayub, *Understanding Islamic Finance*, Hoboken, NJ, Wiley 2007, p. 348.
192 Marifa Academy, *Islamic Banking and Finance: Principles and Practices,* 2014, p. 64; Muhammad Ayub, *Understanding Islamic Finance*, Hoboken, NJ, Wiley 2007, p. 348.
193 Muhammad Ayub, *Understanding Islamic Finance*, Hoboken, NJ, Wiley 2007, p. 348.
194 Muhammad Ayub, *Understanding Islamic Finance*, Hoboken, NJ, Wiley 2007, p. 348.
195 Muhammad Ayub, *Understanding Islamic Finance*, Hoboken, NJ, Wiley 2007, p. 348.
196 Marifa Academy, *Islamic Banking and Finance: Principles and Practices*, 2014, p. 61; Bala Shanmugam and Zaha Rina Zahri, *A Primer on Islamic Finance*, Charlottesville, VA, The Research Foundation of CFA Institute 2009, p. 21; Muhammad Ayub, *Understanding Islamic Finance*, Hoboken, NJ, Wiley 2007, p. 169.
197 Mohammed Obaidullah, *Islamic Financial Services*, 2005, p. 114.
198 Mohammed Obaidullah, *Islamic Financial Services*, 2005, p. 114.
199 Mohammed Obaidullah, *Islamic Financial Services*, 2005, p. 115.
200 Bala Shanmugam and Zaha Rina Zahri, *A Primer on Islamic Finance*, Charlottesville, VA, The Research Foundation of CFA Institute 2009, p. 47; Zamir Iqbal and Abbas Mirakhor, *An*

usufruct, services, assets of a particular project, or any specified investment activity.[201] Sukuk are often regarded as one the most promising Islamic financial products.[202] Governments, corporations, and other entities have issued sukuk.[203]

Sukuk are neither shares nor bonds.[204] While sukuk represent particular assets and are issued for a particular period of time, shares represent the ownership of a company as a whole and are issued for an indefinite period of time.[205] Unlike bonds, sukuk carry returns based on the cash flow originating from the assets on the basis of which they are issued.[206] Also, while bonds represent debt, sukuk represent ownership.[207] Thus, sukuk can be referred to as "Islamic investment certificates."[208]

Following are the key parties in sukuk:

1. The issuer or the originator of sukuk, who sells its asset to the SPV and utilizes the realized funds.[209]
2. The Special Purpose Vehicle, which is an entity that purchases the asset from the originator and funds the purchase price by issuing sukuk.[210] It is

---

Introduction to Islamic Finance, Singapore, Wiley 2011, p. 184; Hans Visser, *Islamic Finance: Principles and Practice*, Northampton, MA, Edward Elgar Pub 2013, p. 79; Usman Hayat and Adeel Malik, *Islamic Finance: Ethics, Concepts, Practice*, CFA Institute Research Foundation 2014, p. 37.

201 Muhammad Ayub, *Understanding Islamic Finance*, Hoboken, NJ, Wiley 2007, p. 392; Mohd Azmi Omar, Muhamad Abduh and Raditya Sukmana, *Fundamentals of Islamic Money and Capital Markets,* Singapore, Wiley 2013, pp. 117–118.

202 Usman Hayat and Adeel Malik, *Islamic Finance: Ethics, Concepts, Practice*, CFA Institute Research Foundation 2014, p. 37; Bala Shanmugam and Zaha Rina Zahri, *A Primer on Islamic Finance*, Charlottesville, VA, The Research Foundation of CFA Institute 2009, p. 47.

203 Usman Hayat and Adeel Malik, *Islamic Finance: Ethics, Concepts, Practice*, CFA Institute Research Foundation 2014, p. 38; Zamir Iqbal and Abbas Mirakhor, *An Introduction to Islamic Finance*, Singapore, Wiley 2011, p. 192.

204 Muhammad Ayub, *Understanding Islamic Finance*, Hoboken, NJ, Wiley 2007, p. 392.

205 Muhammad Ayub, *Understanding Islamic Finance*, Hoboken, NJ, Wiley 2007, p. 392; Mohd Azmi Omar, Muhamad Abduh and Raditya Sukmana, *Fundamentals of Islamic Money and Capital Markets,* Singapore, Wiley 2013, p. 79.

206 Bala Shanmugam and Zaha Rina Zahri, *A Primer on Islamic Finance*, Charlottesville, VA, The Research Foundation of CFA Institute 2009, p. 47; Obiyathulla Ismath Bacha and Abbas Mirakhor, *Islamic Capital Markets: A Comparative Approach,* Hoboken, New Jersey, Wiley 2013, p. 174; Muhammad Ayub, *Understanding Islamic Finance*, Hoboken, NJ, Wiley 2007, p. 392.

207 Usman Hayat and Adeel Malik, *Islamic Finance: Ethics, Concepts, Practice*, CFA Institute Research Foundation 2014, p. 38; Mohd Azmi Omar, Muhamad Abduh and Raditya Sukmana, *Fundamentals of Islamic Money and Capital Markets*, Singapore, Wiley 2013, p. 79; Zamir Iqbal and Abbas Mirakhor, *An Introduction to Islamic Finance*, Singapore, Wiley 2011, p. 185.

208 Usman Hayat and Adeel Malik, *Islamic Finance: Ethics, Concepts, Practice*, CFA Institute Research Foundation 2014, p. 38; Maha-Hanaan Balala, *Islamic Finance and Law: Theory and Practice in a Globalized World*, New York, I.B.Tauris 2011, p. 30.

209 Muhammad Ayub, *Understanding Islamic Finance*, Hoboken, NJ, Wiley 2007, p. 393.

210 Muhammad Ayub, *Understanding Islamic Finance*, Hoboken, NJ, Wiley 2007, p. 393.

established specifically for the securitization process and managing the issue.[211] Sometimes, it is also referred to as the issuer.[212] The legal structure of an SPV is devised keeping in view the regulatory and legal environment in which it is intended to operate.[213]
3. Investment banks, which provide underwriting, lead managing, and book making services for sukuk in return for a fee or commission.[214]
4. The Subscribers of sukuk.[215]

According to the nature of the asset, usufruct of the asset, or the services involved, the sukuk can be structured as Murabaha sukuk, Ijara sukuk, Salam sukuk, Istisna sukuk, Musharaka sukuk, etc.[216] Certain sukuk can be traded in the secondary market.[217] Sukuk that create debt obligations cannot be traded in the secondary market; sukuk that represent an ownership stake in the underlying asset can be traded in the secondary market.[218]

Both Muslims and non-Muslims can invest in sukuk.[219] Similarly, both Muslims and non-Muslims can issue sukuk.[220]

3.5.2. *Takaful*

Takaful is an agreement among a group of persons, referred to as participants, who collectively agree to compensate each other in case of specified loss.[221]

---

211 Muhammad Ayub, *Understanding Islamic Finance*, Hoboken, NJ, Wiley 2007, p. 393.
212 Muhammad Ayub, *Understanding Islamic Finance*, Hoboken, NJ, Wiley 2007, p. 393.
213 Muhammad Ayub, *Understanding Islamic Finance*, Hoboken, NJ, Wiley 2007, p. 393.
214 Muhammad Ayub, *Understanding Islamic Finance*, Hoboken, NJ, Wiley 2007, p. 393.
215 Muhammad Ayub, *Understanding Islamic Finance*, Hoboken, NJ, Wiley 2007, p. 393.
216 Zamir Iqbal and Abbas Mirakhor, *An Introduction to Islamic Finance*, Singapore, Wiley 2011, p. 187; Muhammad Ayub, *Understanding Islamic Finance*, Hoboken, NJ, Wiley 2007, p. 396.
217 Zamir Iqbal and Abbas Mirakhor, *An Introduction to Islamic Finance*, Singapore, Wiley 2011, p. 187; Bala Shanmugam and Zaha Rina Zahri, *A Primer on Islamic Finance*, Charlottesville, VA, The Research Foundation of CFA Institute 2009, pp. 48–49; Muhammad Ayub, *Understanding Islamic Finance*, Hoboken, NJ, Wiley 2007, p. 407.
218 Zamir Iqbal and Abbas Mirakhor, *An Introduction to Islamic Finance*, Singapore, Wiley 2011, pp. 187–188; Muhammad Ayub, *Understanding Islamic Finance*, Hoboken, NJ, Wiley 2007, p. 407.
219 Hans Visser, *Islamic Finance: Principles and Practice*, Northampton, MA, Edward Elgar Pub 2013, p. 80.
220 Hans Visser, *Islamic Finance: Principles and Practice*, Northampton, MA, Edward Elgar Pub 2013, p. 80.
221 Mohammed Obaidullah, *Islamic Financial Services*, 2005, p. 127; Bala Shanmugam and Zaha Rina Zahri, *A Primer on Islamic Finance*, Charlottesville, VA, The Research Foundation of CFA Institute 2009, pp. 64–65; Brian Kettell, *Introduction to Islamic Banking and Finance*, London, Harriman House 2011, pp. 128–129; M. Kabir Hassan, Rasem N. Kayed and Umar A. Oseni, *Introduction to Islamic Banking and Finance*, Harlow, Pearson Education Limited 2013, pp. 293–294; Muhammad Ayub, *Understanding Islamic Finance*, Hoboken, NJ, Wiley 2007, p. 422.

Takaful, which is also referred to as Islamic insurance, is based on the notions of shared responsibility, cooperation, and mutual help.[222] Each Takaful participant is the insurer as well as the insured.[223] The participants contribute money to create a common fund.[224] Whenever a participant suffers the specified loss, it receives financial compensation from the fund.[225] A Takaful operator manages the fund.[226] The fund is allowed to invest in avenues and ventures that are acceptable to Islam.[227] This way, the fund can generate income and grow.[228]

Though Takaful is considered a non-profit activity, it can be undertaken as a commercial venture.[229] There are different models of Takaful.[230]

Under the Mudaraba model, the participants act as Rab-al-Mal and the operator acts as Mudarib.[231] The operator, who is responsible for asset management and underwriting, shares the profit with the participants.[232]

Under the Wakala model, the participants act as principal and the operator acts as agent.[233] The operator, who is responsible for asset management and underwriting, is paid an agreed fee.[234]

---

222 Mohammed Obaidullah, *Islamic Financial Services*, 2005, p. 125; Bala Shanmugam and Zaha Rina Zahri, *A Primer on Islamic Finance*, Charlottesville, VA, The Research Foundation of CFA Institute 2009, p.64; Brian Kettell, *Introduction to Islamic Banking and Finance*, London, Harriman House 2011, p. 129; Muhammad Ayub, *Understanding Islamic Finance*, Hoboken, NJ, Wiley 2007, p. 420.

223 Bala Shanmugam and Zaha Rina Zahri, *A Primer on Islamic Finance*, Charlottesville, VA, The Research Foundation of CFA Institute 2009, p. 65; Zamir Iqbal and Abbas Mirakhor, *An Introduction to Islamic Finance*, Singapore, Wiley 2011, p. 221.

224 Mohammed Obaidullah, *Islamic Financial Services*, 2005, p. 127; M. Kabir Hassan, Rasem N. Kayed and Umar A. Oseni, *Introduction to Islamic Banking and Finance*, Harlow, Pearson Education Limited 2013, pp. 293–294; Brian Kettell, *Introduction to Islamic Banking and Finance*, London, Harriman House 2011, p. 130.

225 Mohammed Obaidullah, *Islamic Financial Services*, 2005, p. 127; Brian Kettell, *Introduction to Islamic Banking and Finance*, London, Harriman House 2011, p. 130.

226 Usman Hayat and Adeel Malik, *Islamic Finance: Ethics, Concepts, Practice*, CFA Institute Research Foundation 2014, p. 40.

227 Mohammed Obaidullah, *Islamic Financial Services*, 2005, p. 127.

228 Mohammed Obaidullah, *Islamic Financial Services*, 2005, p. 127.

229 Mohammed Obaidullah, *Islamic Financial Services*, 2005, p. 127.

230 Mohammed Obaidullah, *Islamic Financial Services*, 2005, p. 128; Zamir Iqbal and Abbas Mirakhor, *An Introduction to Islamic Finance*, Singapore, Wiley 2011, p. 219; Muhammad Ayub, *Understanding Islamic Finance*, Hoboken, NJ, Wiley 2007, p. 423.

231 Zamir Iqbal and Abbas Mirakhor, *An Introduction to Islamic Finance*, Singapore, Wiley 2011, p. 219; Bala Shanmugam and Zaha Rina Zahri, *A Primer on Islamic Finance*, Charlottesville, VA, The Research Foundation of CFA Institute 2009, p. 66; Ibrahim Warde, *Islamic Finance in the Global Economy*, Edinburgh, Edinburgh University Press 2010, p. 154.

232 Zamir Iqbal and Abbas Mirakhor, *An Introduction to Islamic Finance*, Singapore, Wiley 2011, p. 219; Brian Kettell, *Introduction to Islamic Banking and Finance*, London, Harriman House 2011, p. 132; Bala Shanmugam and Zaha Rina Zahri, *A Primer on Islamic Finance*, Charlottesville, VA, The Research Foundation of CFA Institute 2009, p. 66.

233 Zamir Iqbal and Abbas Mirakhor, *An Introduction to Islamic Finance*, Singapore, Wiley 2011, p. 220.

234 Zamir Iqbal and Abbas Mirakhor, *An Introduction to Islamic Finance*, Singapore, Wiley 2011, p. 220; Bala Shanmugam and Zaha Rina Zahri, *A Primer on Islamic Finance*, Charlottesville,

Under the Wakala-Mudaraba model, Wakala is used for running the operations and for underwriting activities, and Mudaraba is utilized for asset-management.[235]

Muslim scholars consider conventional insurance to be un-Islamic as it involves Riba, Gharar, and Maisir.[236] Most forms of conventional insurance have a Takaful equivalent.[237]

4. DEVELOPMENTS IN ISLAMIC FINANCE

4.1. EMERGENCE OF MODERN ISLAMIC FINANCIAL INSTITUTIONS

It is wrong to assume that Islamic finance has always existed in its current form or that Islamic finance emerged fully formed in the 1970s.[238] Islamic finance can be aptly described as a work in progress.[239]

While it is generally believed that the first modern Islamic financial institution, MitGhamr, was established in Egypt in 1963[240], there is evidence of an Islamic financial institution, Anjuman Mowodul Ikhwan, offering interest-free loans to Muslims in India in the 1890s.[241] Also, another Islamic financial

VA, The Research Foundation of CFA Institute 2009, p. 67; Brian Kettell, *Introduction to Islamic Banking and Finance*, London, Harriman House 2011, p. 132; Ibrahim Warde, *Islamic Finance in the Global Economy*, Edinburgh, Edinburgh University Press 2010, p. 154.

235 Zamir Iqbal and Abbas Mirakhor, *An Introduction to Islamic Finance*, Singapore, Wiley 2011, pp. 220–221; Brian Kettell, *Introduction to Islamic Banking and Finance*, London, Harriman House 2011, p. 132.

236 Bala Shanmugam and Zaha Rina Zahri, *A Primer on Islamic Finance*, Charlottesville, VA, The Research Foundation of CFA Institute 2009, p. 64; Brian Kettell, *Introduction to Islamic Banking and Finance*, London, Harriman House 2011, p. 127; Hans Visser, *Islamic Finance: Principles and Practice*, Northampton, MA, Edward Elgar Pub 2013, p. 128.

237 Ibrahim Warde, *Islamic Finance in the Global Economy*, Edinburgh, Edinburgh University Press 2010, p. 154.

238 Ibrahim Warde, *Islamic Finance in the Global Economy*, Edinburgh, Edinburgh University Press 2010, p. 2.

239 Ibrahim Warde, *Islamic Finance in the Global Economy*, Edinburgh, Edinburgh University Press 2010, p. 2.

240 Frank E. Vogel and Samuel L. Hayes, *Islamic Law and Finance*, Boston, Mass, Springer 1998, p. 4; Zamir Iqbal and Abbas Mirakhor, *An Introduction to Islamic Finance*, Singapore, Wiley 2011, p. 15; Islamic Development Bank Group, *Islamic Finance: A Catalyst for Shared Prosperity?*, Washington, D.C, World Bank Publications 2016, p. 57; Munawar Iqbal and Philip Molyneux, *Thirty Years of Islamic Banking*, 2005, p. 37; Natalie Schoon, *Modern Islamic Banking*, West Sussex, Wiley 2016, p. 5; Bala Shanmugam and Zaha Rina Zahri, *A Primer on Islamic Finance*, Charlottesville, VA, The Research Foundation of CFA Institute 2009, p. 3.

241 Bala Shanmugam and Zaha Rina Zahri, *A Primer on Islamic Finance*, Charlottesville, VA, The Research Foundation of CFA Institute 2009, p. 3; Zamir Iqbal and Abbas Mirakhor, *An Introduction to Islamic Finance*, Singapore, Wiley 2011, p. 14.

institution, AnjumanImdad-e-BahmiQardhBilaSud, was established to offer interest-free loans in India in 1923.[242]

In 1963, an Islamic financial institution, Tabung Haji, was established in Malaysia as well to offer interest-free loans to Muslims for the performance of Haj.[243] In the 1970s, many Islamic financial institutions, both public and private, emerged in different countries.[244] In 1971, the first state-sponsored Islamic financial institution, Nasser Social Bank, was established in Egypt[245]; in 1975, the first Islamic commercial bank, Dubai Islamic Bank, was established in the United Arab Emirates[246], and the first multilateral Islamic development finance institution, Islamic Development Bank, was established in Saudi Arabia[247]; in 1979, the first Islamic insurance company, Islamic Insurance Company, was established in Sudan.[248]

From 1975 to 1990 is regarded as the most significant period in the history of Islamic finance as it witnessed the evolution of Islamic finance into a viable alternative to conventional finance.[249] Not only a large number of Islamic financial institutions were established in the private sector, but many Islamic financial products were also developed and Islamic financial institutions showed good results while using these products.[250]

There are more than three hundred Islamic financial institutions, with assets close to $1.9 trillion, in fifty economies, both Muslim and non-Muslim, across the globe.[251] Islamic finance has experienced growth in Muslim as well as non-Muslim countries.[252]

---

242 Bala Shanmugam and Zaha Rina Zahri, *A Primer on Islamic Finance*, Charlottesville, VA, The Research Foundation of CFA Institute 2009, p. 3; Zamir Iqbal and Abbas Mirakhor, *An Introduction to Islamic Finance*, Singapore, Wiley 2011, p. 14.

243 Zamir Iqbal and Abbas Mirakhor, *An Introduction to Islamic Finance*, Singapore, Wiley 2011, p. 15; Usman Hayat and Adeel Malik, *Islamic Finance: Ethics, Concepts, Practice*, CFA Institute Research Foundation 2014, p. 8.

244 Frank E. Vogel and Samuel L. Hayes, *Islamic Law and Finance*, Boston, Mass, Springer 1998, p. 4.

245 Munawar Iqbal and Philip Molyneux, *Thirty Years of Islamic Banking*, 2005, p. 37; Frank E. Vogel and Samuel L. Hayes, *Islamic Law and Finance*, Boston, Mass, Springer 1998, p. 4; Zamir Iqbal and Abbas Mirakhor, *An Introduction to Islamic Finance*, Singapore, Wiley 2011, p. 15.

246 Usman Hayat and Adeel Malik, *Islamic Finance: Ethics, Concepts, Practice*, CFA Institute Research Foundation 2014, p. 8; Zamir Iqbal and Abbas Mirakhor, *An Introduction to Islamic Finance*, Singapore, Wiley 2011, p. 15.

247 Usman Hayat and Adeel Malik, *Islamic Finance: Ethics, Concepts, Practice*, CFA Institute Research Foundation 2014, p. 8; Zamir Iqbal and Abbas Mirakhor, *An Introduction to Islamic Finance*, Singapore, Wiley 2011, p. 15.

248 Bala Shanmugam and Zaha Rina Zahri, *A Primer on Islamic Finance*, Charlottesville, VA, The Research Foundation of CFA Institute 2009, p. 64; Usman Hayat and Adeel Malik, *Islamic Finance: Ethics, Concepts, Practice*, CFA Institute Research Foundation 2014, p. 8.

249 Munawar Iqbal and Philip Molyneux, *Thirty Years of Islamic Banking*, 2005, p. 37.

250 Munawar Iqbal and Philip Molyneux, *Thirty Years of Islamic Banking*, 2005, pp. 37–38.

251 Islamic Development Bank Group, *Islamic Finance: A Catalyst for Shared Prosperity?* Washington, D.C, World Bank Publications 2016, p. 57.

252 Islamic Development Bank Group, *Islamic Finance: A Catalyst for Shared Prosperity?* Washington, D.C, World Bank Publications 2016, p. 63; Timothy Spangler, *Islamic Funds* –

4.2. ISLAMIC FINANCIAL STANDARDS

There are two main entities, based in different Muslim countries, aiming for the harmonization of standards and principles concerning Islamic finance. One is Accounting and Auditing Organization for Islamic Financial Institutions (AAOIFI) and the other is Islamic Financial Services Board (IFSB). The standards or guidelines prescribed by these entities are not binding; however, they are taken into account by governments, national regulators, Islamic financial institutions, and conventional financial institutions that offer Islamic financial services.[253] There are also other entities, which do not make standards and guidelines, but are working for the development of the Islamic finance globally. These include Islamic Development Bank (IDB), International Islamic Financial Market (IIFM), General Council for Islamic Banks and Financial Institutions (CIBAFI), etc.

4.2.1. *Accounting and Auditing Organization for Islamic Financial Institutions (AAOIFI)*

Accounting and Auditing Organization of Islamic Financial Institutions (AAOIFI) was set up in 1991 in Bahrain.[254] It is an entity that develops and issues standards for the global Islamic financial industry.[255] In other words, it standardizes and harmonizes international Islamic financial practices and reporting in accordance with Sharia.[256]

AAOIFI has issued a hundred standards regarding accounting, auditing, ethics, and governance.[257] These standards are developed as result of a thorough process comprised of various steps.[258] These standards are not only implemented by Islamic Development Group, but are also a part of the mandatory regulatory requirements in various countries.[259] On the other hand, some countries use them as guidelines for policy making or as voluntary guidelines.[260] At present,

---

Sharia Law and Investment Structures, Forbes, Apr. 5, 2011. https://www.forbes.com/sites/timothyspangler/2011/04/05/islamic-funds-sharia-law-and-investment-structures/#39a28f9ac526.

253 Zulkifli Hasan, *Shari'ah Governance in Islamic Banks*, Edinburgh, Edinburgh University Press2012, p. 67, Ahmad A. Alkhamees, *A Critique of Creative Shari'ah Compliance in the Islamic Finance Industry*, Leiden, Brill | Nijhoff 2017, p. 238.

254 AAOIFI, http://aaoifi.com/our-history/?lang=en (last visited May. 31, 2018).

255 AAOIFI, http://aaoifi.com/our-history/?lang=en (last visited May. 31, 2018).

256 AAOIFI, http://aaoifi.com/our-mission/?lang=en(last visited May. 31, 2018).

257 AAOIFI, http://aaoifi.com/about-aaoifi/?lang=en(last visited May. 31, 2018).

258 AAOIFI, http://aaoifi.com/standards-development-and-revision-processes/?lang=en (last visited May. 31, 2018).

259 AAOIFI, http://aaoifi.com/adoption-of-aaoifi-standards/?lang=en (last visited May. 31, 2018).

260 AAOIFI, http://aaoifi.com/adoption-of-aaoifi-standards/?lang=en (last visited May. 31, 2018).

these standards are being followed by a large number of leading Islamic financial institutions across the globe.[261]

AAOIFI has more focus on individual role players or individual Islamic financial institutions.[262] AAOIFI has four categories of membership for the various institutions.[263] Currently, it has members from forty-five different jurisdictions.[264]

4.2.2. Islamic Financial Services Board (IFSB)

Islamic Financial Services Board (IFSB) was inaugurated in 2002 in Malaysia.[265] It started operations in 2003.[266] Its mission is "to promote the stability and resilience of Islamic financial industry."[267] In order to fulfil this mission, it "promotes the development of a prudent and transparent Islamic financial services industry through introducing new, or adopting existing international standards consistent with Shari'ah principles, and recommend them for adoption."[268]

So far, IFSB has issued twenty-seven standards, guiding principles, and technical notes[269], which are prepared through a thorough process comprised of various steps.[270] IFSB is more concerned with the regulatory and supervisory bodies.[271] It has three categories of membership.[272] Currently, it has members from fifty-seven jurisdictions.[273]

---

261 AAOIFI, http://aaoifi.com/adoption-of-aaoifi-standards/?lang=en (last visited May. 31, 2018); AAOIFI, http://aaoifi.com/about-aaoifi/?lang=en (last visited May. 31, 2018).

262 Zulkifli Hasan, *Shari'ah Governance in Islamic Banks*, Edinburgh, Edinburgh University Press 2012,p. 67; Ahmad A. Alkhamees, *A Critique of Creative Shari'ah Compliance in the Islamic Finance Industry*, Leiden, Brill | Nijhoff 2017, p. 238.

263 AAOIFI, http://aaoifi.com/?lang=en (last visited May. 31, 2018).

264 AAOIFI, http://aaoifi.com/about-aaoifi/?lang=en (last visited May. 31, 2018).

265 The Islamic Financial Services Board, www.ifsb.org/background.php (last visited May. 31, 2018).

266 The Islamic Financial Services Board, www.ifsb.org/background.php (last visited May. 31, 2018).

267 The Islamic Financial Services Board, www.ifsb.org/mission.php (last visited May. 31, 2018).

268 The Islamic Financial Services Board, www.ifsb.org/mission.php, (last visited May. 31, 2018).

269 The Islamic Financial Services Board, www.ifsb.org/background.php, (last visited May. 31, 2018).

270 The Islamic Financial Services Board, www.ifsb.org/standard.php, (last visited May. 31, 2018).

271 Zulkifli Hasan, *Shari'ah Governance in Islamic Banks*, Edinburgh, Edinburgh University Press 2012, p. 67; Ahmad A. Alkhamees, *A Critique of Creative Shari'ah Compliance in the Islamic Finance Industry*, Leiden, Brill | Nijhoff 2017, p. 238.

272 The Islamic Financial Services Board, www.ifsb.org/requirement.php (last visited May. 31, 2018).

273 The Islamic Financial Services Board, www.ifsb.org/background.php (last visited May. 31, 2018).

4.3. ISLAMIC FINANCE IN THE MUSLIM WORLD

4.3.1. Indonesia

In Indonesia, Bank Indonesia is a statutory body, which started its operations in 1953.[274] The bank was established under the central bank Act No.11 of 1953.[275] The functioning of the bank is governed by the UU No. 23/1999 on Bank Indonesia.[276]

The bank is responsible for supervising and regulating the financial sector, which includes Islamic finance.[277] Act No.21/2008 on Sharia (Islamic) Banking empowers the bank to supervise and regulate the Islamic financial institutions.[278]

In 2016, the share of Islamic banking, in the total banking assets in Indonesia, was 5%[279] it had a share of 1.6% in the total global Islamic banking assets[280]; its share in the total sovereign sukuk issuance globally was 14.7%, while it was 1.8% in corporate sukuk issuance[281]; its overall share in the global issuance of sukuk was 12.1%[282]; it possessed 3% of the total global Islamic funds.[283]

4.3.2. Kingdom of Saudi Arabia

In Kingdom of Saudi Arabia (KSA), Saudi Arabian Monetary Authority (SAMA) started its operations in 1952.[284]

The agency is responsible for supervising and regulating the financial sector, which includes Islamic finance.[285] However, there is no separate legislation for the supervision and regulation of Islamic financial institutions.[286] It regulates

274 Bank Indonesia, www.bi.go.id/en/tentang-bi/museum/sejarah-bi/bi/Pages/historybi1.aspx (last visited May. 31, 2018).

275 Bank Indonesia, www.bi.go.id/en/tentang-bi/museum/sejarah-bi/bi/Pages/historybi1.aspx (last visited May. 31, 2018).

276 "Status and Position of Bank Indonesia" available at www.bi.go.id/en/tentang-bi/fungsi-bi/status/Contents/Default.aspx.

277 "Objectives and Tasks of Bank Indonesia Function" available at www.bi.go.id/en/tentang-bi/fungsi-bi/tujuan/Contents/Default.aspx.

278 "Bank Indonesia Acts" available at www.bi.go.id/en/tentang-bi/uu-bi/Contents/Default.aspx.

279 Islamic Financial Services Board, Islamic Financial Services Industry Stability Report 8 (2017), https://www.ifsb.org/docs/IFSB%20IFSI%20Stability%20Report%202017.pdf.

280 Islamic Financial Services Board, Islamic Financial Services Industry Stability Report 9 (2017), https://www.ifsb.org/docs/IFSB%20IFSI%20Stability%20Report%202017.pdf.

281 Islamic Financial Services Board, Islamic Financial Services Industry Stability Report 16, 18 (2017), https://www.ifsb.org/docs/IFSB%20IFSI%20Stability%20Report%202017.pdf.

282 Islamic Financial Services Board, Islamic Financial Services Industry Stability Report 19 (2017), https://www.ifsb.org/docs/IFSB%20IFSI%20Stability%20Report%202017.pdf.

283 Islamic Financial Services Board, Islamic Financial Services Industry Stability Report 25 (2017), https://www.ifsb.org/docs/IFSB%20IFSI%20Stability%20Report%202017.pdf.

284 "SAMA's Functions" available at www.sama.gov.sa/en-US/About/Pages/SAMAFunction.aspx.

285 "SAMA's Functions" available at www.sama.gov.sa/en-US/About/Pages/SAMAFunction.aspx.

286 *Fitch: Islamic Banking Is Dominant in Saudi Arabia*, Reuters, Feb. 2, 2016, https://www.reuters.com/article/idUSFit947384 (last visited May. 31, 2018); *see also* Speech of H.E. The

conventional financial institutions and Islamic financial institutions in the same manner, without making any distinction between the two.[287]

In 2016, the share of Islamic banking, in the total banking assets in Kingdom of Saudi Arabia (KSA) was 51.1%[288]; it had a share of 20.6% in the total global Islamic banking assets[289]; its share in the total sovereign sukuk issuance globally was 6.7%, while it was 11.6% regarding corporate sukuk issuance in 2016[290]; its overall share in the global issuance of sukuk was 7.7%[291]; it possessed 38% of the total global Islamic funds.[292]

4.3.3. Malaysia

In Malaysia, Bank Negara Malaysia is a statutory body, which started its operations in1959.[293] Central Bank of Malaysia Act, 2009, governs the functioning of the bank.[294]

The bank is responsible for supervising and regulating the financial sector, which includes Islamic finance.[295] Islamic Financial Services Act, 2013, empowers the bank to supervise and regulate Islamic financial institutions.[296]

In 2016, the share of Islamic banking, in the total banking assets in Malaysia, was 23.8%[297]; it had a share of 9.3% in the total global Islamic banking assets[298]; its share in the total sovereign sukuk issuance globally was 50.8%, while it was 50.2% in corporate sukuk issuance[299]; its overall share in

---

Governor of SAMA at the First Islamic Banking and Finance Research Conference www.sama.gov.sa/en-US/News/Pages/News14032016.aspx (last visited May 31, 2018).

287 *Fitch: Islamic Banking Is Dominant in Saudi Arabia*, Reuters, Feb. 2, 2016, https://www.reuters.com/article/idUSFit947384 (last visited May. 31, 2018); *see also* Speech of H.E. the Governor of SAMA at the First Islamic Banking and Finance Research Conference www.sama.gov.sa/en-US/News/Pages/News14032016.aspx (last visited May 31, 2018).

288 Islamic Financial Services Board, Islamic Financial Services Industry Stability Report 8 (2017), https://www.ifsb.org/docs/IFSB%20IFSI%20Stability%20Report%202017.pdf.

289 Islamic Financial Services Board, Islamic Financial Services Industry Stability Report 9 (2017), https://www.ifsb.org/docs/IFSB%20IFSI%20Stability%20Report%202017.pdf.

290 Islamic Financial Services Board, Islamic Financial Services Industry Stability Report 16, 18 (2017), https://www.ifsb.org/docs/IFSB%20IFSI%20Stability%20Report%202017.pdf.

291 Islamic Financial Services Board, Islamic Financial Services Industry Stability Report 19 (2017), https://www.ifsb.org/docs/IFSB%20IFSI%20Stability%20Report%202017.pdf.

292 Islamic Financial Services Board, Islamic Financial Services Industry Stability Report 25 (2017), https://www.ifsb.org/docs/IFSB%20IFSI%20Stability%20Report%202017.pdf.

293 "About the Bank" available at www.bnm.gov.my/index.php?ch=en_about&pg=en_intro&lang=en.

294 "Legislation" available at www.bnm.gov.my/index.php?ch=en_legislation&lang=en.

295 "Legislation" available at www.bnm.gov.my/index.php?ch=en_legislation&lang=en.

296 "Legislation" available at www.bnm.gov.my/index.php?ch=en_legislation&lang=en.

297 Islamic Financial Services Board, Islamic Financial Services Industry Stability Report 8 (2017), https://www.ifsb.org/docs/IFSB%20IFSI%20Stability%20Report%202017.pdf.

298 Islamic Financial Services Board, Islamic Financial Services Industry Stability Report 9 (2017), https://www.ifsb.org/docs/IFSB%20IFSI%20Stability%20Report%202017.pdf.

299 Islamic Financial Services Board, Islamic Financial Services Industry Stability Report 16, 18 (2017), https://www.ifsb.org/docs/IFSB%20IFSI%20Stability%20Report%202017.pdf.

the global issuance of sukuk was 50.6%[300]; and it possessed 29% of the total global Islamic funds.[301]

4.3.4. *Pakistan*

In Pakistan, State Bank of Pakistan is a statutory body, which started its operations in 1956.[302] The bank was established under State Bank of Pakistan Act, 1956, which also governs the functioning of the bank.[303]

The bank is responsible for supervising and regulating the financial sector, which includes Islamic finance.[304] However, there is no separate legislation for the supervision and regulation of Islamic financial institutions.[305] The bank's Islamic Banking Department is responsible for the development and promotion of Islamic finance in the country.[306]

In 2016, the share of Islamic banking, in the total banking assets in Pakistan, was 11.7%[307]; it had a share of 1.1% in the total global Islamic banking assets[308]; its share in the total sovereign sukuk issuance globally was 4.8%[309]; its overall share in the global issuance of sukuk was 3.8%[310]; it possessed 3% of the total global Islamic funds.[311]

4.3.5. *United Arab Emirates*

In United Arab Emirates (UAE), Central Bank of the UAE is a statutory body, which started its operations in 1980.[312] Union Law No. (10) of 1980 governs the functioning of the bank.[313]

300 Islamic Financial Services Board, Islamic Financial Services Industry Stability Report19 (2017), https://www.ifsb.org/docs/IFSB%20IFSI%20Stability%20Report%202017.pdf.

301 Islamic Financial Services Board, Islamic Financial Services Industry Stability Report25 (2017), https://www.ifsb.org/docs/IFSB%20IFSI%20Stability%20Report%202017.pdf.

302 "Introduction" available at www.sbp.org.pk/about/Intro.asp.

303 "Introduction" available at www.sbp.org.pk/about/Intro.asp.

304 "Functions of SBP" available at www.sbp.org.pk/about/Func.asp.

305 Www.sbp.org.pk/departments/ibd/Regulation_Supervision.pdf.

306 "Islamic Banking Department" available at www.sbp.org.pk/departments/ibd.htm.

307 Islamic Financial Services Board, Islamic Financial Services Industry Stability Report8 (2017), https://www.ifsb.org/docs/IFSB%20IFSI%20Stability%20Report%202017.pdf; *see also* www.sbp.org.pk/ibd/bulletin/2017/Mar.pdf.

308 Islamic Financial Services Board, Islamic Financial Services Industry Stability Report 9 (2017), https://www.ifsb.org/docs/IFSB%20IFSI%20Stability%20Report%202017.pdf.

309 Islamic Financial Services Board, Islamic Financial Services Industry Stability Report 16, 18 (2017), https://www.ifsb.org/docs/IFSB%20IFSI%20Stability%20Report%202017.pdf.

310 Islamic Financial Services Board, Islamic Financial Services Industry Stability Report 19 (2017), https://www.ifsb.org/docs/IFSB%20IFSI%20Stability%20Report%202017.pdf.

311 Islamic Financial Services Board, Islamic Financial Services Industry Stability Report 25 (2017), https://www.ifsb.org/docs/IFSB%20IFSI%20Stability%20Report%202017.pdf.

312 "Objectives" https://www.centralbank.ae/en/index.php?option=com_content&view=article&id=68&Itemid=107#(last visited May. 31, 2018).

313 "Objectives" https://www.centralbank.ae/en/index.php?option=com_content&view=article&id=68&Itemid=107#(last visited May. 31, 2018).

The bank is responsible for supervising and regulating the financial sector.[314] Federal Law No.6 of 1985 Regarding Islamic Banks, Financial Institutions and Investment Companies empowers the bank to supervise and regulate Islamic financial institutions.[315]

In 2016, the share of Islamic banking, in the total banking assets in United Arab Emirates (UAE), was 19.6%[316]; it had a share of 9.0% in the total global Islamic banking assets[317]; its share in the total sovereign sukuk issuance globally was 8.1%, while it was 18.3% regarding corporate sukuk issuance[318]; its overall share in the global issuance of sukuk was 10.5%[319]; it possessed 0.41% of the total global Islamic funds.[320]

4.4. ISLAMIC FINANCE IN EUROPE

4.4.1. United Kingdom

The United Kingdom is the leader in Islamic finance in Europe.[321] A conducive regulatory framework, a supportive government, and a vast experience of financial innovation are the factors that attract Islamic financial institutions to the country.[322]

Islamic finance saw its dawn in the UK in the 1980s when different investment banks started offering customized Islamic financial services to their clients from the Middle East.[323] In 1981, the International Association for Islamic Economics was set up.[324] In 1982, the first Islamic bank, Al Barakara International, was

314 "Objectives" https://www.centralbank.ae/en/index.php?option=com_content&view=article&id=47&Itemid=105(last visited May. 31, 2018).

315 Available at https://www.centralbank.ae/pdf/LawNo6-1985-IslaminBanks.pdf.

316 Islamic Financial Services Board, Islamic Financial Services Industry Stability Report 8 (2017), https://www.ifsb.org/docs/IFSB%20IFSI%20Stability%20Report%202017.pdf.

317 Islamic Financial Services Board, Islamic Financial Services Industry Stability Report 9 (2017), https://www.ifsb.org/docs/IFSB%20IFSI%20Stability%20Report%202017.pdf.

318 Islamic Financial Services Board, Islamic Financial Services Industry Stability Report 16, 18 (2017), https://www.ifsb.org/docs/IFSB%20IFSI%20Stability%20Report%202017.pdf.

319 Islamic Financial Services Board, Islamic Financial Services Industry Stability Report 19 (2017), https://www.ifsb.org/docs/IFSB%20IFSI%20Stability%20Report%202017.pdf.

320 Islamic Financial Services Board, Islamic Financial Services Industry Stability Report 25 (2017), https://www.ifsb.org/docs/IFSB%20IFSI%20Stability%20Report%202017.pdf.

321 Manu Mair, *Britain to lead the world in Islamic finance*, Feb. 26, 2015, https://www.telegraph.co.uk/finance/newsbysector/banksandfinance/11435465/Britain-to-lead-the-world-in-Islamic-finance.html (last visited May. 31, 2018).

322 "UK Excellence in Islamic Finance" https://assets.publishing.service.gov.uk/government/uploads/system/uploads/attachment_data/file/367154/UKTI_UK_Excellence_in_Islamic_Finance_Reprint_2014_Spread.pdf (last visited May. 31, 2018).

323 "UK Excellence in Islamic Finance" https://assets.publishing.service.gov.uk/government/uploads/system/uploads/attachment_data/file/367154/UKTI_UK_Excellence_in_Islamic_Finance_Reprint_2014_Spread.pdf (last visited May. 31, 2018).

324 Ahmed Belouafi, AbdelkaderChachi, *Islamic Finance in the United Kingdom: Factors Behind its Development and Growth*, 22 IES. 37, 37–78 (2014). www.irti.org/English/Research/Documents/IES/002.pdf.

established.[325] In 1983, Takaful UK Limited was set up for the local Muslims.[326] In 1995, the Loughborough University became the first British university to offer Islamic banking and finance at the graduate level.[327] In 1997, the first Islamic mutual fund was launched.[328] In 2001, the Bank of England established the Islamic Finance Working Group to enable the development of Islamic finance in the UK.[329] Among other things, it explores different ways to ensure that Islamic financial institutions and their clients receive the same treatment as their conventional counterparts.[330] In 2005, the first corporate Sukuk was launched.[331] In 2007, the first Sukuk was listed on the London Stock Exchange.[332] In 2010, the second corporate Sukuk was launched.[333] In 2013, the Islamic Finance Task Force was set up to promote the UK as a centre of Islamic finance.[334] In 2014, the UK became the first non-Muslim country to issue sovereign Sukuk.[335]

Islamic financial institutions are regulated by the Financial Conduct Authority and the Prudential Regulation Authority.[336]

In the UK, the laws have been modified in order to facilitate Islamic financial transactions.[337] For instance, the law was amended to remove the imposition of

---

325 "UK Excellence in Islamic Finance" https://assets.publishing.service.gov.uk/government/uploads/system/uploads/attachment_data/file/367154/UKTI_UK_Excellence_in_Islamic_Finance_Reprint_2014_Spread.pdf (last visited May. 31, 2018).

326 Ahmed Belouafi, AbdelkaderChachi, *Islamic Finance in the United Kingdom: Factors Behind its Development and Growth*, 22 IES. 37, 37–78 (2014). www.irti.org/English/Research/Documents/IES/002.pdf.

327 Ahmed Belouafi, AbdelkaderChachi, *Islamic Finance in the United Kingdom: Factors Behind its Development and Growth*, 22 IES. 37, 37–78 (2014). www.irti.org/English/Research/Documents/IES/002.pdf.

328 "UK Excellence in Islamic Finance" https://assets.publishing.service.gov.uk/government/uploads/system/uploads/attachment_data/file/367154/UKTI_UK_Excellence_in_Islamic_Finance_Reprint_2014_Spread.pdf (last visited May. 31, 2018).

329 "UK Excellence in Islamic Finance" https://assets.publishing.service.gov.uk/government/uploads/system/uploads/attachment_data/file/367154/UKTI_UK_Excellence_in_Islamic_Finance_Reprint_2014_Spread.pdf (last visited May. 31, 2018).

330 "UK Excellence in Islamic Finance" https://assets.publishing.service.gov.uk/government/uploads/system/uploads/attachment_data/file/367154/UKTI_UK_Excellence_in_Islamic_Finance_Reprint_2014_Spread.pdf (last visited May. 31, 2018).

331 Islamic Finance In Europe, (Filippo di Mauro et al. eds., 2013). https://www.ecb.europa.eu/pub/pdf/scpops/ecbocp146.pdf?50223aa58804d7b4f32f4f302534672d.

332 "UK Excellence in Islamic Finance" https://assets.publishing.service.gov.uk/government/uploads/system/uploads/attachment_data/file/367154/UKTI_UK_Excellence_in_Islamic_Finance_Reprint_2014_Spread.pdf (last visited May. 31, 2018).

333 Islamic Finance In Europe, (Filippo di Mauro et al. eds., 2013). https://www.ecb.europa.eu/pub/pdf/scpops/ecbocp146.pdf?50223aa58804d7b4f32f4f302534672d.

334 Https://www.gov.uk/government/uploads/system/uploads/attachment_data/file/367154/UKTI_UK_Excellence_in_Islamic_Finance_Reprint_2014_Spread.pdf; Islamic Finance In Europe, (Filippo di Mauro et al. eds., 2013). https://www.ecb.europa.eu/pub/pdf/scpops/ecbocp146.pdf?50223aa58804d7b4f32f4f302534672d.

335 Https://www.gov.uk/government/news/government-issues-first-islamic-bond.

336 Islamic Finance & Markets 2015, https://www.milbank.com/images/content/1/7/17969/Getting-the-Deal-Through-Islamic-Finance-Markets.pdf.

337 Islamic Finance & Markets 2015, https://www.milbank.com/images/content/1/7/17969/Getting-the-Deal-Through-Islamic-Finance-Markets.pdf.

double stamp duty on Islamic mortgages.[338] Similarly, the law has been amended to provide similar tax treatment to Sukuk and conventional bonds.[339]

In the UK, there is no central authority that monitors if Islamic financial products and services are indeed Islamic.[340] Also, there is no legal requirement for an Islamic financial institution to have a Sharia supervisory board.[341]

The UK has Islamic financial Institutions as well as conventional financial institutions operating Islamic windows.[342] Various universities, institutions, and other entities are offering programs, courses, and trainings in Islamic finance.[343] More than 25 law firms are providing legal services related to Islamic finance.[344]

4.4.2. Luxembourg

Luxembourg is one of the major European financial markets.[345] The existing legal and regulatory framework in the country is conducive to Islamic finance and the government is trying to promote it as a hub for Islamic finance.[346]

In 1978, the first Islamic financial institution was established.[347] In 1982, the first Islamic insurance was established.[348] In 2002, it listed its first Sukuk.[349] In 2008, the government set up a task force for the development of Islamic finance

338 "UK Excellence in Islamic Finance" https://assets.publishing.service.gov.uk/government/uploads/system/uploads/attachment_data/file/367154/UKTI_UK_Excellence_in_Islamic_Finance_Reprint_2014_Spread.pdf (last visited May. 31, 2018).

339 Islamic Finance & Markets 2015, https://www.milbank.com/images/content/1/7/17969/Getting-the-Deal-Through-Islamic-Finance-Markets.pdf.

340 Islamic Finance & Markets 2015, https://www.milbank.com/images/content/1/7/17969/Getting-the-Deal-Through-Islamic-Finance-Markets.pdf.

341 Islamic Finance & Markets 2015, https://www.milbank.com/images/content/1/7/17969/Getting-the-Deal-Through-Islamic-Finance-Markets.pdf.

342 Islamic Finance & Markets 2015, https://www.milbank.com/images/content/1/7/17969/Getting-the-Deal-Through-Islamic-Finance-Markets.pdf.

343 "UK Excellence in Islamic Finance" https://assets.publishing.service.gov.uk/government/uploads/system/uploads/attachment_data/file/367154/UKTI_UK_Excellence_in_Islamic_Finance_Reprint_2014_Spread.pdf (last visited May. 31, 2018).

344 "UK Excellence in Islamic Finance" https://assets.publishing.service.gov.uk/government/uploads/system/uploads/attachment_data/file/367154/UKTI_UK_Excellence_in_Islamic_Finance_Reprint_2014_Spread.pdf (last visited May. 31, 2018).

345 Islamic Finance In Europe, (Filippo di Mauro et al. eds., 2013). https://www.ecb.europa.eu/pub/pdf/scpops/ecbocp146.pdf?50223aa58804d7b4f32f4f302534672d.

346 Arendt and Medernach, Islamic Finance 6 (2015); Islamic Finance In Europe, (Filippo di Mauro et al. eds., 2013). https://www.ecb.europa.eu/pub/pdf/scpops/ecbocp146.pdf?50223aa58804d7b4f32f4f302534672d.

347 Bishr Shiblaq, Developing an Islamic Finance Hub in Europe: Luxembourg (2009) www.arendt.com/publications/documents/lawyerspublications/2009.08.28%20-%20developing%20an%20islamic%20finance%20hub%20in%20europe%20luxembourg%20-%20*bis*hr%20shiblaq.pdf.

348 Islamic Finance In Europe, (Filippo di Mauro et al. eds., 2013). https://www.ecb.europa.eu/pub/pdf/scpops/ecbocp146.pdf?50223aa58804d7b4f32f4f302534672d.

349 Islamic Finance In Europe, (Filippo di Mauro et al. eds., 2013). https://www.ecb.europa.eu/pub/pdf/scpops/ecbocp146.pdf?50223aa58804d7b4f32f4f302534672d.

in Luxembourg.[350] In 2009, the government declared Islamic finance as one of the key areas for development.[351] Also in 2009, the Central Bank of Luxembourg became a member of IFSB.[352] In 2011, Luxembourg hosted the 8th IFSB summit and became the first non-Muslim country to do so.[353] In 2014, Luxembourg issued its first sovereign Sukuk.[354]

In Luxembourg, there is no central authority that monitors if Islamic financial products and services are indeed Islamic.[355] Also, there is no legal requirement for an Islamic financial institution to have a Sharia supervisory board.[356]

Murabaha, Ijara, Istisna, and Musharaka are the frequently used Islamic financial transactions.[357] The government has ensured that these transactions receive tax treatment similar to their conventional counterparts.[358] Therefore, many Islamic financial transactions can be conducted tax efficiently.[359]

5. CRITIQUE OF ISLAMIC FINANCE

While there are people who have absolute faith in Islamic finance, there are those who question its various features and practices. The following are some of the main concerns and objections raised about Islamic finance:

1. The theory and practice of Islamic finance are not consonant with each other.[360]
2. While striving to provide Islamic alternatives to conventional financial products and transactions, Islamic financial institutions often simply

---

350 Bishr Shiblaq, Developing an Islamic Finance Hub in Europe: Luxembourg (2009) www.arendt.com/publications/documents/lawyerspublications/2009.08.28%20-%20developing%20an%20islamic%20finance%20hub%20in%20europe%20luxembourg%20-%20*bi*shr%20shiblaq.pdf.

351 Bishr Shiblaq, Developing an Islamic Finance Hub in Europe: Luxembourg (2009) www.arendt.com/publications/documents/lawyerspublications/2009.08.28%20-%20developing%20an%20islamic%20finance%20hub%20in%20europe%20luxembourg%20-%20*bi*shr%20shiblaq.pdf.

352 Islamic Finance In Europe, (Filippo di Mauro et al. eds., 2013). https://www.ecb.europa.eu/pub/pdf/scpops/ecbocp146.pdf?50223aa58804d7b4f32f4f302534672d.

353 Oliver R. Hoor and Pierre Kreemer, Luxembourg aims at becoming the first non-Muslim country to issue sovereign sukuk, AGEFI Luxembourg 27 (January 2014).

354 Arendt and Medernach, *Islamic Finance*, 2015, p. 7.

355 Bishr Shiblaq, Developing an Islamic Finance Hub in Europe: Luxembourg (2009) www.arendt.com/publications/documents/lawyerspublications/2009.08.28%20-%20developing%20an%20islamic%20finance%20hub%20in%20europe%20luxembourg%20-%20*bi*shr%20shiblaq.pdf.

356 Bishr Shiblaq, Developing an Islamic Finance Hub in Europe: Luxembourg (2009) www.arendt.com/publications/documents/lawyerspublications/2009.08.28%20-%20developing%20an%20islamic%20finance%20hub%20in%20europe%20luxembourg%20-%20*bi*shr%20shiblaq.pdf.

357 Arendt and Medernach, *Islamic Finance*, 2015, p. 6.

358 Arendt and Medernach, *Islamic Finance*, 2015, p. 6.

359 Oliver R. Hoor and Pierre Kreemer, Luxembourg aims at becoming the first non-Muslim country to issue sovereign sukuk, AGEFI Luxembourg 27 (January 2014).

360 Muhammad Ayub, *Understanding Islamic Finance*, Hoboken, NJ, Wiley 2007, p. 435.

replicate, in substance, conventional financial products and transactions.[361] Consequently, Islamic financial products and transactions are similar, in substance, to conventional financial products and transactions.[362]

3. Islamic financial products and transactions, compared to their conventional counterparts, are often inefficient.[363]
4. While the pioneers of Islamic finance stressed on using participatory modes, i.e., mushāraka and mudaraba, the debt-creating modes are also being used to earn fixed returns.[364]
5. Islamic financial institutions routinely conduct business on the basis of fixed rates and earn fixed returns.[365] Even in participatory modes, Islamic financial institutions charge market-based rates on their investment.[366]
6. Islamic financial institutions routinely use interest-based benchmarks, e.g., LIBOR, etc., to price their products.[367]
7. Islamic financial institutions routinely take collateral while conducting business.[368] They do not facilitate people who are unable to offer collateral.[369]
8. Islamic financial institutions are never lenient towards clients who are genuinely defaulting.[370]
9. Islamic financial services and products are not standardized.[371]
10. Islamic financial institutions usually work in the same regulatory environment as conventional financial institutions.[372]

---

361 Habib Ahmed, *Product Development in Islamic Banks,* Edinburgh, Edinburgh University Press 2011, p. 192.

362 Bala Shanmugam and Zaha Rina Zahri, *A Primer on Islamic Finance*, Charlottesville, VA, The Research Foundation of CFA Institute 2009, p. 94; Habib Ahmed, *Product Development in Islamic Banks,* Edinburgh, Edinburgh University Press 2011, p. 195.

363 Habib Ahmed, *Product Development in Islamic Banks,* Edinburgh, Edinburgh University Press 2011, p. 193.

364 Muhammad Ayub, *Understanding Islamic Finance,* Hoboken, NJ, Wiley 2007, p. 435.

365 Muhammad Ayub, *Understanding Islamic Finance*, Hoboken, NJ, Wiley 2007, p. 435.

366 Muhammad Ayub, *Understanding Islamic Finance*, Hoboken, NJ, Wiley 2007, p.435.

367 Muhammad Ayub, *Understanding Islamic Finance*, Hoboken, NJ, Wiley 2007, p. 435; Hossein Askari, Zamir Iqbal and Abbas Mirakhoe, *New Issues in Islamic Finance and Economics,* 2009, pp. 57, 179; Natalie Schoon, *Modern Islamic Banking,*West Sussex, Wiley 2016, pp. 36, 139.

368 Muhammad Ayub, *Understanding Islamic Finance*, Hoboken, NJ, Wiley 2007, p. 436.

369 Muhammad Ayub, *Understanding Islamic Finance*, Hoboken, NJ, Wiley 2007, p. 436.

370 Muhammad Ayub, *Understanding Islamic Finance*, Hoboken, NJ, Wiley 2007, p. 436.

371 Muhammad Ayub, *Understanding Islamic Finance*, Hoboken, NJ, Wiley 2007, p. 441; Bala Shanmugam and Zaha Rina Zahri, *A Primer on Islamic Finance,* Charlottesville, VA, The Research Foundation of CFA Institute 2009, p. 92–93; Zamir Iqbal and Abbas Mirakhor, *An Introduction to Islamic Finance,* Singapore, Wiley 2011, p. 362; Natalie Schoon, *Modern Islamic Banking,*West Sussex, Wiley 2016, p.158.

372 Muhammad Ayub, *Understanding Islamic Finance*, Hoboken, NJ, Wiley 2007, p. 435; Bala Shanmugam and Zaha Rina Zahri, *A Primer on Islamic Finance*, Charlottesville, VA, The Research Foundation of CFA Institute 2009, p. 95; Natalie Schoon, *Modern Islamic Banking,* West Sussex, Wiley 2016, p. 135.

11. While setting up Islamic windows or Islamic branches, conventional financial institutions allocate interest-tainted funds as the base capitol.[373]

6. CONCLUSION

Islamic finance has had tremendous growth.[374] While Islamic financial institutions are offering a large number of products and services that are similar to the ones offered by conventional financial institutions[375], Islamic financial institutions are constantly trying to come up with new ideas in order to remain competitive. However, while trying to prove Islamic finance as a viable alternative to conventional finance, Islamic financial experts must ensure that it remains Islamic in substance.

---

373 Muhammad Ayub, *Understanding Islamic Finance*, Hoboken, NJ, Wiley 2007, pp. 435–436; Natalie Schoon, *Modern Islamic Banking*, West Sussex, Wiley 2016, pp. 73–74.

374 Muhammad Ayub, *Understanding Islamic Finance*, Hoboken, NJ, Wiley 2007, 433; Bala Shanmugam and Zaha Rina Zahri, *A Primer on Islamic Finance*, Charlottesville, VA, The Research Foundation of CFA Institute 2009, p. 92; Brian Kettell, *Case Studies in Islamic Banking and Finance*, West Sussex, UK, Wiley 2011, p. 13; Habib Ahmed, *Product Development in Islamic Banks*, Edinburgh, Edinburgh University Press 2011, p. 223; Natalie Schoon, *Modern Islamic Banking*, West Sussex, Wiley 2016, p. 157.

375 Muhammad Ayub, *Understanding Islamic Finance*, Hoboken, NJ, Wiley 2007, p. 433; Habib Ahmed, *Product Development in Islamic Banks*, Edinburgh, Edinburgh University Press 2011, pp. 192–195, 223; Natalie Schoon, *Modern Islamic Banking*, West Sussex, Wiley 2016, p. 158.

ISLAMIC FINANCE IN NON-MUSLIM-MAJORITY JURISDICTIONS: REGULATORY ISSUES

Hans Visser
Professor Emeritus of Monetary Economics, Vrije Universiteit Amsterdam

1. INTRODUCTION

Over the last three decades or so, Islamic finance has been slowly spreading from Muslim-majority jurisdictions to other countries. It has not exactly been a triumphal progress, certainly not for retail banks, though banks specialising in wealth management or real estate investment are doing better, first of all in the United Kingdom. The main hurdles preventing a faster rise of Islamic banking outside Muslim-majority countries probably are the following:

(i) politicians have become afraid of negative public reactions to specifically Islamic initiatives;
(ii) surveys indicate that significant parts of the Muslim population in non-Muslim-majority countries are, like the rest of the population, financially illiterate and have hardly any idea what Islamic finance is about[1];
(iii) part of the Muslim population is critical of Islamic finance because in their view it may obey the letter of Islamic law, but flouts the spirit of Islamic law, in particular because it is largely debt-based. This is for instance the case with the followers of Hizb ut-Tahrir[2];
(iv) devising a regulatory framework that fits both Islamic finance and conventional finance and creates a level playing field is a complex task.

The fourth hurdle is the subject of this chapter. Administrative hurdles or regulatory issues seem to hit Islamic commercial banking more than Islamic

1 H.A. Dar, 'Demand for Islamic financial services in the UK: chasing a mirage?', (2004) *Economics Research Paper* no. 04–11, Loughborough University, http://hdl.handle.net/2134/335, accessed 15.08.2007; T. Coolen-Maturi, 'Islamic insurance (takaful): demand and supply in the UK', (2013) *International Journal of Islamic and Middle Eastern Finance and Management* 6:2.

2 *Gold Standard; The Future for a Stable Global Currency*, Hizb ut-Tahrir Britain, 2011 www.hizb.org.uk/solutions/gold-standard-the-future-for-a-stable-global-currency, accessed 29.03.2012.

wealth management and real-estate investment. It's not surprising that Islamic commercial banking, in particular retail banking, has not yet really taken off outside the Muslim-majority world. The focus of this chapter is on Islamic commercial banks, with an emphasis on Europe. Questions surrounding the capital market are left on one side, as the hurdles there appear to be much lower. Pension funds and takaful would require separate treatment and are also left out of account. It may be noted that regulatory issues facing Muslim-majority jurisdictions do not differ fundamentally from those elsewhere, but generally the hurdles are lower, as their governments often are more willing to facilitate Islamic finance than other governments and the population is likely to be more receptive to Islamic financial products.[3] We start with a couple of general issues which supervisors see themselves confronted with and which are central to the character of Islamic financial products. These are followed by a number of specific issues that bear on the application of supervisory measures to Islamic financial products. The distinction is perhaps not watertight, but may still be workable.

2. GENERAL ISSUES

2.1. SINGLE OR SEPARATE SET OF RULES

The first question that must be answered by governments and banking supervisors is whether Islamic finance should fall under a separate set of rules and laws or that there should be a single set of rules for Islamic finance and conventional finance. The leading idea of the economics discipline is that there is no such thing as a free lunch, or, in technical language, there are always opportunity costs: if you want to have one thing, you will have to give up something else. So both solutions have their pros and cons. Single regulation, as in Bahrain, Singapore, the United Arab Emirates (UAE) and the UK, makes it at first sight easier to maintain a level playing field, but care must be exerted to avoid undue restrictions on the activities of Islamic financial institutions. Separate legislation, as in Malaysia, on the other hand makes it easier to take account of the special nature of Islamic financial institutions. Separate regulation could for instance provide for a specification of the role and tasks of an Islamic bank's sharia supervisory board, or for special liquidity support channels, given the lack of Islamic money market paper. Also, separate regulation could solve the problem that Islamic commercial banks do not fit in a system where full-fledged commercial banks, or clearing banks, have to keep interest-bearing deposits at the central bank and borrow against interest from the central bank. The downside is that it requires more legislative work and runs the risk of losing

3 See M.K. Hassan, J. Brodmann and B. Rayfield, 'The Current Status of Islamic Bank Regulation in the World' (2017) *Journal of Islamic Economics, Banking and Finance* 13:1.

sight of the level playing field.[4] But the lines between the two approaches are blurred. In a survey conducted by the IMF in 2011 among 30 non-EU countries plus the UK it was found that only three had a separate regulatory framework for Islamic banking, but the majority of the others supplemented the Basel Committee framework fully or partly applicable to all banks with additional provisions for Islamic banks. These sometimes consisted of prudential standards and guiding principles developed by the Islamic Financial Service Board (IFSB). Some countries, such as Bahrain, Indonesia, Jordan, Lebanon and Pakistan, have separate supervisory units within a single supervisory authority.[5]

2.2. LEGAL ISSUES: SUBSTANCE OVER FORM?

A crucial question is whether lawmakers and law courts follow an *economic* or a *legal* approach, in other words, a *substance over form* approach or not. A strict legal approach would make life extremely difficult for Islamic banks. The United States tends to be very liberal in this regard.[6] In Europe, the British government, eager to promote London as a centre of Islamic finance, included a provision in the 2003 *Finance Act* treating returns and income payments on debt as if they were interest. This helped stimulate the market for sukuk (Islamic certificates).[7] Luxembourg and the Netherlands likewise stand out as champions of the substance-over-form approach.[8] Nevertheless, the Dutch tax authorities do not feel free to treat Islamic substitutes for conventional interest payments on home finance contracts as equivalent to interest. This is because Dutch real estate law gives a very narrow and exact definition of interest. If a lease element is involved, as is the case in *ijara wa iqtina* or hire purchase and *musharaka mutanaqisah* or diminishing partnership home finance, the law for instance explicitly requires the financier to state which amount of the rental serves as interest payment. *Murabaha* contracts, discussed below, are subject to the same requirement. As an aside, applying a substance over form approach would not help much if a lease element is involved, as tax deductibility of interest and other costs of home

4 A. Lopez Mejia, S. Aljabrin, R. Awad, M. Norat and I. Song, 'Regulation and Supervision of Islamic Banks' (2014) *IMF Working Paper* No. 14/219.

5 I. Song and C. Oosthuizen, 'Islamic Banking Regulation and Supervision: Survey Results and Challenges' (2014), *IMF Working Paper* No. 14/220.

6 A. Thomas, 'Methods of Islamic home finance in the United States: beneficial breakthroughs' (2001), www.failaka.com, accessed 21.02.2006; M.J.T. McMillen, 'The Arcapita Group Bankruptcy: A Restructuring Case Study', in *Islamic Commercial Law Report 2016*, International Shari'ah Research Academy for Islamic Finance (ISRA), Kuala Lumpur, and Thomson Reuters 2015, pp. 136–142.

7 A.U.F. Ahmad, 'Regulatory Impediments to Islamic Finance: The UK and Australia Compared' (2013) *Journal of Islamic Economics, Banking and Finance* 9:4, 201.

8 N. Muller, 'Islamic Finance and Taxation: A Level Playing Field in Sight?', in *Derivatives & Financial Instruments*, Volume 12, International Bureau of Fiscal Documentation (IBFD), Amsterdam 2010, pp. 7–9.

finance is only available to Dutch home buyers if they own at least 50% of the object. A revision of the laws and regulations pertaining to tax and real estate issues would be complex and time-consuming, which does little to convince politicians and civil servants that it is worth pursuing, given also the poor prospects for Islamic mortgages and other products in the retail market. After all, in the United Kingdom, with a much larger potential market and no such legal restrictions, Islamic retail banks or Islamic retail windows of conventional financial institutions closed down after making losses or low profits or now concentrate on wholesale banking and wealth management.

Obviously, tax issues are inextricably bound up with the substance-over-form question. If Islamic finance is to have a sporting chance in non-Muslim-majority countries, an economic rather than a legal approach is called for, not only with regard to deductibility of financing costs but also in the areas of indirect taxes and international tax agreements. A couple of examples will make this clear.

The most popular Islamic finance form is *murabaha*. The banker buys a good that is needed by a customer and sells it to the customer with a markup, usually against deferred payment. The markup roughly equals the contant value of all future interest payments on an equivalent conventional financing. However, the markup is added to the purchase price of the good and this may increase the purchase price considerably. Under a legal approach VAT will be charged over the purchase price including the markup, putting murabaha purchases at a competitive disadvantage. An economic approach, as applied by the US Internal Revenue Service, would leave room for treating the markup as a financing cost, just like conventional interest. There is an additional problem with murabaha in that the financial institution acts as a trader. Banks are not always allowed to buy and resell merchandise, which severely restricts the use of murabaha. A case in point is Bosnia and Herzegovina, where in addition banks face limitations on using profit-and-loss sharing arrangements (PLS, that is, *mushāraka* or full partnerships and *mudaraba* or sleeping partnership) and ijara or leasing, making life for Islamic banks extremely difficult.[9] In the European Union, very few activities are forbidden for banks, but for non-financial activities such as merchandise trading very high capital-asset ratios apply, in fact 100 per cent. The way out for Islamic banks is to create a holding with both a bank and a

---

9 D. Klepić and F. Hadžić, 'Experience of Normative Regulation of Islamic Banking in United Kingdom and Possibility of Applying in Bosnia and Herzegovina' (2009) *Zbornik radova Ekonomskog fakulteta u Sarajevu* (Collection of Papers of School of Economics in Sarajevo) 29, 279–297 www.ceeol.com/search/article-detail?id=110688, accessed 12.09.2016. More recent information is hard to come by, as the supervisor, the Banking Agency of the Federation of Bosnia and Herzegovina, publishes exclusively in Bosnian. The only Islamic bank in Bosnia, Bosna Bank International, is making its business mostly of long-term financing of acquisitions, construction and adaptation of real estate, R. Komorowski and K. Kubiszewska, 'An Assessment of Islamic Banking in Bosnia and Herzegovina – comparative analysis using the Camels approach' (2016) *Ekonomia Międzynarodowa* 16, 376.

murabaha credit company. The holding is a mixed activity financial holding, which is subject to less onerous capital-asset ratios.[10]

Murabaha home finance, with a longer tenor, is especially hard hit by a legal approach. Because murabaha home finance has a longer tenor than *murabaha* trade finance or consumption good finance, the markup will add substantially to the purchase price. A real-life example will make this clear.[11] A home buyer takes out a mortgage loan of £100,000 in order to be able to buy a £150,000 home, with a £50,000 down payment. The financier charges £61,789.09 for a 15-year tenor, a usual maturity. The home buyer thus has to pay £211,789.09, more than 40 per cent higher than the price for the same home under a conventional mortgage loan. This also leads to over 40 per cent higher real estate transfer taxes. Those real estate transfer taxes are more generally a burden on all Islamic forms of home finance, as these usually involve more than one transfer of ownership where under conventional finance one suffices. This is the case with murabaha finance, where the financier buys the home and sells it on to its customer, and also with *ijara wa iqtina* (hire purchase) and *musharaka mutanaqisa* (diminishing ownership, with the home buyer gradually increasing her share of the joint ownership and the financier thus seeing its share diminish). A level playing field would require only single payment of stamp tax (real estate transfer tax). The UK 2003 *Finance Act*, which was introduced to remove obstacles to Islamic forms of finance, requires only a single payment of Stamp Duty Land Tax on Islamic real estate transactions.[12] In the Netherlands, however, multiple transfers of ownership have a similar provision only for transactions taking place within six months of each other. Tax issues are extremely complicated and unforeseen problems are sure to crop up. The 2003 *Finance Act* for instance stipulates that under an ijara wa iqtina contract the initial transfer of the property is relieved from Stamp Duty Land Tax if the customer is the registered

---

10 See on capital-asset ratios Directive 2013/36/EU of the European Parliament and of the Council of 26 June 2013 on access to the activity of credit institutions and the prudential supervision of credit institutions and investment firms, amending Directive 2002/87/EC and repealing Directives 2006/48/EC and 2006/49/EC, *Official Journal of the European Union* 27.06.2013, and Regulation (Eu) No 575/2013 of the European Parliament and of the Council of 26 June 2013 on prudential requirements for credit institutions and investment firms and amending Regulation (EU) No 648/2012, *Official Journal of the European Union* 27.06.2013. Lower ratios apply generally for holdings, or financial conglomerates, because supervisors have not yet succeeded in imposing rules on financial conglomerates preventing double or multiple gearing, that is, the same capital being used for fulfilling solvability rules in different entities. See on this siubject L. van Goor, 'It's easy to miss something you're not looking for – why some banks will get in trouble again', (2015) https://glocomnet.com, accessed 19.03.2018. I am indebted to Dr Linda van Goor for information on these issues.

11 Derived from information obtained by Ms. Rachida Talal from a British provider of Islamic home finance in the early 2010s, which she was kind enough to share with me.

12 UK Government, 'Practice guide 69: Islamic financing, update' (2015) www.gov.uk/government/publications/islamic-financing/practice-guide-69-islamic-financing, accessed 03.08.2016.

proprietor.[13] That would imply it does not extend to the financier. The UK Court of Appeal indeed concluded it does not.[14]

As for trans border transactions, these would be stimulated if tax treaties replaced 'interest' by 'income from debt claims', in order to take account of Islamic forms of debt, as in the tax treaty between Bahrain and the Netherlands. Furthermore, it may make sense to include *zakat mal*, the obligatory wealth tax for the benefit of mainly the poor, in treaties as a tax, which Kuwait and Saudi Arabia insist on.[15]

2.3. DEPOSIT INSURANCE AND THE NATURE OF ISLAMIC BANK DEPOSITS

Islamic banks offer deposits that have different characteristics from those offered by conventional banks. Consider demand deposits, or current accounts. These may be held under a *qard hasan* or interest-free loan contract, as in Iran, the UAE, Bahrain and Kuwait, or under a *wadia* or safe custody contract, as in South East Asian countries. Another variant is the *mudaraba* contract, as applied in Malaysia, which involves profit sharing between the bank as the *mudarib* or agent, who invests the funds, and the customer as the *rabb al-mal*, the financier or sleeping partner.[16] Losses should thus be borne by the depositors, which is clearly at odds with deposit guarantees.[17] Under a qard hasan or a wadia contract the bank guarantees the principal amount of the demand deposits, but a mudaraba contract requires the rabb al-mal to absorb any losses, unless the mudarib is guilty of culpable negligence. In many jurisdictions supervisors require demand deposits to be capital-certain, and if Islamic banks and their customers deem mudaraba demand deposits incompatible with capital certainty, they will have to choose another form.

Now the bank may guarantee the principal amount of a demand deposit, but what if a bank fails? Is deposit insurance acceptable from an Islamic point of view? Qard hasan and wadia accounts should not present any difficulty. Islamic law allows guarantees by an external guarantor against a fee, according to many, though not all, *fiqh* or Islamic jurisprudence scholars. One argument in

---

13 UK Government (2015).

14 D. Hunter, 'Chelsea Barracks: Tax consequences of Islamic Finance product heard by the Court of Appeal' (2016) *DAC Beachcroft Banking & Finance Disputes Update*, 4 July, http://sites-dacb.vuturevx.com, accessed 07.07.2016.

15 Muller (2010).

16 Md D. Bakar, S.M. Alhabshi and E. Rahaman, *Islamic Banking and Takaful – Products and Services*, CIMA Certificate in Islamic Finance, Study Guide 2, Chartered Institute of Management Accountants (CIMA), London 2008, p. 74.

17 S.E. Hidayat, 'The Application of International Financial Reporting Standards (IFRS) by Islamic Financial Institutions (IFIs): Benefits and Challenges' (2016) *Journal of Islamic Economics, Banking and Finance* 12:2.

favour of a guarantee is that the preservation of wealth is one of the *maqasid al-sharia* or objectives of divine law, as formulated by Abu Hamid al-Ghazali (1058–1111).[18] The former Dutch system would have been attractive to Islamic banks, as it provided for guarantees by the banks collectively to come to the rescue of depositors of a failed bank, without any pre-paid contributions to a fund. Islamic banks and their sharia boards could interpret this construction as *takaful* or, literally, mutual support. A deposit insurance fund with pre-paid contributions, such as the European Banking Union fund, is much more difficult for sharia boards to swallow. The funds are mainly invested in interest-bearing securities, which goes against the prohibition of riba. Islamic banks will have to stomach a riba-based fund, accepting it as a case of *darura* or necessity, that is, force majeure. Supervisors and regulators could alternatively consider a separate fund for Islamic banks that would invest its money in sharia-compliant ways. The downside is that less money would be available to deal with any given calamity. The solution suggested by Gimigliano that Islamic banks mimic the mutual assistance character of takaful or Islamic insurance by agreeing to make voluntary instead of compulsory contributions does not address the problem of riba-tainted investments by the guarantee fund.[19]

Savings accounts could be structured in the same way as demand deposits, that is, as a wadia, as in Malaysia, or as a qard hasan account, as in Iran. Banks could provide a yield on wadia or qard hasan savings accounts in the form of a *hiba* or gift. Of course, such a gift cannot be promised in advance, not formally at least, because that would taint the account with riba. With *mudaraba* accounts, however, conflicts between sharia and prevailing banking law arise again. Banks would generally be obliged by regulators to provide capital certainty, but that would conflict with the character of *mudaraba* as a profit-sharing arrangement where any loss is solely borne by the *rabb al-mal*, in this case the holder of the savings account. The Islamic Bank of Britain came to an agreement with the Financial Services Authority and resolved this conflict by offering full repayment of the savings deposits while informing account holders how much they would receive in a loss-making situation if the character of a *mudaraba* were fully maintained. Clients who let their obedience to sharia prevail had the option to refuse full repayment.[20]

In practice banks try to prevent a situation where depositors would be confronted with a negative return. To this end they set part of their profits aside

18 S.F. Najeeb and M.M. Mustafa, 'Strengthening the Financial Safety Net: the Role and Mechanisms of *Sharī'ah*-compliant Deposit Insurance Schemes (SCDIS)', (2016) IFSB Working Paper WP-06/03/2016, 18 www.ifsb.org/docs/2016-03-31%20Working%20Paper%20on%20SCDIS%20(WP-06)(Final).pdf, accessed 10.01.2017.

19 G. Gimigliano, 'Investigating Islamic banking in Italy', (2016) *International Journal of Islamic and Middle Eastern Finance and Management* 9:3.

20 M. Ainley, A. Mashayekhi, R. Hicks, A, Rahman and A. Ravalia, *Islamic Finance in the UK: Regulation and Challenges*, Financial Services Authority, London 2007; A.U.F. Ahmad, 'Regulatory Impediments to Islamic Finance: The UK and Australia Compared' (2013) *Journal of Islamic Economics, Banking and Finance* 9:4, 105.

in a Profit Equalization Reserve, enabling them in lean years to pay a return on deposits comparable with the interest rate paid by conventional banks on their time and savings deposits. In cases where banks face restrictions on funding a Profit Equalization Reserve, supervisors might consider loosening these, in order to enable Islamic banks to compete on equal terms with conventional banks. This might, however, conflict with the rules formulated by the International Accounting Standards Board (IASB) and adopted by those supervisors. Moreover, there is a corporate governance issue involved in that investors at any one time may profit or lose with past or future investors and shareholders losing respectively profiting.[21]

It may be noted in passing that the Sharia Advisory Council of Bank Negara Malaysia, the Malaysian central bank, in 2002 resolved that a deposit insurance scheme for Islamic banks is permissible, even for mudaraba accounts. In 2005 the scheme got off the ground. Malaysia stands apart in applying *maslaha* or public interest in a relatively liberal way in financial regulation, and the ground for this decision was that without an insurance scheme Islamic banks would hardly be able to compete on equal terms with conventional banks.[22] Gulf States find such wide applications of maslaha abhorrent. Regulators in non-Muslim-majority countries can point to Malaysia if they do not want to follow the example of the UK Financial Services Authority. In view of the Malaysian position on maslaha, based on the maqasid al-sharia, it is no surprise that the Islamic Financial Services Board, being based in Kuala Lumpur, deems guarantees given by banks on their murabaha time deposit contracts fully compatible with sharia.[23]

Another kind of accounts peculiar to Islamic banks is the *profit-sharing investment account* (PSIA), structured as a mudaraba, mushāraka or *wakala* (agency). There are two varieties, *unrestricted investment accounts* and *restricted investment accounts*, offered for fixed periods. Unrestricted investment accounts, *mudaraba mutlaqa* accounts, leave the bank a free hand as to the investments it makes with the available funds; restricted investment accounts, or *mudaraba muqayyada* accounts, restrict the portfolio that the bank can invest in. The latter, in other words, define the subset of investments whose yields, that may be negative, are shared with the deposit holder. The bank in this case is deemed to act as an agent for the depositor, or investor, and should not run any risk itself (unless it is found guilty of fraud or culpable negligence). The standard-setting body Accounting and Auditing Organization for Islamic Financial Institutions (AAOIFI) recognizes neither restricted nor unrestricted investment accounts as

21 B. Kettell, *Case Studies in Islamic banking and finance*, Wiley: Chichester 2011, Chapter 10.

22 M. Khairuddin Bin Hj Arshad, 'Implementation of an Islamic Deposit Insurance System for the Islamic Financial Services Industry', paper presented at the Fourth Islamic Financial Stability Forum, 'Strengthening Financial Safety Nets in the Islamic Financial Services Industry' Kuala Lumpur 17 November 2011 www.ifsb.org/docs/IFSF4_Md%20 Khairuddin%20Hj%20Arshad_paper_FINAL_pdf, accessed 19.03.2013.

23 Najeeb and Mustafa (2016).

liabilities of the bank, but in practice both banks and clients tend to see little difference between unrestricted accounts and savings deposits.[24] That could be an argument for granting holders of restricted investment accounts recourse to the assets financed by their deposits in case of default of the bank, but not holders of unrestricted investment accounts. In line with this way of thinking, there are jurisdictions, not only Malaysia but also for example Turkey, that provide deposit insurance for unrestricted investment account holders, in the interest of financial stability, that is, using the argument of maslaha.[25] Such accounts have in fact lost their mudaraba character. National regulators will have to decide whether or not to provide deposit insurance to unrestricted investment account holders only or to all investment account holders, plus mudaraba savings account and time deposit holders. They should bear in mind that the practice of Islamic banking does not always conform to the ideal. A survey by the Asian-Oceanian Standard-Setters Group (AOSSG) found that many banks do not distinguish between unrestricted and restricted accounts nor between deposits that are pure liabilities and investment accounts.[26] This would provide an argument for supervisors to deny all such accounts any prior ranking and instead impose deposit insurance, with the client having the right to renounce payment in case of default.

3. SPECIFIC ISSUES

3.1. BASEL III SOLVENCY REQUIREMENTS

The special character of Islamic financial products may complicate the application of supervisory measures or demand special provisions in order to create a level playing field. One important set of measures are the Basel III solvency requirements.

A case in point are sukuk. AAOIFI accepts 14 different varieties. Decisions must be made which of these can be used to fulfil Basel III capital-asset ratios, and if so, to what degree. The central bank of the UAE accepts perpetual sukuk issued by Abu Dhabi Islamic Bank as Tier 1 capital. This looks eminently sensible at first sight, provided the sukuk have a clear PLS profile, as with sukuk based on an underlying PLS contract, that is, *sukuk mudaraba* and *sukuk mushāraka*. Others have followed in the footsteps of Abu Dhabi. Saudi Arabia's National Commercial Bank and Qatar Islamic Bank both raised Tier 1 capital by issuing

24 Asian-Oceanian Standard-Setters Group, 'Financial Reporting by Islamic Financial Institution' (2015), www.aossg.org, accessed 15.02.2016.

25 E. Addo Awadzi, C. Chartouni and M. Tamez, 'Resolution Frameworks for Islamic Banks' (2015) IMF Working Paper No. 15/247, 24.

26 Asian-Oceanian Standard-Setters Group, 'Financial Reporting by Islamic Financial Institution' (2015).

perpetual sukuk mudaraba.[27] But before other bank regulators and supervisors agree on assigning Tier 1 status on such sukuk, whether 100% or less, they should check whether sukuk holders do have recourse to the assets of the bank in case of default. If so, even if it is decided they receive Tier 1 status, they certainly cannot be counted as Tier 2 capital. Accepting subordinated sukuk as Tier 2 capital, popular in the Gulf States, Malaysia and Turkey, looks less problematic. As a general rule, Tier 1 capital is meant to absorb shocks for a bank as a going concern, whereas Tier 2 capital serves to compensate creditors of a distressed bank. Tier 1 is divided into Common Equity Tier 1 and Additional Tier 1 (AT1). AT1 includes unsecured instruments with a minimum of five year maturity that rank senior to common equity but junior to Tier 2 instruments and to depositors, general creditors and holders of subordinated debt of the bank, plus debt instruments that are converted into common equity or written down when a pre-specified trigger event occurs. Bank Negara Malaysia includes unrestricted mushāraka, mudaraba and wakala sukuk under AT1. A case could be made for including unrestricted mushāraka sukuk under common equity, which is what IFSB basically does. It is a moot point whether mudaraba and wakala sukuk are suitable for AT1 purposes. IFSB says they are not and Sairally et al. concur, arguing that mudaraba and wakala sukuk holders have a first claim on the residual value of the portion of the assets financed by their funds. Supervisors will have to take a decision.[28]

Next we have the investment accounts discussed above. In principle, unrestricted investment accounts share in the total risk of the bank and thus can be accepted as a form of risk capital, whereas restricted investment accounts only share the risks of their specific investments and should not be included in the institution's risk capital. However, Islamic financial institutions tend not to shift losses to their clients in practice but apply income smoothing with the help of a Profit Equalization Reserve and perhaps also an Investment Risk Reserve that covers any future investment losses, specifically meant for investment account holders and funded out of their income.[29] That would be an argument against assigning these accounts risk capital status, what anyhow would be incongruent if holders have recourse to the assets financed by their funds. To deal with this on-the-one-hand – on-the-other situation the IFSB provides two formulas for calculating the capital-asset ratio: (i) a standard formula, for cases where the investment account holder fully bears the credit and market risks of the assets funded by the investment account; and (ii) a discretionary formula, where a correction factor is applied to take account of the degree in which account holders share the losses.[30] Of course, these formulas only provide a tool and not a ready-made set of regulations.

---

27 'Basel III Tier 1 sukuk regaining momentum', (2015) IFN Alerts 2 July IslamicFinanceNews@redmoneygroup.com, accessed 02.07.2015.

28 B.S. Sairally; M. Muhammad and M.M. Mustafa, 'Additional Tier 1 Capital Instruments under Basel III: A Sharīʿah Viewpoint' (2016) *Arab Law Quarterly* 30:2.

29 Bakar et al. 2008, 194.

30 Lopez Mejia et al. (2014).

3.2. BASEL III LIQUIDITY REQUIREMENTS

Supervisors and regulators have to ask themselves whether Islamic banks should be subject to different required minimum liquidity ratios than conventional banks. Murabaha loans figure large on Islamic banks' balance sheets, resulting in a high volume of receivables. These are very illiquid. Sharia law only allows them to be sold at par, though Malaysia's regulator is more lenient, on the ground of maslaha. Another issue calling for attention is the *run-off rate* to be applied to PLS funding. Islamic banks rely for their funding to a large extent on short-term investment accounts structured as mudaraba contracts, which are said to be more volatile than conventional time deposits.[31] The run-off rate thus may be high, which translates into a low net stable funding eligibility of PLS funds.[32] This would under Basel III imply an obligation to hold more high-quality liquid assets in order to cover net cash outflows (a run-off) for a 30-day period under a high-stress scenario. It is up to national regulators to apply weights to the different funding sources. An IFSB Guidance Note may provide help.[33]

A serious problem for Islamic banks is that they have far fewer instruments at their disposal for liquidity management than conventional banks, as interest-free short-term investment objects other than cash or current-account deposits are few and far between. sukuk might provide a way out, but the secondary market for sukuk is very thin. For the small volume available, supervisors would have to decide which sukuk should be eligible as a liquidity buffer and whether any haircuts should apply. Perhaps other banks or the central bank can help Islamic banks with their liquidity management by offering *tawarruq* and *reverse tawarruq* facilities, like the central bank of the UAE does.[34] A tawarruq starts with a murabaha contract including a credit sale. The financier, bank B, buys a good, sells it to the customer, in this case the bank needing cash, bank A, against deferred payment and with a markup. Next, bank A, or bank B as its agent, sells the good against cash payment to a third party. Such transactions usually involve platinum or aluminium contracts on the London Metal Exchange or palm oil contracts on the Kuala Lumpur Commodities Exchange, as such transactions can be made very quickly at low cost and with little risk of substantial price fluctuations during the short period of time required for the transactions. If

31 B. Vizcaino, 'Basel III deposit challenge looms over Islamic banks' (2014) Reuters, 2 September, in.reuters.com/article/2014/09/02/islam-banking-deposits-idINKBN0GX0JU20140902, accessed 04.09.2014.

32 'Roundtable – The Basel III challenge' (2014) *The Banker*, November.

33 IFSB, 'Guidance Note on Quantitative Measures for Liquidity Risk Management in Institutions Offering Islamic Financial Services [Excluding Islamic Insurance (Takāful) Institutions and Islamic Collective Investment Schemes]' (2015) www.ifsb.org/standard/GN-6%20GN%20on%20LRM%20(December%202015)%20(final).pdf, accessed 22.07.2016.

34 Central Bank of the UAE), 'Collateralized Murabahah Facility, Notice 4119/2011 (2010) www.centralbank.ae/en/pdf/Notice-No4119–2011-Collateralized-Murabahah-Facility.pdf, accessed.

bank A wants to deposit money it works the other way, with a reverse tawarruq. Bank A buys, as agent for bank B, a commodity contract against immediate payment, sells it to bank B with a markup against deferred payment, and next sells it as agent of bank B on the commodities exchange. Bank B receives the revenue of the sale. The result is that A after a number of months will receive a larger sum from bank B than it has paid for the metals contract, comparable with a conventional time deposit.

Though tawarruq and reverse tawarruq are widely practiced by Islamic financial institutions, it is frowned upon by fiqh scholars, as they involve real transactions solely to meet the letter of Islamic law, as the intention is to borrow or invest money for a time-dependent yield. Generally, following the medieval jurist Taqi al-Din Ibn Taymiyya (1263–1328), they deem tawarruq transactions not forbidden, but nevertheless *makruh*, undesirable.[35] Darura, or force majeure, is about the only exception they are willing to make, but darura proves to be a very elastic notion. Other solutions are available. The Basel III liquidity rules require the banks to hold a buffer of high-quality liquid assets and recognise that Islamic financial institutions have difficulty in meeting the rules other than by holding cash. This gives them a competitive disadvantage and Basel III allows them to choose from a wider range of assets than conventional banks, be it subject to haircuts in order not to disadvantage the conventional institutions. The Bank of England is concretising the approach and is expected to launch a *wakala* or agency-based deposit fund in Spring 2018. Islamic banks will be able to place deposits in this fund which the Bank of England as their agent will invest in sharia-compliant assets. Instead of the interest earned by conventional banks on their highly liquid required reserves, the Islamic banks will receive a return from the wakala fund.[36]

3.3. ACCOUNTING RULES

Islamic-majority jurisdictions follow different accounting rules. Some have adopted standards developed by AAOIFI, but important players such as Malaysia, the UAE and Saudi Arabia follow the International Financial Reporting Standards (IFRS) of the IASB, like most countries.[37] This should make it easy for supervisors outside the Muslim-majority countries to impose the IFRS on Islamic banks.

---

35 M.S. Gassner, 'Islam & hedge funds', (2007) www.islamica-me.com, February, accessed 13.02.2007. Ibn Taymiyya is held in high esteem by the Saudi Wahhabites in particular. Malaysian scholars are less inclined to follow his slant on the fiqh.

36 'New Shariah compliant facility to expand options for UK Islamic banks' (2017) *UK Islamic Finance* 1:4 www.ukislamicfinance.com, accessed 07.02.2018.

37 M. Amin, 'Accounting and Reporting Practices for Islamic Banks in UK and Overseas' (2015) *New Horizon* 192.

An important subject on which AAOIFI and IASB differ is financial lease, *ijara muntahia bittamleek* in the Islamic variant. A general difference between ijara and a conventional lease is that under an ijara contract the lessor is responsible for maintenance, whereas a conventional lease leaves maintenance to the lessee. But the relevant standards, Financial Accounting Standard 8 (FAS 8) of AAOIFI and International Accounting Standard 17 (IAS 17) of IASB differ in more respects.[38] To cite a few, IAS 17 recommends fair value while under FAS 8 assets are recorded at historical cost at commencement of the lease term. Further, under a finance lease IAS 17 has an asset recorded in the books of the lessor as Receivables, as if it is sold, but under FAS 8 an asset is recorded as Investment in Ijara Assets. This is because FAS 8 sticks to the form of the contract, which is strictly a lease contract (Islamic law does not allow combining two transactions, in this case a lease and a sale, in one contract, it does not even allow conditioning one contract on another), whereas IAS 17 follows a substance-over-form approach and treats a finance lease as if the asset has been purchased by the lessee. In line with this, FAS 8 treats lease rentals as revenue and depreciation as an expense while IAS-17 has lease rentals allocated between interest earnings and amortization of principal. Thus, FAS 8 has earnings spread evenly over the lease term but IAS 17 results in higher earnings in earlier years and lower earnings in later years (the value of Receivables falls in step with the received principal payments, interest earnings consequently fall too and a larger part of the rental is used for amortization). This may impact taxable income. There are no such differences between FAS 8 and IAS 17 in the treatment of operating leases. It may be noted in passing that as per 1 January 2019 IFRS 16 has replaced IAS 17, but for the lessor not much did change.[39]

Another issue is how lenders treat expected losses. AAOIFI standards only recognise incurred losses, whereas IFRS 9, which became effective on 1 January 2018, requires lenders to book expected losses in advance.[40] However, AAOIFI's FAS 30 'Impairment, Credit Losses and Onerous Commitments', which will supersede FAS 11 'Provisions and Reserves' as per 1 January 2020, looks set to minimize the difference between FAS and IFRS, as it provides for allowances for expected credit losses to be shown on the balance sheet as a deduction for the respective asset.[41] Perhaps this is a result of the consultative group on Sharia-compliant transactions set up by the IASB that commenced work in July 2013. The AAOIFI first declined the invitation to join, but in December 2014 they decided to join after all.[42]

---

38 M. Hanif, 'Ijarah Accounting: A Comparison of Conventional IAS-17 and Islamic FAS-8' (2016) *Journal of Islamic Economics, Banking and Finance* 12:1.

39 IASB, 'IFRS 16 – Leases' (2016) www.iasplus.com/en/standards/ifrs/ifrs-16, accessed 18.10.2017.

40 B. Vizcaino, 'Islamic banks adapting to IFRS accounting rules' (2016) Reuters 28 November www.arabnews.com/node/1016786/business-economy, accessed 10.04.2017.

41 AAOIFI, 'Financial Accounting Standard No. 30, Impairment and credit losses, Exposure Draft (ver. 5.0)' (2017) aaoifi.com, accessed 30.11.2017.

42 M. Amin (2015).

3.4. RESOLUTION

If an Islamic bank has been placed in resolution, its Islamic character is likely to add to the worries. The sharia board of the bank may, for instance, judge the resolution measures not sharia-compliant. If another Islamic bank is interested in acquiring the bank in resolution, the sharia boards of the two banks may disagree on the sharia compliance of the measures. A legal framework should be in place that provides for such conflicts and decides whether the resolution authorities have the power to suspend or remove sharia board members of a bank in resolution, in addition to its directors. The resolution authority might be given the right to establish its own sharia board for advice on resolution measures.[43]

Another issue calling for attention is what triggers should be in place for activating resolution powers, in view of the special character of Islamic banks' products. The conventional capital adequacy and liquidity thresholds do not always seem appropriate for ijara or PLS financing, which are not pure lending. On the liabilities side of the balance sheet, it should be made clear whether deposits, in particular the investment accounts discussed above, have the legal status of client assets. In that case account holders have recourse to the bank's assets in a resolution. Their deposits are not available for absorbing losses and should be segregated. General guidelines for dealing with resolution (not specifically for Islamic banks) have been published by the Financial Stability Board (FSB).[44]

The ban on riba puts an obstacle in the way of an acquisition of an Islamic bank in resolution by another bank. The ban on riba implies that debt can only be sold at its nominal value and not every sharia board will accept the maslaha argument as applied by the Malaysian regulators. Moreover, resolutions may also find obstacles in their way because mandatory debt write-offs, or 'haircuts' in the industry's lingo, do not seem to be sharia-compliant. According to Islamic law, debt can only be discharged if it is paid in full or if it is forgiven voluntarily by the creditor. Circumstances may arise where the resolution authority, or the sharia board it appointed, can only force a decision with an appeal to the principle of darura. There is, however, no unanimity among sharia scholars how far the applicability of this principle can be stretched.

3.5. SHARIA RISK

Finally, we have *sharia risk*. This is the risk of loss because an Islamic financial institution's claims, products or activities are found or judged to be not sharia-compliant. Customers may withdraw deposits on the mere rumour that an

43 Addo Awadzi et al. (2015).

44 FSB, 'Key Attributes of Effective Resolution Regimes for Financial Institutions', revised edition (2014) www.fsb.org, accessed 01.02.2018.

institution or its personnel do not fully comply with Islamic law. If a contract party suspects non-compliance with sharia it may want to nullify a contract. A lawsuit might impair the bank's viability, because of damages to be paid and because the loss of reputation makes customers leave. In addition, if a court finds for the complainant, the losing Islamic bank will have to donate any profits from the transactions found to be non-compliant with sharia to a charity.[45] A bank or other financial institution may also face losses if a debtor declares its debt not sharia-compliant and stops making payments, as Dana Gas in 2017 did on its mudaraba sukuk, notwithstanding an injunction of the London High Court where the case was tried to pay back the sukuk principal and the accrued unpaid profit rates.[46]

In European countries law courts will likely only apply national law to any dispute (if the governing law of the contract is national law) and refuse to consider sharia compliance, though US bankruptcy courts are reported to be more willing to consider sharia considerations.[47] Where that is not the case parties can decide to take their case to an arbitration body.[48] Still, that does not solve problems such as cropped up in the Dana Gas case, where the judgement of the UK court on the sukuk issued by Dana Gas conflicted with the judgement of a UAE court on the underlying mudaraba transaction. IFSB is working on a standard for the Islamic capital market preventing such conflicts.[49]

Regulators may reduce sharia risk by requiring Islamic banks to have a sharia board that meets, for instance, AAOIFI Governance Standards. Usually, Islamic banks appoint a sharia board of their own accord, in order to give themselves a reliable image, and Muslim-majority countries tend to oblige them to do so, but there are exceptions, such as Tunisia and Turkey. Kenya is another country without obligatory sharia boards. Better not to leave it to the banks. Regulators might also consider imposing minimum requirements as to the educational background of the employees of Islamic financial institutions. A lack of knowledge of Islamic law on the side of employees increases the risk of breaches of Islamic law. The Malaysian *Islamic*

---

45 K. Ginena, 'Shari'ah risk and corporate governance of Islamic banks', (2014) *Corporate Governance* 14:1. For the complexities of litigation concerning sharia compliance see K. Howladar, 'Shari'ah Risk: Understanding Recent Compliance Issues in Islamic Finance' (2010) *Moody's Investor Service Report*, May www.moodys.com, accessed 02.06.2010.

46 A. Winning and D. Barbuscia, 'Creditors tell High Court that Dana Gas sukuk get-out is "absurd"' (2017) 25 September www.reuters.com/article/dana-gas-sukuk-trial/creditors-tell-high-court-that-dana-gas-sukuk-get-out-is-absurd, accessed 26.09.2017.

47 M.J.T. Mcmillen, 'The Arcapita Group Bankruptcy: A Restructuring Case Study', in *Islamic Commercial Law Report 2016*, International Shari'ah Research Academy for Islamic Finance (ISRA), Kuala Lumpur, and Thomson Reuters, 2015, pp. 136–142, www.salaamgateway.com, accessed 17.11.2016.

48 F. Mohammad, 'The Adjudication of Islamic Finance Cases: The UK Experience', in *Islamic Commercial Law Report 2016*, International Shari'ah Research Academy for Islamic Finance (ISRA), Kuala Lumpur, and Thomson Reuters, 2015, pp. 130–132, www.salaamgateway.com, accessed 17.11.2016.

49 B. Vizcaino, 'Islamic finance body IFSB throws down gauntlet on sukuk' (2018) www.reuters.com, 29 March.

Financial Services Act 2013, in particular Part IV on sharia requirements, provides an example of how to lay down rules for minimizing sharia risk.[50] Regulators should look critically at the composition and the role of a bank's sharia board. If they have a directorship role, their capability as bankers may not meet a supervisor's standard. Furthermore, given the scarcity of competent sharia board members, there is a high probability that board members also serve on the sharia boards of other financial institutions, which may lead to conflicts of interest if they act as directors. And if sharia board members hold no directorships but are paid by the firm they may easily yield to pressure from directors, because if they do not follow the wishes of the firm's board the firm may tell them their services are no longer required and go *sharia shopping*, that is, look around till they find sharia scholars willing to okay the firm's products and services, which increases sharia risk.[51]

An Islamic financial institution's sharia risk can never be reduced to zero and regulators and supervisors would have to ask themselves whether to impose higher capital-asset and liquidity ratios to cope with that risk. These might be variable, depending for instance on the track record of any parent companies.

3. FINAL OBSERVATIONS

It will be clear that providing for Islamic financial institutions in a country's banking laws and regulations is a complicated and time-consuming business. It may not always be possible to fit all forms of Islamic finance in the national regulatory framework and sometimes compromises will be inevitable, with Islamic financial institutions having to apply darura and maslaha considerations. When considering special capital-asset and liquidity ratios it should be taken into account that Islamic banks weathered the 2008 financial crisis relatively well[52], that they do not engage in complicated derivatives deals and that there is some indication of low credit risk. However, the evidence is mixed.[53] Some Islamic financial institutions were as severely hit by the real estate crisis that followed in the wake of the 2007–2008 credit crisis as their conventional counterparts. It can therefore not be said that Islamic financial institutions in general are significantly less crisis-prone than conventional ones. Devising supervisory rules involves a lot of work, but the task for any supervisory body can be made more manageable by learning from the experience of others and by applying available standards and guidelines.

---

50 Bank Negara Malaysia, *Islamic Financial Services Act 2013* (2013) www.bnm.gov.my/documents/act/en_ifsa.pdf, accessed 18.08.2016.

51 U.A. Oseni, 'Fatwā shopping and trust: towards effective consumer protection regulations in Islamic finance' (2017) *Society and Business Review* 12:3.

52 TH. Beck, A. Demirgüç-Kunt and O. Merrouche, 'Islamic vs. conventional banking: Business model, efficiency and stability (2013) *Journal of Banking and Finance* 37:2.

53 Md.N. Kabir, A. Worthington and R. Gupta, 'Comparative credit risk in Islamic and conventional banks' (2015) *Pacific-Basin Finance Journal* 34.

ISLAMIC FINANCE TRANSACTIONS IN GERMANY

A Practitioners Report

Martin BÜNNING
Lawyer and Tax Advisor, partner Ashurst LLP, Frankfurt

Aryanaz REZAIAN
Student of law at Goethe Universität in Frankfurt, legal researcher Ashurst LLP, Frankfurt

1. INTRODUCTION

In western jurisdictions most investors are focused on the use of leverage. In particular in real estate and M&A (mergers and acquisition) transactions the use of debt is a key element of acquisition structures which helps to improve the return on the equity for the investors (leverage). The financing of transactions with bank and shareholder debt also is in the focus of the tax planning for the majority if not all investors irrespective of the nature of the target asset (real estate, private equity, renewable energy etc.). In particular the deductibility of the resulting interest expenses (and potential tax arbitrage achievable by the use of shareholder loans) is an important item in the tax planning for investors. The availability of bank financing and tax planning opportunities allows investors to offer more competitive consideration compared to those investors who may not use debt to the same extent (i.e. certain regulated investors like insurance companies, mutual funds etc.) or not at all due to religious or other ethical restrictions. Hence, investors who may not rely on (conventional) bank financing seem to have a competitive disadvantage compared to other investors who are not subject to the same restrictions.

Investors who follow religious or other ethical rules which prevent them to use conventional bank financing seem to be in a less favourable position compared to other investors who may rely on the conventional leverage strategy. This seems to apply in particular to those investors who follow

Shari'ah rules and the explicit ban of interest ("riba") incorporated therein. Under Shari'ah compliant Islamic finance instruments no interest must be charged or paid.[1] The basic principle of those products is that the "lender" only is entitled to remuneration provided the "borrower" can generate income or a profit with the funding granted under the instrument.[2] This concept obviously is different from the concept of an interest-bearing loan provided by conventional financial institutions.[3] The ban of interest apparently is the central distinguishing factor between the western economy and an Islamic oriented economic model.[4] Nevertheless, investors adherent to Shari'ah principles are investing in the same markets like investors applying conventional financing structures.

Over the last fifteen years Germany's real estate market was in the focus of international investors, including investors from the Middle East and the gulf region. Some of these investors made their investments in compliance with Shari'ah principles aiming at the same IRR (internal rate of return) as investors using conventional financing structures. The lack of a particular legal and tax regime for those transactions results, however, in a number of practical issues related to the need to adapt Islamic finance instruments to a tax and legal system based on different principles.

In the absence of Islamic banks, providing Shari'ah-compliant instruments for financing transactions in Germany may be complex but yet feasible: The German state of Saxony-Anhalt (*Sachsen-Anhalt*), in July 2004, took an unprecedented step by issuing a "sukuk" debt instrument, compliant with Islamic principles.[5] The "Saxony-Anhalt sukuk", as it was named, was structured as a sukuk Al Ijara and was backed by a portfolio of tax offices owned by the Federal State of Saxony-Anhalt. Indeed, the 5-year 100-million-euro asset-backed sukuk was considered as a success and also lead to a second issue.

Following the experience with the Saxony-Anhalt sukuk, Ijara-Leasing has become the most common structure for Islamic Finance transactions in Germany in relation to German real estate. The German portfolio of the most active Islamic investor is structured on the basis of a (modified) Ijara

1 Ayub, Understanding Islamic Finance (2007), p. 157: "Contemporary Shariah scholars have reached the consensus that modern commercial interest comes under the purview of Riba and no form of loan/debt based on interest is exempt from this prohibition". On the other hand it is fairly obvious that Islamic finance techniques and products replace the function of credit and interest, David / Jauffret-Spinosi, Les grands systèmes de droit contemporains (12e ed.), p. 382; Zweigert / Kötz, Einführung in die Rechtsvergleichung (3. Ed.), p. 302.

2 Makhlouf, L'émergence d'un droit international de la finance islamique: Origines, formation et integration en droit francais (2015), pp. 161 f.; Grieser, WM 2009, p. 586.

3 Heckel, ZVglRWiss 111 (2012), p. 311 (312 s., 314).

4 Cf. Ashfaq, Islamic Banking and Finance in Europe: the Case of Germany and United Kingdom (2017), p. 16.

5 Fawzy, VuR 2009, p. 39 (40).

lease structure. But also other Islamic financing schemes have been applied. Under these structures it is possible to combine conventional bank financing with Shari'ah principles, in particular the "riba" or ban of interest. Obstacles under Germany's tax accounting principles, its VAT regime and its real estate transfer tax law require particular attention by the parties involved in order to avoid undesired tax exposure and result in rather complex corporate and tax structures. Tax authorities have, however, approved those investment schemes in a number of tax field audits.

The following shall provide for a summary of the salient issues investors following Shari'ah principles will need to bear in mind in case they want to achieve similar commercial results as conventional investors. The analysis of real estate transactions seems to be most appropriate for this purpose and of most practical relevance.

2. CONVENTIONAL (TAX) STRUCTURING FOR INBOUND REAL ESTATE TRANSACTIONS

Conventional structures for the acquisition of German real estate focus on the following elements.[6] For this type of transactions a standard market practice has been developed by international investors which uses no-German entities for their acquisitions:

2.1. REAL ESTATE TRANSFER TAX (RETT, GRUNDERWERBSTEUER)

RETT is levied on each acquisition of real estate when a contractual obligation is created to transfer the legal title in the property, or in case legal title passes by operation of law following a corporate reorganization etc.[7] RETT is also levied on transactions in which the contractual right to acquire real property is assigned to another party before legal title actually passes to the initial acquirer (so-called interim transaction, *Zwischengeschäft*). Taxable transactions do also include arrangements under which a party may dispose of the real estate asset owned by another person for its own account. Also the creation of a trust arrangement under which the legal owner agrees to hold the real property on behalf of the principal will be subject to RETT provided the nominee undertakes to transfer the legal title to the principal upon his request. The applicable tax

6 The following explanations are limited to so-called asset deals in which the property itself is the subject of the transaction. So-called share deals, in which shares in real estate companies are acquired, are not dealt with here.

7 Fischer, Boruttau, GrEStG, 18. Edition (2016), §1 recital 200.

rate varies from 3.5% to 6.5% depending on the Federal State in which the real property is located.

Also the transfer of interest in partnerships or corporate entities which own real estate can be subject to RETT provided, in the case of partnerships, at least 95% of the capital interest in a partnership directly or indirectly is transferred to one or several (unrelated) acquirers within a five year period or in the case of corporate entities and partnerships at least 95% of the shares or the capital interest is acquired by a single acquirer or a qualifying group of acquirers. The German lawmaker recently has introduced anti-avoidance rules in relation to these share deals which tackle structures in which commercially 95% or more of the economic interest in the real property owning company or partnership is transferred without triggering a RETT charge. Currently, there are plans to make these provisions even more restrictive.

On the other hand lease agreements are not taxable transactions for RETT purposes even in case the beneficial ownership in the real estate asset is transferred from the legal owner / landlord to the tenant according to the terms of the agreement. Under German tax accounting rules the beneficial ownership in a real estate asset is transferred to the tenant when the tenant acquires the majority of the risks and rewards arising during the useful lifetime of the property. The German tax administration has issued detailed guidelines on the allocation of the beneficial ownership under real estate leasing contracts. Basically, these rules provide that the beneficial ownership in real estate will pass to the tenant in case the fixed term of the lease agreement is at least 90% of the useful lifetime of the real estate asset (building) and when the lessor benefits from any increase in value and suffers from any reduction of the value of the asset. Since the beneficial ownership may pass without legal title no RETT would arise in these circumstances.

2.2. VALUE ADDED TAX (VAT, UMSATZSTEUER)

Real estate transactions typically are exempt from VAT provided they are subject to RETT in order to avoid double taxation. Hence real estate transactions under which legal title does not pass and which, therefore, are not subject to RETT would in principle be subject to VAT (i.e. transfer of beneficial ownership in leasing transactions described in the preceding paragraph). However, also VAT exempt transactions can become subject to VAT by election of the supplier (technically the election is a waiver of the VAT exemption). The waiver of the VAT exemption can make sense for the seller of real estate in case he records input VAT correction amounts (*Vorsteuerberichtigungsbeträge*) which would have to repaid to the tax administration in case of a tax exempt sale of the real property.

Also the renting of real property is a VAT exempt supply unless the landlord elects to waive the VAT exemption for the individual lease agreement to the extent possible in order to protect the input VAT refunds. However, in case the tenants use the property for services which are not subject to VAT (i.e. banks, insurance companies, doctors, public services, post office etc.) or in case the property is used for residential purposes no waiver of the VAT exemption is permissible.

In the context of real estate transactions the going concern VAT exemption is relevant in many instances. Such exemption provides that the transfer of a going concern is not a taxable transaction for VAT purposes. The exemption applies in particular to the acquisition of fully let real properties (unless the transaction qualifies as a project development).

The parties of real estate transactions aim to avoid that input VAT refunds need to be repaid to the tax administration as a result of the transaction or that VAT needs to be paid (and financed) which subsequently will be repaid by the tax administration.

2.3. TAXATION OF INCOME

The net income derived from the renting of real estate and from the disposition of real estate is subject to corporate or personal income tax at ordinary rates (corporate income tax: 15.825% incl. solidarity surcharge, personal income tax: 47.475% marg. rate incl. solidarity surcharge plus church tax in case the individual belongs to a religious congregation entitled to levy tax).

The taxable income is calculated on the basis of the gross income less depreciation of the assets and less business expenses, in particular interest. Generally, interest payable under bank loans or under shareholder loans is fully deductible unless the annual net interest expense of a business is EUR 3,000,000 p.a. or more. In that case interest will only be deductible up to 30% of the taxable EBITDA of the business (so-called interest barrier rule, *Zinsschranke*). In cross border situations the interest deductions often are increased by interest payable under shareholder loans which are provided by related parties resident abroad. Provided the recipient of the interest receivable under shareholder loans is resident in a jurisdiction with a favourable tax regime where interest is not effectively taxed (due to lower tax rates or personal tax exemptions, different classification of the income or specific tax structuring) the investor may achieve a beneficial tax arbitrage. Interest payable on shareholder loans must be at arm's length and not excessively high. Otherwise the income would be adjusted to the appropriate amount as a constructive dividend.

Therefore, the use of interest-bearing loans and the reduction of the taxable income by interest expenses is a key element in many transactions and has become a very effective tax planning tool.

Germany knows a second tax which is levied on trading income by the municipalities. Such trade tax (*Gewerbesteuer*) is charged on businesses which maintain a German fixed place of business. Renting income and the income from the disposition of real estate typically do not qualify as a trade or business. Nevertheless, the income derived from real estate is included in the trading income of corporate entities (e.g. limited liability companies and stock corporations) and partnerships which pursue (other) trading activities or have a trading imprint (*gewerbliche geprägte Personengesellschaft*) provided they have established a German principal place of management and control.

Foreign entities which own German real estate and rent it to third parties typically neither create a German principal place of management and control or another fixed place of business (permanent establishment) which would cause a trade tax liability. Hence, foreign investors are used not to acquire German real estate with German domestic entities but rather use non-resident entities for their real estate acquisitions.

For trade tax purposes the taxable income is adjusted by the add-back of 25% of any interest expense provided it is a deductible item under the interest barrier regime (see above).

The capital gain realized on the disposal of the real estate asset is subject to ordinary taxation (including trade tax in case the seller has established a German fixed place of business). Should the real property be held by a German corporate entity, 95% of the capital gain from the disposal of the shares would be exempt under German domestic tax law in case the seller is a corporate entity. The sale of a non-resident entity (neither a German corporate seat nor a German principal place of management and control) owning German real estate by a foreign shareholder would not be taxable in Germany at all.[8]

2.4. PARTNERSHIP TAXATION

The use of special purpose vehicles (SPV) in the legal format of (limited) partnerships often is considered in real estate transactions. Due to the fiscally transparent status of partnerships there are a number of planning opportunities associated with this legal concept. In particular under German partnership taxation rules any expenses incurred by a partner in relation to his capital interest in the partnership or in relation to the partnership's business in general is a deductible item at the level of the partnership itself. On the other hand, contractual relationships and the resulting income and expenses between a partner and his partnership are ignored for taxation purposes.

A particularity of the German legal and tax system is that the partnership can be undisclosed (*stille Gesellschaft*). In this case the owner of the business would

8 Töben / Lohbeck, Birk (Hrsg.) Transaktion Vermögen Pro Bono (2008), p. 211 (232).

receive a capital contribution from a partner in exchange for the transfer of a notional interest in the business (current income [profit and loss], capital gains and liquidation proceeds) and certain limited management rights. Depending on the terms of the partnership agreement the undisclosed partnership would qualify as a debt instrument with a consideration for the lender which is contingent on the profits of the business. In this case the lender would be taxed on interest income and the borrower may claim a deduction for interest paid (within the general limitations, so called typical undisclosed partnership, *typische stille Gesellschaft*). The undisclosed partnership may also be structured as a trading partnership where the partners share the profits of the business on the basis of the partnership agreement and are taxed on their respective share (so called atypical undisclosed partnership; *atypische stille Gesellschaft*).

2.5. WITHHOLDING TAXES

Investors also want to avoid that withholding taxes are levied on cross border payments. Germany, as many other tax jurisdictions, does not levy withholding taxes on cross border rent payments or on interest payments as long as the interest is not contingent on profits (also interest payable under a typical undisclosed partnership arrangement would fall into this category). Profit distributions by corporate entities are subject to withholding tax at a rate of 26.375% unless the recipient of the distribution is entitled to protection from German withholding tax under a double taxation treaty of the EU parent subsidiary directive. Such protection typically is not available to holding companies with no other economic purpose than holding the shares in a German subsidiary.

3. ISLAMIC BANKING IN GERMANY

Currently there are about 15 banks that are owned by shareholders in Muslim countries and operating in Germany. Most of these banks do not offer Islamic banking services in relation to transactions but are engaged in the business of import and export finance or retail banking.

Also some of the German banks[9] have already addressed the special financial needs of Muslim customers but the focus of most banks was on retail products and customers and the scope of the activities remained limited. Hence, Islamic investors need to rely on conventional financing for their German activities and adapt the Islamic finance structures to the financial (and legal) environment they operate in.[10]

---

9 Cf. Fawzy, VuR 2009, p. 39 (40).

10 Due to the relatively low importance of Islamic banking in Germany, the statements are confined to cross-border issues in which Islamic investors from abroad operate in Germany.

4. ANALYSIS OF CERTAIN ISLAMIC FINANCE INSTRUMENTS UNDER GERMAN (TAX) LAW

The use of Islamic finance instruments in the context of the acquisition of German real estate needs to analyzed in the context of the applicable German tax regime. In general the German tax system does not provide a special tax regime for tax payers who invest in accordance with certain religious or ethical principles unless the investor qualifies for a general tax exemption which is available for certain charitable organizations. In the context of commercial transactions which are set up with the intention to create a profit for the personal benefit of the investors such general tax exemption cannot be achieved. The current German tax regime is not flexible and in general cannot be adapted to special religious and / or ethical requirements of specific tax payers.[11] In order to render a comparable economic return structures applied by Islamic investors need to be as tax efficient as structures applied by conventional investors.[12] This requires that, in case of a conflict or undesired fiscal results Islamic finance instruments need to be adjusted to the German tax environment. In particular the applied structures should (i) not trigger real estate transfer tax more than once per transaction, (ii) not create a VAT payable or a non-refundable input VAT charge, (iii) allow a full interest deduction, (iv) not be subject to trade tax (v) allow for the repatriation of proceeds without withholding tax, and (vi) allow for a tax efficient exit at the end of the investment term.

4.1. SAXONY-ANHALT SUKUK

The Saxony-Anhalt sukuk[13] has been one of the first practical experiences with Islamic finance instruments in Germany. In this structure the German Federal State of Saxony Anhalt monetized its tax offices by renting them under a long term lease with a term of 99 years to a special purpose vehicle incorporated as a Dutch limited liability company (*besloten Vennootschaap*, BV). This entity was wholly owned by a Dutch foundation (*Stichting, the "Sachsen Anhalt Trust"*).[14]

Under the long term lease the Federal State was entitled to an upfront payment of the lease payments for the entire term. The BV refinanced itself by

11 There apparently is a basic conflict which results from the fact that the (tax) laws in a western jurisdiction is created and can be changed by a lawmaker, whereas the rules of Islamic law are derived from divine sources which cannot be changed but can only be construed and explained differently by man, Zweigert / Kötz Einführung in die Rechtsvergleichtung (3. Ed.), p. 297.

12 Heckel, ZVglRWiss 111 (2012), pa. 311 (314).

13 A description of transaction can be found in: Kugler, Islamic Finance – Neue Ansätze bei Immobilientransaktionen und deren Finanzierung in Deutschland (2009), pp. 78 f.

14 The issuance of the sukuk via a Dutch issuer was carried out to avoid the German withholding tax on interest and the addition of interest in accordance with Art. §8 No. 1 GewStG.

issuing an "Islamic" bond to the capital markets. In a further step the BV let the tax offices back to the tax administration of the Federal State under a short term lease agreement in consideration for regular rent payments. This lease agreement had a fixed termination date after 5 years. The BV then used the proceeds from the rents to make the payments due under the bond.

At the end of the five year term of the lease agreement the Federal State and BV had the mutual right to terminate the long term lease and to cancel the long term right to use granted to the BV. Upon the termination of the long term lease agreement the Federal State had to make a last payment corresponding to the pro rata upfront payment attributable to the remaining term of the long term lease agreement.

The combination of the long term lease and the short term lease agreement (lease and lease back) was qualified as an Ijara arrangement (see below) and the bonds issued by the BV qualified as a sukuk Al Ijara which was considered suitable for Islamic investors.

Since legal title in the property did not pass to the BV there was no taxable event for RETT purposes. As the Federal State is not subject to income taxation no capital gains tax became due either. The parties did not elect to make the respective supplies subject to VAT so that the VAT was neutral to the economics of the transaction.

The use of a Dutch BV is a typical feature of bond issues for German issuers. By using a Dutch entity the German withholding tax regime was avoided which might have required that the issuer makes a withholding at a rate of 26.375% of the gross (notional) interest. Even though the Islamic bond did not provide for an interest coupon the payment would have to be split into a repayment of principal portion and a notional interest portion under German tax accounting rules. The notional interest portion would have been treated as interest for all taxation purposes (including withholding tax).[15]

4.2. MUDARABA AND MUSHARAKA

In a Mudaraba arrangement a bank would agree to enter into a (undisclosed) partnership agreement with an investor under which the bank undertakes to provide funding for the acquisition of a real estate asset by an investor in exchange for a participation in the proceeds derived from the real estate asset, i.e. current rent income and capital gains (including a loss participation).[16] Typically, the investor would not contribute capital but rather would provide

[15] Pohlmann / Beck, IStR 2010, p. 225 (233 f.); incorrect, however, Kugler, Islamic Finance – Neue Ansätze bei Immobilientransaktionen und deren Finanzierung in Deutschland (2009), p. 71.

[16] Grieser, WM 2009, p. 586 (587 f.); Heckel, ZVglRWiss 111 (2012), pa. 311 (321).Obviously, it is unclear whether the profit share of Musharaka transactions must match the capital ratios,

know how and would remain in charge to run the business. In contrast, in a Musharaka arrangement both, the investor and the bank would make a capital contribution and would share the income accordingly. In a Musharaka transaction the management of the project would be shared between the Investor and the bank.[17]

In the context of the acquisition of German real estate one might consider that the Islamic investor establishes a non-resident acquisition vehicle for the acquisition of the property. After signing of the acquisition contract the vehicle could enter into an undisclosed partnership agreement with a bank under which the bank undertakes to provide the funding (or a portion thereof) in consideration for a participation in the proceeds derived from the property. The payment obligations under the undisclosed partnership agreement can be secured by land charges and further security as appropriate.[18]

The formation of such undisclosed partnership structure would not trigger real estate transfer tax as the creation of an undisclosed partnership is not a taxable transaction for RETT purposes. Further, the creation of the undisclosed partnership is not subject to VAT and, hence there would not be a risk to create a VAT payable at the time of the acquisition.[19]

Going forward, both the investor and the bank would be subject to income taxation as follows: In the case of a typical undisclosed partnership the investors would be taxed on the net rent income (after deduction of the interest payable to the bank). Provided the bank has no taxable presence in Germany no German tax would arise. In particular no German withholding tax would apply on the interest payments.[20]

Should the arrangement qualify as an atypical silent partnership the investors and the bank would be subject to German corporate income tax with their respective profit share.[21] Both parties may deduct any expense they incurred in relation to the acquisition of the real property and / or the undisclosed partnership interest. Whether or not the taxable income can be reduced by interest deductions depends on how the bank has financed its interest. Should the bank refinance its undisclosed partnership interest with interest-bearing debt the interest would be deductible from the taxable income.

In case of an exit at the end of the investment term by selling the real estate asset the SPV would be subject to corporate income tax purposes. The sale of

while in Mudaraba transactions it does not have to., Usmani, An Introduction to Islamic Finance (2002), p. 7 and p. 14.

17 Heckel, ZVglRWiss 111 (2012), pa. 311 (322).

18 Ayub, Understanding Islamic Finance (2007), p. 168 ff.

19 Blaurock, Handbuch stille Gesellschaft, 7. edition (2010), 28.06; Robisch, Bunjes USTG Kommentar, 16. edition (2017), §1 recital 68.

20 Cf. Momen, Vertragsmodelle – Islamic Finance (2010), pp. 23 ff.

21 Grieser / Penndorf, IBFD Derivatives & Financial Instruments, volume 12-2010, S. 25 (29); Momen, Vertragsmodelle –Islamic Finance (2010), pp. 73, 74.

the SPV itself would not trigger a taxable capital gain in Germany. However, in case the undisclosed civil law partnership is structured as an atypical silent partnership the winding up of the financing structure invariably would lead to the crystallization of capital gains and trigger a corresponding income tax liability.

Whether or not the application of a Mudaraba or Musharaka structure leads to comparable results as a conventional financing structure depends on the availability of debt financing. Since conventional banks typically are reluctant to enter into silent partnership agreements for regulatory reasons the structure would have to be amended in order to facilitate conventional bank financing. This would require that a further layer of entities is introduced into the structure between the SPV and the financing institution.[22] An "orphan" entity (held by a charitable foundation) could be established which would enter into the undisclosed civil law partnership agreement and would finance the contribution with a conventional loan. The remuneration under the conventional loan would have to match the income derived by the orphan entity from the undisclosed partnership interest which might give raise to leakage. The use of orphan entities is a customary tool to separate conventional financing structures from the structure held by the Islamic investors. However, the use of an orphan structure commercially requires that there is no loss of income for the Islamic investors. Since the remuneration under the undisclosed partnership agreement is not fix because it is linked to the performance of the real estate asset and the interest payable to the conventional bank is a fixed percentage there might not be a perfect match which may result in a profit or loss for the orphan entity which is not appropriate for the structuring. Finally, the conventional bank would not benefit from a direct security over the real estate asset but rather needs to rely on the assignment of the security interest by the orphan entity which might make the transaction less attractive for a conventional bank.

4.3. MURABAHA[23]

In a Murabaha structure a bank would acquire a certain asset at the request of an investor. The investor would then acquire the asset from the bank and indemnifies the bank for the acquisition cost incurred plus a profit margin. In contrast to an interest-bearing loan the bank in this situation would not provide cash financing to its client in consideration for interest but would rather purchase the asset on behalf of the client and then transfer it to the client with a mark-up.

---

22 Kugler, Islamic Finance – Neue Ansätze bei Immobilientransaktionen und deren Finanzierung in Deutschland (2009), p. 69.

23 Ayub, Understanding Islamic Finance (2007), pp. 213 ff.; Wurst, Immobilienfinanzierung und Islamic Banking (2011), pp. 83 ff.; Grieser, WM 2009, p. 586 (589 f.).

The client would pay the remuneration due to the bank in instalments.[24] For accounting purposes the remuneration would have to be discounted and each instalment would have to be split into settlement of the outstanding amount and a notional interest amount.[25]

In the context of German real estate transactions the Murabaha structure would lead to an unfavourable result since the acquisition of the property by the bank and the transfer of the same property to the investor would each trigger a RETT charge.[26] The same would apply in case the bank would assign its right to acquire the property prior to actual transfer of legal title or in case the parties enter into a trust arrangement. Further, the amount of deductible interest available to reduce the taxable income going forward would depend on the accounting treatment of the instalment payments and not on an actual agreed interest payment.

Nevertheless the Murabaha scheme can be applied in a modified form as a commodity Murabha. In this scheme the Islamic investors would create an acquisition structure in which they provide equity and shareholder debt to a special purpose vehicle which shall acquire the real estate property. Under Sharia principles interest payable under shareholder loans is not considered as a detrimental remuneration which would be subject to the ban of interest. The interest payable under the shareholder loan would be deductible from the German taxable income according to general taxation rules.

The remaining financing would be provided under a commodity Murabaha in which the Islamic investors would acquire commodities (copper, gold or certificates representing such commodities) from a commodity trading company. The special purpose vehicle would sell the commodities in the general market for cash which it would use to settle the balance of the purchase price. In this case the special purpose vehicle would still owe to the commodity trading company the outstanding purchase price in instalments. The receivable of the commodity trading company would be secured by a standard security package. The commodity trading company itself would finance the transaction with conventional debt. The financing bank would benefit from an assignment of the security package including a land charge on the real property acquired by the special purpose vehicle.

---

24 Ayub, Understanding Islamic Finance (2007), p. 161: "The Shariah recognizes a difference in value due to a time element, and does not prohibit realizing the time value of money in a business"; Heckel, ZVglRWiss 111 (2012), pa. 311 (321).

25 Grieser / Penndorf, IBFD Derivatives & Financial Instruments, Volume 12–2010, p. 25 (30); Thurow, IRZ 2011, p. 277 (279, 281); Pohlmann / Beck, IStR 2010, p..225 (229); Momen, Vertragsmodelle – Islamic Finance (2010), pp. 27 f.

26 Grieser / Penndorf, IBFD Derivatives & Financial Instruments, Volume 12–2010, p. 25 (30); Thurow, IRZ 2011, p. 277 (280); Kugler, Islamic Finance – Neue Ansätze bei Immobilientransaktionen und deren Finanzierung in Deutschland (2009), pp. 70 f.; cf. Momen, Vertragsmodelle – Islamic Finance (2010), pp. 32 ff.; Wurst, Immobilienfinanzierung und Islamic Banking (2011), pp. 95 f.: Wurst's suggested way of avoiding land transfer tax through simple interpretation of the law is unlikely to be feasible.

In this constellation the Islamic investors would be in a very similar position than conventional investors apart from the financing which is structured with a commodity trading element which presumably will increase the cost for the transaction. Also banks might be reluctant to lend against this structure since they are remote from the security over the land.

4.4. IJARA[27]

In an Ijara transaction a certain asset is let to the customer of the bank for a certain period of time, which basically corresponds to a conventional leasing arrangement.[28] In consideration for making available the asset the bank is entitled to a fee agreed between the parties which can be settled in cash or by providing other services and may be paid in a single payment or in instalments for certain intervals.[29] The bank's customer may use the property to let it to third parties under a rent contract. At the end of the lease term the parties may agree to transfer the asset to the investor.

In conventional structures it is not practical that the bank would acquire the property and lease it to the investor. The absence of bank financing and the leverage effect would prevent the Islamic investors to invest commercially in the same fashion as a western competitor. A conventional acquisition structure would require that the transaction is carried out by a special purpose vehicle which is financed with bank and shareholder debt and equity provided by the Investors.[30] Since the Islamic investors may not enter into transactions involving conventional bank financing the transaction practice has developed a modified Ijara scheme which allows the use of conventional bank financing and at the same time is compliant with Shari'ah principles.[31]

In this modified Ijara lease structure the Islamic investors would establish their acquisition structure and fund it with shareholder loans and equity. In parallel to the structure owned by the Islamic investors an orphan structure would be established held by a Dutch foundation or another suitable vehicle. A subsidiary of this parallel structure would acquire the real property (including the rent agreements) and enter into the conventional bank loan agreement. Under the financing documentation the special purpose vehicle would also provide a full security package to the financing conventional bank.

---

27 Ayub, Understanding Islamic Finance (2007), pp. 279 ff.

28 Pohlmann / Beck, IStR 2010, p. 225 (230); Heckel, ZVglRWiss 111 (2012), p. 311 (322).

29 Grieser, WM 2009, p. 586 (590).

30 Kugler, Islamic Finance – Neue Ansätze bei Immobilientransaktionen und deren Finanzierung in Deutschland (2009), p. 71 with a simplified description of the structuring and inaccurate tax assessment on the pp. 61 f.

31 Cf. Kugler, Islamic Finance – Neue Ansätze bei Immobilientransaktionen und deren Finanzierung in Deutschland (2009), p. 75.

At the same time the "conventional" SPV would enter into an Ijara lease agreement with two elements. The first element provides for a long term lease under which the beneficial ownership the asset is transferred to the special purpose vehicle owned by the Islamic investors. In consideration for the long term lease the Islamic investors pay the entire lease sum in advance. The amount of the advance lease payment is equal to the balance of the purchase price and further acquisition cost due by the "conventional" special purpose vehicle.

The second element of the Ijara arrangement in this case is a short term lease agreement under which the conventional special purpose vehicle has the right to use the property in particular by renting it to third parties in consideration for a leasing fee. The fee is calculated as the balance of the gross rent income less any expenses incurred by the conventional special purpose vehicle (including interest payable to banks).

As a result the financing conventional bank would only have to deal with the conventional special purpose vehicle and also the tenants and service provider would exclusively have to deal with this entity.

The structure can be wound up when the Islamic investors decide to exit from the investment. In that case the investors will terminate the Ijara lease arrangement which results in an obligation of the conventional special purpose vehicle to repay the outstanding balance of the long term lease payment received in advance and the accrued built in capital gains. Commercially, the conventional special purpose vehicle will be forced to sell the property in order to be able to settle its payment obligations.

The entering into the Ijara arrangement should not trigger RETT as there is no transfer of legal title involved and the transfer of the beneficial interest does not trigger a RETT charge.[32] The classification of the transaction for VAT purposes, however, is not evident as it is not clear whether the transaction can be considered as the combination of two lease agreements (which can be subject to VAT by election) or whether the transfer of the beneficial ownership needs to be considered as a taxable supply of property. In the latter case the VAT would be due at the time the Ijara arrangement is entered into which would result in additional financing requirements until and to the extent the input VAT is eventually refunded.[33]

For income taxation purposes the vehicle owned by the Islamic investors would be considered as the beneficial owner of the property. This entity would be taxed on the net rent income after deduction of interest payable under the bank loan and interest payable under any shareholder loan provided to the Islamic investors' vehicle. The conventional special purpose vehicle on the other hand would be considered as a nominee with no own income from the renting activity. It should, however, be entitled to a service fee which should leave it with a marginal profit.

32 Fischer, Boruttau, GrEStG 18. edition (2016), §1 recital 200.

33 OFD Hannover, Vfg. V. 17.02.2009, S 7100 – 611 – StO 172, UR 2009, p. 466.

This modified Ijara lease structure has been applied by Islamic investors in the course of their acquisition of a major portfolio of real estate assets in the Berlin region and the eastern part of Germany primarily in the first decade of the millennium. These transactions in the meantime were reviewed by the German tax administration which accepted the structuring without adjustments to the material and decisive features.

5. GENERAL ANTI-AVOIDANCE RULES

The German tax administration will not accept "artificial" structures under which a tax payer creates a tax advantage which would not have been available in case the artificial structure was not applied. It seems, however, obvious that the structures primarily are not driven by the intention to create an unjustified tax advantage. In contrast the structures aim to achieve a tax treatment which at least is comparable to the outcome for investors who are not bound by the principles of Shari'ah and Islamic finance but it is neither intended nor achieved that the structures result in an even more advantageous tax regime.

Further, the structures described in this paper could only be challenged as abusive in case there are no other (valid) grounds besides the intention to create a more beneficial tax position. In the context of Islamic finance the intention clearly is to create an investment scheme which is compatible with the principles of Shari'ah and Islamic finance. The observance of religious rules is considered as a justification for "artificial" structures under German tax law. Hence, there should be no practical risk that the structures would not be accepted for taxation purposes. As described in this paper there are, however, risks and downsides in the implementation of Islamic finance schemes which are due to the fact that the German tax regime does not provide any specific rules which would facilitate the implementation of Shari'ah compliant structures.

6. CONCLUSION

The (tax) planning for acquisitions of assets, in particular real estate, in western jurisdictions focuses on the use of debt (leverage) and the deduction of interest expenses from the taxable revenue. Notwithstanding recent attempts of international organizations (OECD and EU) to limit the permissible deductions of interest expenses, the use of (shareholder) debt and the corresponding interest expenses remains an important planning tool for conventional investors. Investors who decided to use Islamic finance instruments need to find ways to adapt accepted Islamic finance structures to the requirements of the jurisdictions in which they operate. It is obvious that a number of issues arise in this context which to a large extent result from the tax systems in the target jurisdictions. Certain jurisdictions have introduced special regimes to facilitate the investments by Middle East and other Islamic investors.

This includes in particular the United Kingdom[34] and its approach to implement Islamic financial transactions. Building on the principle that "all financial institutions authorized by the FSA and operating in the UK, or seeking to do so, are subject to the same standards, regardless of their country of origin, the sectors in which they wish to specialize, or their religious principles"[35], Islamic financial structures were adopted within the UK legal system.[36] In practice, the focus has mainly centered on the modification of tax measures to include Islamic financial structures within the UK's (complex) tax regime ensuring that transactions will not receive less favourable tax treatment due to their multi-tiered architectures.[37]

In Luxembourg[38], there was no need for the adoption of Islamic financial structures within the legal system. The existing regulatory and tax frameworks have proven flexible enough to implement various Shari'ah-compliant structures. Luxembourg law further allows to combine its elements with agreements concluded under foreign law.[39]

Germany is, however, not considering the introduction of a special tax regime for Islamic investors so that they will need to operate in the same environment in future. It is, however, possible to find structures which are compliant with Islamic finance principles and at the same time achieve a tax position for the investors which is comparable with the tax position of conventional investors. In practice the requirements of Islamic investors and conventional structuring often are separated in two separate strings of entities with one string being held by the Islamic investors which uses Sharia compliant financing tools. The second string of entities would use funds provided under conventional bank financing and make them available to the investors by using Islamic finance instruments which are adapted for the specific purpose. By this technique it is avoided that there is a direct contractual or financial link between conventional banks and Islamic investors. It seems that this technique is widely accepted by the investors (and Islamic scholars and Shari'ah boards)[40] notwithstanding the more complex structures and the increased cost associated with them.

---

34 Fawzy, VuR 2009, p. 39 (40).

35 Ainley, Islamic Finance in the UK: Regulation and Challenges (2007), p. 11.

36 Ercanbrack, The Law of Islamic Finance in the United Kindgom: Legal Pluralism and Financial Competition (2011), p. 256.

37 Ercanbrack, The Law of Islamic Finance in the United Kindgom: Legal Pluralism and Financial Competition (2011), p. 263.

38 Cf. Circulaire du directeur des contributions: L.G.-A nr 55, January 12 2010.

39 The Law Reviews, The Islamic Finance and Markets Review, Edition 2 (2017), Luxembourg, II. Legislative and regulatory framework.

40 Ayub, Understanding Islamic Finance (2007), p. 442. Although it is criticized that Islamic finance products are not standardized due to different Sharia interpretations of its concepts,

Some argue that interest income and therefore income earned from prohibited / illegal sources by conventional banks cannot be the seed capital for business that is based on Shari'ah principles. But this argument disregards the fact that if a person intends, at any time, to stop his misconduct, he should be given the possibility to transform to valid, good and socially useful behaviours. The Quranic verses[41] give a clear principle. Accordingly, the essential requirement is that the operations should be Shari'ah-compliant and completely separated from the interest-based business. Furthermore, initially generated capital of the bank which remains a part of its income, is not necessarily interest income.[42]

---

a consensus on the philosophy and products for business has basically been reached so that insignificant differences in the concepts should no longer a cause of concern.. The mainstream theory of Islamic finance has found acceptance and therefore forms the basis for the development of the industry. The practice of sale and lease-back, inter alia, is one major area where Shari'ah scholars have provided a solution by way of Ijtihad. Until standardizations are realized, settled principles form the basis for the creation of new products in the conventional market. This is supported by the statement of David / Jauffret-Spinosi, Les grands systèmes de droit contemporains (12e ed.): "[…] le *fiqh* laisse un jeu tel à la coutume, à la convention des parties: à la réglementation administrative, aux principes généraux qu'il est possible, sans lui porter atteinte, de parvenir à des solutions qui permettent de construire une société moderne" (p. 380).

41 Ayub, Understanding Islamic Finance (2007), pp. 446 f.: The Quranic verses give the principle that "those who listen to the order of the Almighty and desist from engaging in interest (in future), may keep their previously received gains, their case being entrusted to the Almighty (for accountability in the Hereafter)" (2:275) and "if you repent (on taking interest), you have the right to get your principal" (2:278).

42 Ayub, Understanding Islamic Finance (2007), p. 447.

"ISLAMIC FINANCE" AFTER STATE-SPONSORED CAPITALIST-ISLAMISM

Mahmoud A. El-Gamal
Rice University

1. HISTORICAL BACKGROUND

The industry that exists today under the name "Islamic finance" is an offspring of late twentieth century legal arbitrage and Islamist identity politics. The religious-legal need for such an industry was debunked thoroughly in late nineteenth and early twentieth century Muslim thought, as Muslim societies sought political and economic independence from European, especially British, colonialism. In this regard, Muslim societies struggled to adopt Western education and social methods, including development of their own financial sectors. The quest for economic independence included the establishment of indigenous banks and corporations, with increasingly diminishing levels of Western support.

Various approaches coexisted in the late nineteenth and early twentieth century forms of Muslim liberation theologies, some of which championed greater reform through westernization, such as the Turkish *tanzimat* and the Indian efforts of Syed Ahmed Khan, while others, including, most famously, Jamal al-Din "Al-Afghani," favoured greater independence (c.f. Keddie, 1972, 1983). Muslim jurisprudence that emerged during this period was highly rationalist, and aimed primarily at legitimizing Western financial practices, including banking and the establishment of corporate forms, which were necessary for the programs of all modernizers. Remnants of this jurisprudence have survived into the twenty-first century pronouncements of official and prominent religious scholars, but have generally been shunned by Islamists of all stripes.

Borrowing heavily from Christian liberation theologies of the mid-twentieth century, nationalist-Islamism mutated into a socialist-Islamism, which is exemplified politically in the career of Gamal Abdel-Nasser, and juristically in the writings of the Muslim Brotherhood's most prominent jurist, Mohamed El-Ghazali, among many others; c.f. El-Ghazali (2005), and the later contrast between Islam and Capitalism in Qutb (1993, 2000). The prominent Syrian scholar Mustafa El-Siba`i (1960) wrote the most comprehensive Islamic embrace of Soviet-style nationalization, which, together with Nasser's pro-Arab-republic component of socialist-Islamism, posed significant dangers to the Arab oil monarchies' political and economic models, as well as the geopolitical cold-war interests of their Western patrons.

Oil monarchies countered the socialist-Islamism threat with a pan-Islamist program to export their own forms of legalistic and apolitical Islamism, exemplified in Al-Badri's (1965) rebuttal of Al-Siba`i (1960).

One of the earliest Islamist experiments in finance during the mid-twentieth century was the German-inspired cooperative Mit Ghamr village banking experiment by Ahmed El-Naggar. The focus of this initiative was, characteristically, on local community development, and the mechanics of finance were conventional (although, in what was very likely a revisionist history after the emergence of so-called "Islamic banking" in the late 1970s, El-Naggar, who became a celebrity in this field, before becoming disillusioned with it, claimed that his German sponsors had forced him to charge and pay interest). Consistently with Nasser's socialist program, the Mit Ghamr village bank was nationalized into the Nasser Social Bank, providing El-Naggar with further incentive to adopt the political-economic agendas of alternate patrons in Arab oil monarchies; c.f. El-Naggar (1993). In this regard, although it had been understood, as Rodinson (2007) suggested during the 1960s, that there was no intrinsic incompatibility between Islam and Capitalism, Nasser had chosen to champion the view that "Islam is 100% Socialist;" c.f. Said Aly and Warner (1982).

With the advent of massive petrodollar flows in the 1970s, the pan-Islamic program of the Arab oil monarchies included the export of an "Islamic finance," championed within the United Arab Emirates in the form of Dubai Islamic Bank, and in other countries by the Saudi Prince Muhammad Al-Faisal and businessman Saleh Kamel. Interestingly, while Saudi Arabia promoted so-called "Islamic banking" in Egypt, Turkey, and other countries, the brand name was not tolerated within the Kingdom itself until very recently, and only in reaction to large petrodollar outflows to financial centers in Bahrain and UAE. The latter were only the nearest countries that aimed to benefit from the nexus of petrodollar recycling and capitalist-Islamism. Malaysia, Turkey, and other countries also aimed to reconfigure their financial sectors to become more attractive destinations for Islamist-minded petrodollars, while the bulk of petrodollar recycling was accomplished according to the plan devised by Henry Kissinger in 1973, mostly through New York banks that lent the funds to sovereign states in Latin America and elsewhere. During the early 1980s, a number of Western corporations also sought to attract cheap petrodollar capitals, including in the form of "Islamic finance," especially as the Federal Reserve raised interest in 1982. Eventually, oil prices collapsed after the ensuing recession, contributing to the sovereign debt crisis of the mid 1980s, as oil-reserves used as collateral for various countries' borrowings of recycled petrodollars declined in value.

Seeds of the current formulaic "Islamic finance" can be traced to this period. Thus we can see in the compendium of *fatawa* by the Shari'ah board of Al-Rajhi investment corporation (which was not allowed to practice in Saudi Arabia using an "Islamic" brand name, but nonetheless was then, as now, the strictest adherent to classical Islamic jurisprudence) two consecutive opinions in 1991, the first forbidding the sale of gold on credit, and the second allowing the sale of platinum on credit; c.f. Al-Rajhi (2010, #100 and #101, pp. 170–1). The latter was thus utilized to synthesize an interest-bearing loan to a Western corporation, which had no interest in purchasing the platinum. This rudimentary type of financial engineering created a credit facility through the purchase and then credit sale of a commodity that would be easily resold by the prospective borrower on the spot market. The structure was superficially a *murabaha* financing (mark-up credit sale) agreement, which had been controversial in the late 1970s, resulting in a heated public debate between Drs. Yusuf Al-Qaradawi and Rafiq Yunus Al-Masri, but became increasingly accepted for retail secured financing of actual automobile or real estate purchases; c.f. Abu-Zeid (2004).

This, in turn, set the stage for more creative financial engineering methods to enable recycling of the second wave of petrodollars after the second Iraq War in 2003. This second wave of Islamic finance, which included the rise of elaborate structures for so-called *ṣukūk*, was also a golden opportunity for the armies of English and American legal arbitrageurs who had honed their skills on financial engineering methods aimed at minimizing tax incidence for corporations. Those financial engineers had been stigmatized by the scandalous failure of Enron in 2000, and needed other markets wherein to practice their craft.

The capitalist-Islamism exemplified in today's Islamic finance cannot survive the imminent demise of petrodollars. It has been eclipsed by a terrorist-Islamism, which first emerged in the low oil price period of the late 1990s, before the second Iraq War, and has surged again in recent years after the collapse of oil prices in 2014. It is no surprise that Osama bin Laden, the architect of the worst terrorist attack on New York City in 2001, had denounced the fall of oil prices during the 1990s in his letter to Saudi King Fahd as "the greatest theft in history," c.f. Lawrence (2005, p. 272), and his targeting of the World Trade Centre, as a symbol of global capitalism, was also not coincidental. The fact that bin Laden's "golden chain" of terrorist finance relied heavily on "Islamic finance" institutions is also not a surprise, c.f. Prados and Blanchard (2007), because of the higher presumed level of trust and solidarity within intersecting Islamist social networks, and the "layering"-like methods of Islamic finance.

Another clear link between terrorist-Islamism and so-called "Islamic finance" is exemplified in the darker side of Islamic finance's most widely respected Deobandi "Shari`a scholar," M. Taqi Usmani, who has been a long time supporter of the Afghani Taliban. His overt advocacy for offensive jihadism in the last chapter of his *Islam and Modernism*, which was republished in English in 2006 by Adam Publishers in New Delhi, caused great alarm, especially after attention was drawn to it in a *Times* article; c.f. Norfolk (2007). The anti-modernist, anti-rationalist, message of Usmani's book is consistent with the legal arbitrage nature of the industry for which he has been the foremost pseudo-religious legitimizer.

In this regard, it is no surprise that the methods of so-called "Islamic finance," which merely add superficial degrees of separation between borrower and lender through third parties and traded assets, are identical in many respects to the layering methods of money laundering and terrorist finance. Tolerance of so-called "Islamic finance," therefore, provided governments an opportunity not only to recycle plentiful petrodollars, but also to have a smaller corner of finance on which to focus their efforts in trying to infiltrate and trace Islamist social networks that may sponsor or enable terrorist activities.

Although capitalist-Islamism and terrorist-Islamism have coexisted over the past twenty years, as the former was enabled by the second wave of petrodollars following the second Iraq War, the end of petrodollars means that we are left only with terrorist-Islamism. The highly inefficient medieval-jurisprudence-arbitraging "Islamic finance" industry cannot survive without capitalist-Islamism, which, in turn, cannot survive without petrodollars. However, as Max Weber has noted around the turn of the previous century, institutions rarely die, because they reinvent themselves to serve different purposes. In this regard, "Islamic finance" cannot survive to serve only terrorist-Islamism, because the latter would no longer have the apparently safe cover behind recycled petrodollars and capitalist-Islamism. Therefore, to imagine how the industry can evolve in coming years, we need to envision what other forms of Muslim liberation theology (or Islamism) are likely to fill the vacuum that will be left by capitalist-Islamism. It would be valuable to all humankind if this emergent Islamism can also diminish or eliminate the scourge of terrorist-Islamism, and, to the extent that Muslim and Western governments may agree on this goal, we may be able to limit the range of potential ascendant Islamisms that would be tolerated by those powers.

Understanding the co-evolution of Muslim liberation theology and Western conceptions of justice (socialist in the mid twentieth century, and corporatist legal arbitrage since the late twentieth century) can be helpful in forecasting how Muslims' conceptions of justice may evolve. However, this is a larger research program, well beyond the scope of this paper, which aims only to understand the likely shape of Islamic finance after the age of petrodollars. I fear that there is insufficient data at this time even to envision the latter. However, by tracing the evolution of Islamisms, and understanding the incentive structure that enabled the emergence of today's legal-arbitrage form of "Islamic finance," it may be possible to predict that the current partnership of financial engineers and religious ideologues will come to an end in the near future. The latter are likely to get caught in the dragnet targeting terrorist-Islamism, and the former will fail to find petrodollar-fuelled financial-engineering fees to justify the risk of association with the industry and its increasingly narrower social network of Islamist support. Attempting to predict when this shift will take place, and what will replace it, are also more difficult tasks that require different data and tools than I use in this paper.

2. WHY THERE WAS NO "ISLAMIC FINANCE" BEFORE PETRODOLLARS

The incoherent writings of Mawdudi and his students and followers during the mid-twentieth century postulated an ostensible difference between Islamic and conventional finance that glorified silent partnerships (*mudaraba*) as ideal forms of fair finance, which they contrasted with conventional finance. Of course, partnerships predated Islam and had continued in conventional finance. However, a model that exclusively relies on partnerships failed to provide a practical alternative to debt finance, for obvious moral hazard and adverse selection reasons, and had very shaky juristic grounds. As El-Gamal (2016) has argued, the silent partnership model (wherein profits are shared with the entrepreneur at agreed ratios and losses are borne by the investor) was characterized by many classical jurists as *ijara bi-l-gharar* (or hire with uncertain wages), and, indeed, the contract form can easily lend itself to exploitation of workers by forcing them to carry unwanted risk (of profit sharing) even when they expect to receive an average absolute payment lower than their market wages.

It was for this reason that many distinguished twentieth century Azhari scholars, including most notably the jurist and legal theorist Abdul-Wahhab Khallaf, suggested legitimizing conventional bank transactions, and deemed them to be fairer by fixing the rate of return on investment (including bank loans and deposits in this category). This was one of the main rationales provided in a famous Azhar Islamic Research Institute fatwa on the same, and supported by elaborate scholarly analysis to dismiss all prophetic traditions quoted against the position; c.f. El-Gamal (2006) and the translated fatwas, quotes, and references therein.

Because I had covered the Azhar fatwa and the earlier juristic analyses on which it was based elsewhere, I would like to focus the remainder of this section on a much earlier thorough analysis that showed how banking practices were legitimized very early in the twentieth century. The thought process during that period was summarized in a lengthy fatwa issued by a number of scholars in Hyderabad, India, and forwarded to the Syrian scholar Rashid Rida, who was a close associate-student of Muhammad `Abduh. The latter, of course, was the first holder of the office of Grand Mufti of Egypt and the most famous student of

Jamal el-Din "Al-Afghani" during his stays in Egypt and France. It is clear that the fatwa was sent to numerous scholars around the world, but we have its text and commentary by Rashid Rida thanks to his publications in *Al-Manar* and the subsequent publication in Rida (1986).

The text of the Indian fatwa is rather lengthy (*ibid.*, pp. 19-72). It progressed in four stages: In the first and second, its authors argued, following in the footsteps of a long tradition in the relatively rationalist Hanafi jurisprudence, that the term *riba* (mistakenly translated as "interest" in Islamist discourses) was mentioned in the Qur'an abstractly, and that its explication was provided in prophetic traditions, but did not expand the range of forbidden transactions. In this regard, Qur'anic commentary and exegesis had long established that the *riba* mentioned in the Qur'an is exclusively the *riba al-jahiliya* (unjustified increase in credit during the pre-Islamic age of ignorance; which was only practiced by increasing the amount of matured debts, not as stipulated increments over principal at the inception of a loan). The Hyderabad scholars then proceed in the third and fourth parts of their fatwa to argue that a prespecified interest at the inception of a loan is not the forbidden *riba*, and that the juristic analogy used to forbid it is defective and/or non-binding in the modern age. A partial translation of their conclusions, together with their reasoning based on Qur'anic exegeses as well as scholarly analyses of the prophetic traditions and juristic analyses, follows (p.32, ibid):

> Thus it has become clear that a defined benefit stipulated as a condition in loans is not a form of the riba mentioned in Canonical texts, since the verse mentioned the term only generally and abstractly -- so that the desired meaning cannot be understood from the verse itself -- and the Hadiths [Prophetic traditions] that explain the term are all restricted to sales and no other contracts. Thus, our jurists explicitly stated that riba is only effected in sales and not in voluntary contributions. Perhaps what they meant to say is that it is not the riba that was mentioned in Canonical Texts.
>
> [The authors cite lengthy evidence here from ibn Rushd's *Al-Muqaddima*, wherein he explained `Abdullah ibn `Umar's prohibition of a stipulated increase at the inception of a loan explicitly not as a direct application of the Textual prohibition of *riba*, but rather based on analogical inference. They also cite Al-Baghawi making the same argument: that prohibition of interest on loans is inferred by analogy, not by direct application of the Canonical Texts of Qur'an and Hadith].
> Proof for this assertion is also provided by [Al-Kasani] in Al-Bada'i`, wherein he forbade a stipulated increase in loans by saying: "because the stipulated increase is similar to riba." In this regard, that which is characterized as "similar to riba" cannot itself be characterized simultaneously as riba ...
> As for the Hadith reported in Bulugh al-Maram on the authority of Ali, which everyone among the commoners and the elect have been narrating: "every loan which brings a benefit [to the lender] is riba," this Hadith cannot be used to explain the Qur'an, since it is not well authenticated, and thus has no foundation. In this

> regard, ibn Hajar said: "[the chain of narration for this tradition] includes Al-Harith ibn Usamah, whose narrations are not accepted"...

They provided several other references to Hadith scholars – including Al-Zayla`i, Abi al-Jahm, Al-Bukhari, Al-Nasa'i, and ibn Al-Humam – who rejected the Hadith due to other weak links in its chain of narrators. In particular, ibn al-Humam said that the best one can say about this doctrine is that it is based on the views of the Prophet's companions, and they only agreed that interest on loans was reprehensible – which implies that it is not *riba*, otherwise they should have concluded that it was forbidden. They also dismissed the facts that Al-Ghazali and his teacher Al-Juwaini accepted this Hadith as valid, citing Al-Shawkani in *Nayl Al-Awtar*, who dismissed the claim because they were not experts in Hadith authentication.

In his commentary, Rashid Rida accepted the main scholarly analysis of the Hyderabad jurists – that the prohibition of interest on loans cannot be said credibly to rely directly on Qur'an or valid prophetic tradition. Thus, he agreed with them that its prohibition was based on reasoning by analogy conducted by early companions of the prophet and later jurists. Such analogical reasoning could be overruled in the modern era based on changes in institutions and social needs. Thus, Rida concluded that the juristic analysis of the progressive jurists cannot be deemed invalid. In other words, the conclusion very early in the twentieth century was that the mechanics of banking were not necessarily problematic for Muslims. There is no doubt that Rashid Rida and his contemporaries knew and approved of the efforts to establish indigenous banks, like Tal`at Harb's Banque Misr, in order to finance development and industrialization; c.f. Davis (2014). The legacy of nationalist-Islamism was not to reject the tools of capitalism, but rather to use them for domestic development and economic independence from colonial powers and their banks – an agenda that succeeded to some limited extent.

3. HOW SO-CALLED "ISLAMIC FINANCE" EMERGED SINCE 1970S

However, what followed in the wake of independence in the 1950s and 1960s was the development of Arab socialism, which resulted in the nationalization of some of the existing banks, including Tal`at Harb's industrialization-enabling Banque Misr and Ahmed El-Naggar's village community bank in Mit Ghamr. As Islamists increasingly defined themselves in contrast to the Arab-socialist regimes, an economic component of their separatism was to characterize all banks, including state banks, intentionally pejoratively, as "*ribawi.*"

Thus, the Iraqi jurist and activist M. Baqir Al-Sadr (1981) wrote a juristic treatise on how to create a non-*ribawi* bank in an Islamic society, and the

Jordanian former banker Sami Humud (1976) devised some of the simplest and most practical trade-based means to restructure bank loans. As mentioned in the introduction, those simple financial engineering devices eventually gave rise to more sophisticated forms of structured finance, especially during the second major petrodollar wave in the twenty first century.

So-called "Islamic finance" is first and foremost a Gulf-state-sponsored form of capitalist-Islamism, which was embraced by many other states, both Muslim and otherwise, who were competing for recycled petrodollars. Like other forms of exported Islamism (some more violent than others), the sponsors structured this style of Islamism mainly for export. Thus, Saudi Arabian princes and businessmen sponsored "Islamic finance" in other parts of the world, but were not allowed to operate Islamic banks within Saudi Arabia until the latter was forced to accommodate it because of large private flows to Bahrain and UAE. Before then, the routine answer was that all institutions in Saudi Arabia (including banks) were already Islamic.

Recycled-petrodollars recipient governments were generally happy to accommodate Islamic finance to varying degrees, beyond the obvious financial reasons, also to appease their own domestic Islamists in an arena far from threatening politics. In some countries, like Malaysia and Turkey, Islamist-friendly governments additionally used the growing industry to enrich and empower their own power bases (ethnic Malays and the MUSIAD business association in Istanbul, respectively). In others, like Tunisia and Egypt, secular-minded rulers allowed limited penetration of the industry to appease their Islamists, and simultaneously to gain a better understanding of their social and financial networks. Western governments in Europe and North America have also found the industry to be useful for the same reasons as those secular-minded regimes in majority-Muslim countries.

In countries like Malaysia and Turkey, and increasingly in countries under more secular-minded regimes, Muslims could benefit from this industry's growth both as clients and as practitioners. In the event, Muslims' comparative advantage on the practitioner side was generally limited to retail asset-gathering and the regulatory infrastructure. They worked in partnership with incoherently-pietist marketing by specialized "Shari'ah scholars." The latter constituted the most important marketing vehicles for entrepreneurial efforts to create an isolated market segment of religiously-insecure Muslim clients for this industry, in which they had a comparative advantage. Despite the obvious rationale for this business model, there is scant evidence that so-called Islamic finance has increased financial access and intermediation in Muslim populations. In this regard, the industry's proponents have been very defensive in their argument that their role is not developmental, but merely to "allow pious Muslims [who can afford to pay their fees] to live according to the dictates of their religion."

In propagating a formulaic/juristic understanding of classical Islamic jurisprudence and its potential contemporary applications, proponents of so-called Islamic finance have been aided in their quest by the patterns shown in Pew opinion survey results tabulated in Tables 1 through 5 in the Appendix. These show (Tables 1 and 2) that local, national, and official Imams and Sheikhs in Muslim countries (the norms of whom were copied by Islamic finance "Shari'ah scholars") were deemed to be authoritative figures who guide Muslims in different countries to lead their lives. This was reinforced by the views that Shari'ah is mostly divinely revealed (Table 5), and that it should be enforced strictly, or based on principles (Table 4) that are doubtless interpreted by the same quasi-clergy groups vested with sacred authority (Tables 1 and 2). Needless to say, petrodollar-powered proponents of the industry were able to influence financially the opinions of official and private local religious authorities.

Once the clientele, retail workforce, and brand name juristic authorities of a formulaic-juristic finance industry were in place, the field was ripe for legal arbitrageurs – mostly London and New York based bankers and lawyers, who had previously honed their financial engineering skills to arbitrage tax laws in Western jurisdictions. Especially after the failure of Enron resulted in stricter regulation in these legal arbitrageurs' main domain, they were happy to find a goldmine in so-called "Islamic finance," which was flush with cheap petrodollar liquidity. Earlier, they had taken a company like Enron's debt and interest payments off balance sheets for tax advantage and to boost stock prices with misleading pro-forma financial reports. Now, they could use the same lease-buy-back and similar methods with offshore special purpose vehicles to relabel debt and interest for a different audience and potentially higher fees.

4. AFTER PETRODOLLAR STATE-SPONSORED CAPITALIST-ISLAMISM

The structures of Islamic finance have been clearly flawed throughout their history, but Gulf monarchies generally did not allow high-profile defaults, such as the recent Dana Gas *ṣukūk* debacle, to take place during the peak years of capitalist-Islamism. As I have argued in the previous section, this expensive fiction was possible as long as petrodollars were plentiful to attract legal arbitrage talent and cover up the failures of their flawed structures. Western governments also were willing to support the industry for both its advantages in petrodollar-recycling and intelligence gathering on overlapping Islamist social networks. Gulf monarchies have now changed their attitudes as petrodollars decline, while frustrated Islamist expectations have given rise to terrorist-Islamism and other threatening manifestations of political Islam.

As Gulf monarchies seek to undermine the forces of political Islam, which overlap substantially with the most recent forces of terrorist-Islamism, they find themselves equally compelled to undermine the forces of capitalist-Islamism, which had been empowering the same groups. Thus, for example, they have chosen to undercut Dr. Hussein Hamed Hassan, the long-term chief Shari'ah scholar of Dubai Islamic Bank, and the primary structurer of the Dana Gas *ṣukūk* that have been allowed to fail. Hassan has been a leader of the Muslim Brotherhood who presided over the parliamentary spectacle of approving a short-lived Egyptian constitution during the difficult year of Muslim Brotherhood government. As the Emirates and Saudi Arabia fight the Muslim Brotherhood on all fronts, including the boycott of Qatar and attempt to silence her satellite TV station Al-Jazeera, which has been very friendly to the group, they are, not surprisingly, beginning to undermine the "Islamic finance" industry which has empowered and helped to enrich the same Islamist groups within their borders and beyond.

Therefore, capitalist-Islamism is coming to an end together with its various features, of which "Islamic finance" has been a prominent one. This is the case because the petrodollar fuel for the industry as currently configured is vanishing quickly, and the social networks that the industry has empowered are the same ones that have contributed to terrorist-Islamism in response to growing economic and political pressures. Nonetheless, as Max Weber taught many years ago, institutions are remarkably resilient and find ways to redefine their raison d'être and to survive by fulfilling other functions. Without a doubt, the next mutation of Islamism will determine the direction in which "Islamic finance" will mutate, although the latter may also play a limited role in influencing the shape of the former.

Unfortunately, attempting to forecast the nature of this next mutation is difficult because we lack sufficient data, both in terms of detailed measurement of sentiments and of having such measurements over a sufficiently long time period. The forecasting task requires a more tedious analysis of intellectual and popular writings to understand earlier mutations of Muslim liberation theology (the four Islamisms discussed earlier: nationalist, socialist, capitalist, and terrorist) and suggest potential directions for the next mutation. Nonetheless, it seems safe at this stage to predict that the formulaic/juristic "Islamic finance" that we have observed over the period of petrodollar-and-state-sponsored capitalist-Islamism will soon decline and mutate into other forms that serve heretofore unknown future forms of Islamism.

As the former exporters of capitalist-Islamism and its broader religious-legal worldview, most prominently Saudi Arabia and her Gulf neighbours, continue their soul searching to find an alternative modern-world Muslim worldview to champion, we are likely to suffer through a period of continued confusion in Islamist circles. In many respects, the situation today is similar to that in the early twentieth century, when westernizing modernists and nationalist-Islamists parted ways and left us with the current state of conflict. Modernizers today face the same problems that "Al-Afghani,"' Abduh, Rida, Mawdudi, and others faced as they tried to find a feasible middle between the fastest path to modernization (which is unlikely to work today, as it was then), one the one hand, and "authenticity" to the Muslim tradition and its "salafi" reconstructed fictions, on the other.

Although it is tempting to think that the earlier middle-way program of nationalist-Islamism could have worked, it is likely that it carried the seeds of its own mutation within itself. Thus, Rashid Rida was much more intent on saving the tradition from modernizers than his teachers – who saw modernization as the ultimate goal and authenticity to the tradition as a necessary means to that end. In the event, intellectually, Rida served as a bridge between the type of Salafism that 'Abduh had in mind (based on how progressive he deemed the earliest Muslims to have been) and the eighteenth century Arabian version of Salafism, which yearned to freeze society in a presumed seventh century mould. In the meantime, politically, the Muslim Brotherhood sought power in ways that enabled a small group of young and impressionable officers to transform the program into the socialist-Islamism of the mid-century. The financially ascendant oil monarchies adopted Rida's version of Salafism to empower the capitalist-Islamism with which they countered the threat of socialist-Islamism, and they have dominated Muslim religious discourse to this day.

Needless to say, the current situation is very different from the early twentieth century, both in terms of the different mix of centralization and decentralization of religious authority, and the realities of a Muslim world that was getting surprisingly richer in the past century and that is likely to revert to a much poorer state soon. Those, respectively, are the same problems that have made terrorist-Islamism very difficult to defeat ideologically and financially.

Those forces also mean that "Islamic finance" is likely to evolve in ways that cannot be controlled by its former petrodollar masters, both because they are beginning to endorse a different ideological model and can no longer afford the legal and financial infrastructure that made other governments and communities follow their lead. Some home-grown models, such as mutual housing cooperatives, formal or informal credit unions, and the like, may regain some advantage in leveraging the "Islamic finance" brand name, and they may thus contribute to greater financial integration and modernization of marginalized Muslims in various countries. Although this is far from the ideal of teaching Muslims that there is nothing intrinsically un-Islamic about modern financial practices (and, indeed, that what is often marketed to them as Islamic is in fact overpriced and inferior in every other respect, and, therefore, provably more un-Islamic), it may be a feasible second best from a financial standpoint.

The risks of such a distributed system of religious authority and financial empowerment are also obvious, especially because it emerges at a time when terrorist-Islamism is at its peak. This suggests that financial regulators and law enforcement agencies would be well advised to play a proactive role in steering and monitoring such grassroots initiatives, both to provide entrepreneurs in this domain valuable technical assistance and access to the broader financial sector, and to prevent terrorist-Islamists from abusing the social and financial capital of the much larger populations of Muslims struggling to reconcile their religious tradition with modernity. This may be a costlier risk-management approach than the one championed by the anti-terror industry, and contrary to the myopic self-interest of participants in that lucrative industry, but it may also be more effective in hastening the transition away from today's dominant paradigm of terrorist-Islamism, which has arisen from the ruins of the failing capitalist-Islamist paradigm.

In this effort, Muslim-majority and other governments should be very careful, because attempting to engineer the next mutation of Islamism may backfire in the same manner that state-sponsored capitalist-Islamism has mutated into today's terrorist-Islamism. It is best to think of this problem in terms of dynamic optimal control, albeit in an environment where the target is unknown. The most aggressive anti-terror approaches and the most ambitious modernization approaches use static models that aim at minimizing immediate damage or maximizing immediate reward, without regard for the (often predictable) consequences of their interactions with social forces that react dynamically. Unfortunately, this means that engagement at all levels with the forms of Islamism that exist today, reprehensible and/or incoherent as they may be, remains important.

5. CONCLUDING REMARKS

The analysis that I have provided here is in many respects tentative and overly simplistic. The various brands of Islamism have coexisted in many times and places. For example, many of Mawdudi's Pakistani followers have exhibited prominently a mix of three of the four forms: nationalist-Islamism (their animosity to India, minority sects within the country, etc.), capitalist-Islamism (cynically marketed by a succession of corrupt kleptocrats), and terrorist-Islamism (both within and outside their borders). Likewise, it is very rare to find only one isolated form of Islamism in any large Muslim country or population. Moreover, the transitions to and from socialist-Islamism were clearly influenced by much broader international developments, mainly in Latin America and Asia. This suggests that a more comprehensive and/or sophisticated analysis would have to take into account the global environments in which Islamism is likely to mutate next. However, the main conclusions of this very limited analysis are unlikely to change: capitalist-Islamism is in its final days; terrorist-Islamism is thriving, but hopefully not for long; "Islamic finance" will change; and we need to continue to monitor it and, whenever possible, nudge it in less damaging directions.

REFERENCES

Abu-Zeid, A. *Bay` Al-Murabaha wa Tatbiqatuh Al-Mu`asira* (Murabaha Sale and Its Contemporary Applications), Damascus: Dar Al-Fikr, 2004.

Al-Badri, A. *Hukm Al-Islam fi Al-Ishtirakiya* (Islam's Verdict on Socialism).} Madina, Saudi Arabia: Al-Maktaba Al-`Ilmiya, 1965.

Al-Rajhi Shari`a Board. *Qararat Al-Hay'a Al-Shar`iya bi-Masrif Al-Rajhi* (Opinions of the Shari`a Board of Al-Rajhi bank) Vol.1, Riyad: Kunuz Ishbilya Pub, 2010.

Al-Sadr, M.B. *Al-Bank Al-Laribawi fi Al-'Islam: Utruha lilta`wid `an al-Riba, wa dirasa likafat 'awjuh nashatat al-bunuk fi daw' alfiqh al-Islami* (The Non-Riba Bank in Islam: A Treatise to Replace Riba and A Study of All Bank Activities in Light of Islamic Jurisprudence), Beirut: Dar Al-Taaruf, 1980.
Al-Siba`i, M. *Ishtirakiyat Al-Islam* (The Socialism of Islam).} Cairo: Al-Dar Al-Qawmiya lil Tiba`a wa al-Nashr, third printing, no date (first printing 1959, second 1960).
Davis, E. *Challenging Colonialism: Bank Misr and Egyptian Industrialization 1920--41*, Princeton: Princeton University Press, 2014.
El-Gamal, M. *Islamic Finance: Law, Economics, and Practice*, NY: Cambridge University Press, 2006.
El-Gamal, M. "Mutuality, Reciprocity, and Justice within the Context of a Unified Theory of Riba and Gharar," in Ali, Nazim and S. Nisar (eds.) *Takaful and Islamic Cooperative Finance*, Cheltenham: Edward Elgar, 2016.
El-Ghazali, M. *Al-Islam wa Al-Manahij Al-Ishtirakiya* (Islam and Socialist Systems).} Cairo: Nahdat Misr, fourth printing, 2005.
El-Naggar, A. *Harakat Al-Bunuk Al-Islamiya: Haqa'iq Al-'Asl wa 'Awham Al-Surah* (The Islamic Banks' Movement: Realities of Its Origin and Deslusions of Its Forms), Cairo, Sprint, 1993.
Humud, S. *Tatwir Al-A`mal Al-Masrifiyya bima Yattafiqu wa Al-Shari`ah Al- Islamiyya* (Evolving Banking Operations To Make Them Consistent With Islamic Shari`a), Cairo: Dar Al-Ittihad Al-`Arabi lil-Tiba`a, 1976.
Keddie, N. *An Islamic Response to Imperialism: Political and Religious Writings of Sayyid Jamal ad-Din "al-Afghani"*. Berkeley: University of California Press, 1983.
Keddie, N. *Sayyid Jamal Ad-Din "al-Afgh\={a}n\={\i}": A Political Biography*. Berkeley: University of California Press, 1972.
Lawrence, B. *Messages to The World: The Statements of Osama bin Laden*, NY: Verso, 2005.
Norfolk, A. "Our followers 'must live in peace until strong enough to wage jihad'," *The Times*, September 8, 2007. Retrieved on 11/30/2017 at https://www.thetimes.co.uk/article/our-followers-must-live-in-peace-until-strong-enough-to-wage-jihad-x328fjhsf53.
Prados, A. and C. Blanchard, "Saudi Arabia: Terrorist Financing Issues," Congressional Research Service Issue Brief #RL32499, 2007. Retrieved on 11/30/2017 at https://fas.org/sgp/crs/terror/RL32499.pdf.
Qutb, S. *Ma`rakat Al-Islam wa al-Ra' s Maliya* (The Battle Between Islam and Capitalism).} Cairo: Dar Al-Shuruq, thirteenth printing, 1993.
Qutb, S. *Social Justice in Islam*. (tr: J. Hardie and H. Algar), Oneonta, NY: Islamic Publications International, 2000.
Rida, R. *Al-Riba w al-Mu`amalat fi al-Islam* (Riba and Transactions in Islam), Dar ibn Zaydun (Beirut) and Maktabat Al-Kulliya al-Azhariyyah (Cairo), 1986.
Rodinson, *M. Islam and Capitalism*. (B. Pearce, tr.) London: Saqi Books, 2007.
Rosen, L. *The Justice of Islam*. Oxford: Oxford University Press, 2000.
Said Aly, A. and M. Wenner. "Modern Islamic Reform Movements: The Muslim Brotherhood in Contemporary Egypt." *Middle East Journal* 36(3), 1982, pp. 336-361.

APPENDIX – PEW DATA (GLOBAL ATTITUDES SURVEY, VARIOUS YEARS; AND "THE WORLD'S MUSLIMS," 2012)

Table 1: Pew GAS 2006 – Percentages Responses: Please tell me which of these you trust the most to offer guidance as a Muslim? (Institutions outside such as Azhar, Saudi Imams)

	Local Imam/ Sheikh	National Religious Leaders	Religious Leaders on TV	Imams and Institutions Outside	None
Great Britain (Muslims)	42	4	4	28	16
France (Muslims)	26	18	6	31	19
Germany (Muslims)	18	25	3	12	32
Spain (Muslims)	26	5	4	30	30
Egypt	29	30	22	16	3
Turkey	27	37	6	7	16
Indonesia	60	30	3	4	2
Pakistan	46	19	6	11	7
Jordan	25	24	25	26	0
Nigeria	64	13	3	11	9

Table 2: Pew GAS 2006 – Percentages Responses: Please tell me which one of these you trust SECOND most to offer you guidance as a Muslim?

	Local Imam/ Sheikh	National Religious Leaders	Religious Leaders on TV	Imams and Institutions Outside
Egypt	15	21	29	26
Turkey	27	21	7	7
Indonesia	23	45	20	6
Pakistan	14	28	12	10
Jordan	28	19	19	30
Nigeria	20	26	13	20

Table 3: Pew GAS Percentages Responses: Is the influence of religious leaders very good, somewhat good, somewhat bad or very bad in (survey country)?

Country year	Pakistan 2009	Pakistan 2015	Turkey 2010	Turkey 2015	Egypt 2012	Egypt 2013	Tunisia 2012	Tunisia 2013
Very good	20	27	7	19	36	30	14	12
Somewhat good	43	45	33	22	47	45	36	34
Somewhat bad	18	14	16	18	9	14	27	27
Very bad	11	4	25	23	7	12	14	17
Don't know	9	10	18	18	1	0	8	11
Refused	2		1		1	0	1	0

Table 4: Pew GAS 2015 Percentages Responeses: Which of the following comes closer to your view on laws following the teachings of the Qur'an?

	Strictly	Principles Only	No Influence	DK/Refused
Turkey	13	38	36	13
Jordan	54	38	7	2
Lebanon	15	37	42	6
Palest. ter.	65	23	8	4
Indonesia	22	52	16	9
Malaysia	52	17	17	15
Pakistan	78	16	2	4
Burkina Faso	9	27	60	4
Nigeria	27	17	42	14
Senegal	49	33	16	2

Table 5: Pew 2012 "The World's Muslims" Percentages: Which comes closer to your view?

	Sharia law is revealed word of God	Sharia law is developed by men, based on revelation	Both	DK/Ref
Albania	24	18	8	50
Bosnia-Herz.	52	39	4	6
Kosovo	30	33	3	35
Russia	56	25	8	12
Azerbaijan	53	36	4	6
Kazakhstan	44	31	11	15
Tajikistan	69	20	6	5
Turkey	60	33	6	1
Uzbekistan	49	28	4	19
Indonesia	52	19	6	23
Malaysia	41	35	7	18
Thailand	52	20	2	26
Afghanistan	73	21	4	1
Bangladesh	65	25	7	2
Pakistan	81	8	2	8
Egypt	75	20	3	3
Iraq	69	25	4	2
Jordan	81	18	1	0
Lebanon	49	38	11	1
Morocco	66	13	8	14
Palestinian Ter	75	16	4	5
Tunisia	66	25	6	3

THE TRANSFORMATION OF ISLAMIC LAW: FROM CLASSICAL FIQH TO FINANCIAL FIQH

Dr Amel MAKHLOUF*

Considered to be one of the fastest growing segments of the financial industry, Islamic finance is increasingly viewed as a key component of the financial services sector. But the emergence of Islamic finance in today's globalised world economy has conversely led to limited research on the legal foundations of this new industry.

This publication aims to assess the legal aspects of this alternative banking and financial system known as Islamic finance. It intends to demonstrate that Islamic finance is actually based on a modern Islamic law since the *classical fiqh* – Islamic law in force from the Qur'anic revelations to the early 19th century – is no longer the sovereign law of most Muslim-majority jurisdictions. Whilst the legal foundations of Islamic finance originate from *classical fiqh*, the latter had to be converted progressively over the course of history to meet the needs and realities of societal evolution.

Therefore, the transformation of *classical fiqh* into *financial fiqh* makes the law of Islamic finance *sui generis* as it has emerged without an underlying legal system contrary to *classical fiqh* that used to govern Islamic legal systems towards the end of the 19th century. It would then be interesting to assess the methods of implementing the law of Islamic finance – as a non-state law – to a modern legal system.

---

* Dr Amel Makhlouf is a French qualified lawyer specialised in banking and finance, and in international dispute resolution. She is also a Research Fellow at the Chair for Ethics and Financial Norms at the Sorbonne Law School (Paris, France), a Lecturer in the LL.M Business Law, Arab World and Middle East at the Sorbonne Law School (Paris, France) and a Lecturer at the Institute for Research and Studies on the Mediterranean and the Middle East (Paris, France).
As regards this publication, I wish to express my gratitude to Nicholas H.D. Foster (SOAS, University of London) and Pierre-Charles Pradier (Sorbonne Law School). I am also thankful to my friends Kerime Mahmoud, Anna Foster Vander Elst and Amar Douhane for their tremendous support.
Finally, and most importantly, I am grateful for the love and inspiration I received from my Dad [1952-2019]. This publication is dedicated to Him.

1. THE QUR'ANIC REVELATION TO PROPHET MUḤAMMAD

It would be misleading to characterise the divine revelations made to Prophet Muḥammad – the Messenger of God (Allah) – and recorded in the Qur'an – the sole scripture of the Muslims – as only the beginning of a new religion. More than a religion, Islam is also a faith, a spirituality, a civilisation and, more specifically, an all-encompassing way of life. The Qur'anic revelation also marks the construction of a new law – the classical *Islamic fiqh*[2] – together with the construction of a new legal system – the Islamic legal system – that was in force towards the end of the 19th century.

The Qur'anic revelation to Prophet Muḥammad is divided into two periods: the Meccan revelation (612 CE–621 CE), in which the Prophet's predication was of limited success, and the Medinan revelation (622 CE, after the *hijra*,[3] the emigration of Prophet Muḥammad from Mecca to Medina), symbolising the evolution of Prophet Muḥammad's mission. It is interesting to note that the Meccan verses mainly refer to the fundamental principles of faith since the prime mission of Prophet Muḥammad was to call people to Islam, whereas the Medinan verses convey legal references to the benefit of the *ummah* (the Islamic community), reflecting a new development in Prophet Muḥammad's career. This evolution is noticeable through the rise of legal verses revealed to Prophet Muḥammad in Medina, although they remain a minority in the Qur'an as they are estimated to be around 500 out of 6,236 verses.[4] Far from being a comprehensive legal code,[5] the Qur'an contains relatively few verses with legal significance that *fuqahā'* (legal experts in Islamic law) could readily apply as the foundation for an emerging body of Islamic law.[6]

2. THE EMERGENCE OF CLASSICAL FIQH

The emergence of classical *fiqh* probably occurred around the end of the fifth year of the *hijra*, when the Prophet's mission had gained new momentum.[7] The

2 Literally, *sharī'a* means the way, often interpreted as the highway to good life. In a broader sense, *sharī'a* refers to the legal verses of the Qur'an and the sayings and doings of Prophet Muḥammad (the *sunnan*). It is distinct from the *fiqh* which refers to the understanding and juristic interpretation of the *sharī'a* or of the holy sources of Islamic law, usually described as '*Islamic jurisprudence*'.

3 The emigration of Prophet Muḥammad and his followers from Mecca to Medina in 622 CE also marks the beginning of the Islamic calendar.

4 W.B. Hallaq, *The Origins and Evolution of Islamic Law*, Cambridge: Cambridge University Press, 2005, p. 21. See also E. Geoffroy, *L'Islam sera spirituel ou ne sera plus*, Paris: Seuil, 2009, p. 100.

5 N.H.D. Foster, 'Islamic Commercial Law: An Overview (I)', *InDret Revista para el análisis del derecho*, No. 4, 2006, p. 5.

6 J.G. Ercanbrack, *The Transformation of Islamic Law in Global Financial Markets*, Cambridge: Cambridge University Press, 2015, p. 23.

7 W.B. Hallaq, *The Origins and Evolution of Islamic Law*..., p. 20.

legal subject matter grew increasingly larger and his revelations, containing additional verses of legal significance, marked the beginning of substantive legislation in the Qur'an for the benefit of the *ummah*. The prohibitions of *maysir* (gambling), *gharar* (undue risk), *riba* (interest/usury)[8] and alcohol are probably the most significant prohibited practices as they contrast with the initial Arabic rules in force in pre-Islamic Arabia.

3. THE EMERGENCE OF THE ISLAMIC LEGAL SYSTEM

The emergence of classical *fiqh* led to the development of a legal system, the Islamic legal system, which can be defined as the necessary infrastructure supporting this body of rules.[9] Classical Islamic law had its own legal infrastructure, that is, its own means of making law, amending law, interpreting law, applying law, enforcing law and resolving disputes, and its own *fuqahā'* and doctrinal literature.[10]

For instance, the emergence of Islamic law led to the development of a judicial system in Islam that reflects the growth of an Islamic legal ethic;[11] after all, Prophet Muḥammad himself was raised as the first *qāḍī* (judge) in Islam, the ideal *qāḍī* seen as an example for the *ummah*.

The first century of the *hijra* saw the expansion of Islam through *proto-quḍāh*, the earliest quasi-judges of Islam, who were representatives of the judicial institution. Far from being limited to a legal function, their role included also administrative, financial,[12] religious and military aspects. The fact that some *proto-quḍāh* were illiterate reveals the primitive nature of their legal reasoning and their limited influence '*in terms of both geography and jurisdiction*'.[13]

The expansion of Islam increased the role and the gradual specialisation of the *qāḍī*, which became of central importance from the second year of the *hijra*. Specialisation enhanced the *qāḍī*'s dependence on emerging legal experts advising and assisting the judge prior to rendering a decision.

---

8 Notably Surah 2, Verse 275: '[…] *Allah has permitted trade and has forbidden interest*'; verse 276: '*Allah condemns usury and blesses charities*'.

9 N.H.D. Foster, 'The Emergent Islamic Finance Legal System: A Practical Method or a Dead End?', *New Horizon*, 182, 2011, pp. 36–37.

10 N.H.D. Foster, 'Moving Forward in the Study and Practice of Islamic Finance: Makhlouf's L'émergence d'un droit international de la finance islamique: Origines, formation et intégration en droit français', A lecture delivered at the Collège des Bernardins, Paris, 19 November 2015, *SOAS Law of Islamic Finance Working Papers Series*, Centre of Islamic and Middle Eastern Law, No. 1, 2015.

11 W.B. Hallaq, *The Origins and Evolution of Islamic Law…*, p. 34.

12 *Ibid.*, p. 37: Some of them '*were also charged with the collection of taxes*'.

13 *Ibid.*, p. 37.

4. THE CONSTRUCTION OF CLASSICAL FIQH AND THE DEVELOPMENT OF USUL AL-FIQH

The *fiqh*,[14] that is the collection of Islamic legal opinions regarding the application of the *sharī'a*, acquired its final form approximately two centuries after the *hijra*. *Fiqh* is, first, based on the Qur'an, which is unanimously considered as both the primary and supreme source of Islamic law. It is then supplemented by the *sunnan*, referring to the sayings and doings of Prophet Muḥammad that have been established as an exemplary model for the *ummah* to follow[15] and recorded in short narratives called *ḥādīth*. Muslim jurists refer to the *sunnah*, the secondary source of Islamic law, when a solution cannot be found in the Qur'an because either it is silent or it bears only indirectly on specific matters.

However, even the combination of Qur'an and *sunnah* does not provide comprehensive solutions to every issue.[16] While establishing the substance of an embryonic law, these two sources of Islamic law still leave many open questions and, to some extent, ambiguous guidance. The *fuqahā'* have, therefore, created techniques to develop the *sharī'a* through the establishment of a legal methodology called *uṣūl al-fiqh*[17] based on the four formal sources of Islamic law in Sunni Islam: the primary and secondary sources (the Qur'an and *sunnah*), together with the *ijmā'* (consensus of the scholars) and the *qiyas* (analogical reasoning) that derive validity from the Qur'an and the *sunnah* and are used by jurists to develop nascent law.

In addition, it is worth noting that *'urf* (custom or local established practices) is another concept, though unofficial, that significantly influenced the construction of *fiqh* and, more specifically, commercial *fiqh*.[18] Though not one of the classically recognised sources of *fiqh*, and therefore inadequately mentioned in contemporary literature, *'urf* is a major source of Islamic law.[19] Local practices

14 Literally, *fiqh* means 'in-depth-understanding'.

15 See for example Surah 3, Verse 132: '*Obey Allah and His Messenger so that you may come to be recipients of His mercy*'; Surah 4, Verse 59: '*O you who believe! Obey Allah and obey the Messenger and those in authority among you*' and Surah 4, Verse 80: '*Obeying the Messenger is Obeying Allah*' [English translation of Arabic version of the Qur'an].

16 N.H.D. Foster, 'Islamic Perspectives on the Law of Business Organisations I: An Overview of the Classical Sharia and a Brief Comparison of the Sharia Regimes with Western-Style Law', *European Business Organization Law Review*, 11 (1), 2010, pp. 3–34.

17 Developed from the second century of the *hijra*.

18 A. Shabana, *Custom in Islamic Law and Legal Theory: The Development of the Concepts of 'Urf and 'Ādah in the Islamic Legal Tradition*, New York, Basingstoke: Palgrave Macmillan, 2010, 246 p.

19 J.G. Ercanbrack, *The Transformation of Islamic Law in Global Financial Markets...*, 2015, p. 40. Ercanbrack indicates that '*early Muslim legal literature underscores the supremacy of the concept of "custom" in commercial exchange as a decisive feature of the laws of commerce*', p. 41.

are usually the basis of resolving conflicts, forming contracts and drafting contractual provisions.

The *uṣūl al-fiqh* (sources of Islamic law) allow only *mujtahidūn* (qualified jurists) to practice *ijtihād*,[20] namely, to perform legal reasoning when new cases arise by interpreting the will of Allah as established in the Qur'an and the *sunnah*. *Mujtahidūn* were organised into interpretive communities called *madhāhib*, or schools of law, to wit in sunni Islam, the *maliki*, *hanafi*, *shafi'i* and *hanbali* schools.[21] In that sense, it is interesting to note that whilst in the civil or common law legal systems the state was empowered to legislate, as well as to promulgate law, and constituted the centre of legal authority, it was the doctrinal *madhhab* that produced law in the Islamic legal system and provided its axis of authority.[22] Therefore, legal authority in the Islamic legal system did not emerge from the body politic but from the collective doctrinal work of the *madhhab*.[23]

5. THE EMERGENCE OF COMMERCIAL FIQH

Undoubtedly, the tradition of Islamic commerce features the originality of Islam as a monotheistic religion.[24] Prophet Muḥammad and his Companions were themselves traders, as well as the eponyms of the *madhāhib*[25] who, despite being jurists, heavily influenced the commercial practice and, thus, the commercial aspects of Islamic law.

Over the course of history, the use of unofficial sources of *fiqh* (such as *'urf*) allowed the *fiqh* to be more flexible to meet the needs and realities of societal evolution. The supremacy of *'urf* in commercial exchanges significantly impacted the development of *fiqh al-mu'āmalāt* (Islamic law of transactions).[26]

---

20 On the controversy of the gate of *ijtihād*, see C.T. Chehata, *Études de droit musulman*, Paris: Puf, 1971, p. 40 and W.B. Hallaq, 'Was the Gate of Ijtihad closed?', *International Journal of Middle East Studies*, Vol. 25, No. 4, 1993, pp. 587–605.

21 Four legal schools survived in sunni Islam.

22 W.B. Hallaq, *The Origins and Evolution of Islamic Law…*, 2005, p. 167. See also N. Feldman, *The fall and rise of the Islamic state*, Princeton: Princeton University Press, 2008, 189 p., who considers that '*legal institutions like the schools do not develop in a political vacuum. (…) Although Islamic law was 'jurist's law' in that its content was determined by the jurist-scholars, and not the state, it was also state law in that it had a mechanism for being enforced by the state. That mechanism was the judiciary, appointed by the caliph and serving under his direct authority*', p. 27.

23 *Ibid.*

24 Presentation of J.G. Ercanbrack, 'The Role of Context in the Transformation of Islamic Law in Global Financial Markets", Conference organised by the Chair for Ethics and Financial Norms (Université Paris 1 Panthéon-Sorbonne & King Abdulaziz University, Jeddah), 8 June 2016.

25 Abu Ḥanīfah, Mālik Ibn Anas, Al-Shāfi'ī and Ibn Hanbal.

26 C. Mallat, 'Commercial Law in the Middle East: Between Classical Transactions and Modern Business', *The American Journal of Comparative Law*, Vol. 48, No. 1, 2000, pp. 81–141.

The initial source of the Islamic law of contracts seems to derive from Surah 1, verse 5, which insists on the fulfilment of commitments by stating: '*O you who believe! Fulfill your undertakings*'.[27] This suggests a duty of good faith in Islamic law. Muslims are, therefore, requested to act in accordance with their commitments before entering into an agreement. In addition, the *sharī'a* contains a series of principles governing Islamic commercial law: Parties to a contract are notably required to follow the prohibitions of *riba*, *gharar* and *maysir*; the underlying cause of the contract must be lawful;[28] and the object of the contract must be permissible (*mubah*).[29]

Several commercial transactions were used by traders prior to the revelation of Islam, but Islam ultimately reformed them to follow Islamic criteria, thus allowing Muslims to use commercial transactions throughout the classical period. This is the case for:

- The *mudaraba*, which is a partnership contract, commonly used by the Prophet Muḥammad with his first wife, Khadijah, prior to their marriage. Whereas she acted as a *rab al-māl* (investor) by providing capital, Prophet Muḥammad acted as a *mudarib* (business manager) by investing his skills and efforts. In this structure, profits are shared on a pre-agreed ratio, and losses, if any, are born by the investor alone, unless negligence of *mudarib* is proven.
- The *murabaha*, which is certainly the most popular and most common mode of Islamic financing. The *murabaha* is used today in Islamic finance essentially to circumvent the prohibition of *riba*. It refers to a cost-plus sale contract whereby the seller sells specified assets or commodities to a customer, generally involving an immediate delivery with a deferred payment.[30]
- The *salam*,[31] which is a sale in which the agreed price is paid fully in advance, while delivery of goods is deferred. In order to comply with Islamic contract rules, notably the prohibition of *gharar*, which '*covers all kinds of undue risk*',[32] this agreement must specify the quality and quantity of the goods to be delivered, as well as the date and place of delivery.

---

27 See for example Surah 5, Verse 89: '*Allah will not impose blame upon you for what is meaningless in your oaths, but He will impose blame upon you for [breaking] what you intended of oaths*'.

28 N.H.D. Foster, "Islamic Commercial Law (II): An Overview", *InDret Revista para el análisis del derecho*, No. 1, 2007, p. 12 explaining that '*a contract to buy grapes is invalid if the underlying cause of entering into the transaction is to make wine*'.

29 For instance, the subject-matter of the contract should not imply forbidden commodities such as wine or pork.

30 W.B. Hallaq, *The Origins and Evolution of Islamic Law*..., p. 25.

31 *Ibid.* Hallaq notably explains that '*The ancient Near Eastern contracts of sale, dating back to the second millennium BC, and involving immediate delivery with a later payment, or immediate payment for a later delivery, were prevalent in the pre-Islamic Hejaz and wholly incorporated (under 'arāyā and salam) into Islamic law*'.

32 N.H.D. Foster, 'Islamic Commercial Law (II): An Overview'..., p. 7.

- The *musharaka*, which is a profit-and-loss-sharing contract involving two or more parties that provided capital for the financing of a project or business. In a modern sense, this may refer to a joint enterprise[33] in which all partners share profits on a pre-agreed ratio, but losses, if any, are shared in proportion to the amount invested.

6. THE DECLINE OF THE ISLAMIC LEGAL SYSTEM AND THE DISAPPEARANCE OF COMMERCIAL FIQH

The collapse of the Islamic legal system, together with the disappearance of commercial *fiqh* in the Middle-Eastern world,[34] is intrinsically related to the decline of the Ottoman Empire and its efforts of modernisation through the *Tanzimat* period (6.2) followed by the French colonisation of Algeria (6.3) in the 19th century. Prior to providing an overview of those two historical events, it is worth mentioning the impact of Napoleon's conquest of Egypt on the Egyptian legal system (6.1).[35]

6.1 THE NAPOLEONIC CONQUEST OF EGYPT

After its invasion of Egypt in 1798 under the command of Napoleon and occupying this territory from 1798 to 1801, France influenced the Egyptian law and legal system through, notably, the establishment of commercial courts[36] that were '*composed of Muslims and non-Muslims in equal numbers*'.[37] Though the French invasion of Egypt did not abolish the Islamic legal system, the establishment of commercial courts in Egypt deprived the *qāḍī* of his competence in commercial matters.[38]

---

33 M.T. Usmani, 'The Concept of Musharakah and Its Application As an Islamic Method of Financing', *Arab Law Quarterly*, Vol. 14, 1999, p. 203.

34 This study does not provide an exhaustive analysis of the fall of the Islamic legal system and therefore does not refer to the collapse of that system in India, Malaysia and Indonesia which is intimately intertwined with the British and Dutch colonial empires.

35 Though formally part of the Ottoman Empire, Egypt had a separate legal history from the time of its conquest by Napoleon.

36 J. Goldberg, 'On the Origins of Majālis al-Tujjār in Mid-Nineteenth Century Egypt', *Islamic Law and Society*, Vol. 6, No. 2, 1999, pp. 193–223. Goldberg refers to the introduction of special '*commercial courts in Cairo, Alexandria, Rosetta, and Damietta on 10 September 1798*', p. 198.

37 *Ibid.*, p. 198.

38 *Ibid.* For a better understanding of the French interference into the Islamic legal system in force in Egypt, see J Goldberg, 'L'Europe au-delà de l'Europe. Réflexions sur l'entrée de l'Egypte dans la famille française du droit' *in* G Boetsch, B. Dupret and J.N. Ferrie (eds),

As with the current French judiciary, the appointed judges were merchants and, therefore, '*recruited from the native merchant communities*'.[39] In addition, the dichotomy of the Egyptian private law, also divided between civil law and commercial law, reflects the French influence into Egyptian law since this distinction was unknown in the *sharī'a*.[40] This distinction is of significant interest because '*it was later used, in the Ottoman Empire and systems influenced by the Ottoman Model, to facilitate the introduction of Western style commercial law*'.[41] In the Middle-Eastern and Northern African regions, this distinction seems to have encouraged the broad phenomenon of legal selectivity by importing European law into those legal systems while confining the *sharī'a* to family, inheritance and personal status matters.[42]

6.2 THE DECLINE OF THE OTTOMAN EMPIRE

6.2.1 The Ottoman case

By the mid-19th century, the rise of Western imperialism from military, political, economic and scientific standpoints prevailed over the Muslim world, which led to a series of rapid reforms (known collectively as the *Tanzimat*)[43] undertaken by the Ottoman Empire to reinforce its relative position.

The *Tanzimat* period led to significant legal reforms that influenced the decline of both Muslim scholars and the *sharī'a* through, notably, the establishment of commercial courts in 1840 and the codification of law, namely, the promulgation of a Commercial Code, in 1850.

The codification of the Ottoman Commercial Code was intended to be a replica of the French Commercial Code of 1807, introduced by Napoleon, but it remained insufficient because the provisions of French law were inadequate to the commercial activity of the Ottoman Empire, which at that period was governed by the *sharī'a*. Moreover, Ottoman legislators failed to notice that various regulations of commercial companies were not contained in the French Commercial Code but in the French Civil Code.[44] Absent implementation of the

Droits et sociétés dans le monde arabe (Perspectives socio-anthropologiques), Aix-en-Provence: Presses Universitaires d'Aix-Marseille, 1997, 229 p.

39 *Ibid.*

40 N.H.D. Foster, '*Commerce, Inter-Polity Legal Conflict and the Transformation of Civil and Commercial Law in the Ottoman Empire*' *in* E. Cotran and M. LAU (eds.), *Yearbook of Islamic and Middle Eastern Law*, Vol. 17, 2011–2012, pp 1–49.

41 *Ibid.*, p. 23.

42 See parag. 6.2.2 below. H.A. Hamoudi, 'The death of Islamic law', *Georgia Journal of International and Comparative Law*, Vol. 38, 2010, pp. 322–326.

43 From 1839 to 1876.

44 C. Mallat, 'Commercial Law in the Middle East: Between Classical Transactions and Modern Business'..., p. 102.

French Civil Code into the Ottoman Empire, the Ottoman Commercial Code faced several legal gaps; for instance, it contained several provisions in relation to company law but no definition of 'company' itself. It also contained '*a skeletal chapter of 10 articles on the société anonyme, which was rapidly becoming the most financially important vehicle in company law in France*'.[45]

The enactment of the Ottoman Commercial Code was followed by the enactment of the Penal Code in 1858, the Code of Commercial Procedure in 1861 and the Code of Maritime Commerce in 1863, which were all based on French law. The next step in Ottoman codification was the Mejelle (*Majallat*), which was intended to be a comprehensive codification of both civil law and civil procedure based on the *sharī'a*, mainly influenced by the hanafi madhhab and produced by a distinguished committee of scholars from 1869 to 1876.[46] Such codification contradicts the inherent nature of the *sharī'a*, which is intrinsically an '*uncodified body of legal doctrines, principles, values, and opinions*'[47] and which led to the decline of scholars as '*keepers of the law*'.[48] Indeed, the enactment of the Mejelle deprived the juristic class of its initial role because it was designed not for the *qāḍī* but for secular courts.[49]

The *Tanzimat*, meant to strengthen the relative position of the Ottoman Empire towards European States, appears to have been an expensive undertaking for the Empire that failed to generate enough revenue to pay for all the initiatives. From 1876[50] to 1914, the Ottoman Empire was significantly weakened towards European States, and its defeat in World War I led to the fall of the Ottoman Empire.

6.2.2 The Egyptian case

The legal transplantation of French law also occurred in Egypt, which gained judicial and administrative independence from the Ottoman Empire during the reign of Isma'il Pasha by virtue of the *Khedive Isma'il*, issued in 1874.[51]

The Mixed Courts were introduced in Egypt around 1875, along with the promulgation of a series of codes based solely on French law meant to resolve disputes between Egyptians and foreigners. These were, namely, the Civil Code, the Penal Code, the Commercial Code, the Code of Maritime Commerce, the Code of Civil and Commercial Procedure and the Code of Criminal Procedure.[52]

---

45 *Ibid.*, p. 102.

46 N. Feldman, *The fall and rise of the Islamic state...*, p. 62.

47 *Ibid.*

48 *Ibid.*, p. 63.

49 Schacht Joseph, 'Islamic Law in Contemporary States', *The American Journal of Comparative Law*, Vol. 8, No. 2, 1959, pp. 134–135.

50 Promulgation of the first Constitution of the Ottoman Empire.

51 N. Saleh, 'The Law Governing Contracts in Arabia', *International and Comparative Law Quarterly*, XXXVIII, 1989, p. 767.

52 W.B. Hallaq, *An Introduction to Islamic Law*, Cambridge: Cambridge University Press, 2009, pp. 104-105.

With the Montreux Convention of 1937, the Mixed Courts of Egypt were abolished after a 12-year transitional period. The Mixed Court system was indeed terminated in 1949, and its area of expertise was transferred to the National Courts. This transition prompted the drafting of new codes, to wit, the new Egyptian Civil Code, which was enacted in 1948 and came into force in 1949. Based to a large part on French law, the new Egyptian Civil Code was drafted by a commission headed by 'Abd al-Razzāq al-Sanhūrī, a distinguished Egyptian jurist. This code was used as a model in the Arab–Muslim world, notably in Syria, Iraq and Kuwait.[53]

It is worth noting that '*the totality of provisions based on the sharī'a probably comes to no more than five to ten percent of the whole*'[54] Civil Code. Article 1 of the Egyptian Civil Code of 1948 enjoins a judge to issue judgments in accordance with the letter and spirit of the provisions of the Civil Code itself; failing that, in accordance with custom; and in the absence of custom, in accordance with the principles of Islamic *sharī'a*. In the absence of custom, the judge should apply the principles of natural law and the rules of equity. Therefore, '*for probably the first time in the modern legal history of the Arab Middle East, the sharī'a was officially to back up an important piece of secular legislation. Sharī'a principles were to fill lacunae found in the statutory provisions and in custom*'.[55]

However, such transformation of the Egyptian law and of the judicial system could not conceal the fact that Egypt, as with several Arab-majority countries, practised Islamic law selectively by implementing a secular law based mostly on French law while confining the *sharī'a* to family, inheritance and personal status matters.[56]

6.3 THE FRENCH COLONISATION OF ALGERIA

The French colonisation of Algeria, from 1830 to 1962, is another factor in the decline of the Islamic legal system since a hybrid Islamic French law, known as *droit musulman algérien*,[57] was produced by jurists, most of whom were

---

53 I. Edge, 'Comparative Commercial Law of Egypt and the Arabian Gulf', *Cleveland State Law Review*, Vol. 34, 1985, p. 129.

54 *Ibid.*, p. 133. For a similar view, see also C. Chehata, 'Les survivances musulmanes dans la codification du droit civil égyptien', *Revue internationale de droit comparé*, Vol. 17, n° 4, octobre-décembre 1965, pp. 839–840.

55 N. Saleh, 'The Law Governing Contracts in Arabia'..., p. 768.

56 H.A. Hamoudi, 'The death of Islamic law'..., pp. 322–326.

57 Developed on the same model as the Anglo-Muhammadan law in British India but Hallaq writes that the "*droit musulman algérien*" was '*somewhat cognate to, but larger in scope and academic interest than, the British colonialist notion of Anglo-Muhammadan Law*', W.B. Hallaq, *An Introduction to Islamic Law*..., p. 111. It is also worth mentioning that the French intended to codify Islamic law through the so-called *Code Morand* of 1916 which was mainly based on the maliki *madhhab* but was never enacted due to Algerian resistance.

French.[58] In addition, French judges started to replace the *quḍāh* (judges) and religious courts. This reduced the influence of the *qāḍī*, whose function was to interpret the *sharī'a* as a body of legal doctrines and principles. It also '*led to a dramatic reduction in the number of Muslim courts in the country, from an already reduced 184 in 1870 to 61 in 1890*'.[59]

By the independence of Algeria in 1962,[60] the scope of the *sharī'a* was reduced and confined to family law. This selectivity of Islamic law, prevalent in Muslim-majority countries and criticised by several authors,[61] led to the promulgation in 1984 of a family code distinct from the Algerian Civil Code of 1975.

In 1962, Algerian law became a hybrid or *sui generis* law mostly inspired by French law, notably in the fields of commerce, banking and finance.

7. THE EMERGENCE OF FINANCIAL FIQH

The 19th century is of particular significance in the history of Islamic normativity: the change of commercial activities, together with the need to compete with European States, marked the progressive decline of both the Islamic legal system and Islamic commercial law.[62] While initially being governed by classical *fiqh*, Muslim majority jurisdictions were henceforth governed by a hybrid law based on French law, with only reference to *sharī'a*. As conventional banking and finance systems were introduced into Muslim-majority countries in the contemporary era, it is interesting to assess the law on which Islamic finance is based, as well as the implementation of the law of Islamic finance – as a nonstate law – into a modern legal system.

In today's globalised world economy, Islamic finance is based on the commercial parts of the *fiqh*, which had to be converted into financial *fiqh* to meet the needs of Islamic finance.[63] It notably means to make the commercial contracts initially used in the classical period suitable for financial transactions, that is, to convert them into financial contracts.

---

58 M. Morand, *Introduction à l'étude du droit musulman algérien*, Alger: Jules Carbonel, 1921, 213 p.

59 W.B. Hallaq, *An Introduction to Islamic Law*, Cambridge: Cambridge University Press, 2009, pp. 104-105.

60 *Ibid*., p. 114.

61 Such as H.A. Hamoudi, "The death of Islamic law"..., pp. 293–337.

62 Ercanbrack states that '*the almost complete secularization of Middle Eastern legal systems other than in areas of personal status seems to confirm the notion that the state is now seen as the only viable source of central legal authority*', J.G. Ercanbrack, *The Transformation of Islamic Law in Global Financial Markets*..., p. 112.

63 N.H.D. Foster, 'Moving Forward in the Study and Practice of Islamic Finance: Makhlouf's *L'émergence d'un droit international de la finance islamique: Origines, formation et integration en droit français*'..., p. 4.

Absent an Islamic legal system, financial *fiqh*, therefore, constitutes an emerging body of rules that may be qualified as a law of Islamic finance, regulated by conventional legal systems and relying on them for its effectiveness:[64] '*no Sharia legal system was, nor could be, produced to make Islamic finance operate and it has to function within national legal systems*'.[65]

Yet, the exponential growth of Islamic finance over the last several decades in the modern globalised world economy has contributed to the emergence of a nascent legal system through several initiatives.

One such initiative deals with the standardisation of Islamic financial transactions, which is a historical continuation of the codification of law undertaken in the 19th century in Islamic legal systems.[66] Legal standardisation of financial transactions intends to provide, notably, predictability, certainty, stability, and market transparency and to preserve confidence among legal practitioners.

Another initiative is the development of *sharī'a* standards by the Accounting and Auditing Organization for Islamic Financial Institutions (AAOIFI), consisting of uniform rules and principles governing the Islamic financial industry. Those *sharī'a* standards help to standardise and facilitate the drafting of Islamic finance transactions and have been adopted by Islamic financial institutions across the globe. Additionally, in an attempt to foster and to promote the development of Islamic finance in France by finding a possible combination of French and *sharī'a* law requirements as well as suggesting a comprehensive transcription of *sharī'a* law concepts into French law concepts, the AAOIFI main 20 *sharī'a* standards have been translated into French by Paris Europlace, the organisation in charge of promoting and developing Paris's financial marketplace.[67]

The compilation and issuance of *fatāwa* (Islamic legal opinions) by national *sharī'a* boards,[68] such as in Malaysia and Sudan, may also reduce the risk of uncertainty in legal documentation. However, those legal opinions do not bind other scholars or Courts of law. They are essentially persuasive due to the moral authority of the signing *fuqahā'*.

---

64 N.H.D. Foster, 'Dispute Resolution and Insolvency in Islamic Finance: Problems and Solutions' in N.H.D. Foster, D. Neo (eds) Dispute Resolution and Insolvency in Islamic Finance: Problems and Solutions – Workshop 19 September 2013: Report of Proceedings, *SOAS Law of Islamic Finance Working Papers Series*, 2014, p. 12.

65 N.H.D. Foster, 'Moving Forward in the Study and Practice of Islamic Finance: Makhlouf's *L'émergence d'un droit international de la finance islamique: Origines, formation et integration en droit français*'..., p. 5.

66 J.G. Ercanbrack, *The Transformation of Islamic Law in Global Financial Markets*..., p. 112.

67 Organisation de comptabilité et d'audit des institutions financières islamiques (2013), *Finance islamique: les normes de conformité de l'AAOIFI*, Vol. 1, Paris, Eska, 352 p.

68 Though *sharī'a* scholars are no longer considered as keepers of the law since the *sharī'a* was initially exclusively interpreted by the scholars whilst it is now '*a set of rules defined and applied by authority of the state*', N. Feldman, *The fall and rise of the Islamic state*..., p. 81.

Thus, despite the existence of several initiatives which can be regarded as the first signs of the formation of a legal system for financial *fiqh*, there is still a long way to go before a true system will emerge, if it ever does. Therefore, the potential challenge of an Islamic finance transaction because it does not comply with *sharī'a* remains problematic. A recent example of the serious problems which can arise, and the effect on the market, is the ongoing litigation regarding the Dana Gas *ṣukūk* issues.[69]

69 Dana Gas PJSC v Dana Gas *ṣukūk* Ltd & Ors [2017] EWHC 2928 (Comm) (17 November 2017).

www.ingramcontent.com/pod-product-compliance
Ingram Content Group UK Ltd.
Pitfield, Milton Keynes, MK11 3LW, UK
UKHW051923100926
8556IPUK00021B/1335

9 781780 686196